PERFECT MADNESS

ALSO BY JUDITH WARNER

Hillary Clinton: The Inside Story

Newt Gingrich: Speaker to America

(by Judith Warner and Max Berley)

In and Out of Vogue

(by Grace Mirabella with Judith Warner)

*You Have the Power: How to Take Back Our Country
and Restore Democracy in America*

(by Howard Dean with Judith Warner)

Judith Warner

PERFECT
MADNESS

*Motherhood in
the Age of Anxiety*

RIVERHEAD BOOKS
a member of Penguin Group (USA) Inc.
New York   2005

RIVERHEAD BOOKS
Published by the Penguin Group
Penguin Group (USA) Inc., 375 Hudson Street, New York, New York 10014, USA •
Penguin Group (Canada), 10 Alcorn Avenue, Toronto, Ontario, Canada M4V 3B2 (a division
of Pearson Penguin Canada Inc.) • Penguin Books Ltd, 80 Strand, London WC2R 0RL,
England • Penguin Ireland, 25 St Stephen's Green, Dublin 2, Ireland (a division of Penguin
Books Ltd) • Penguin Group (Australia), 250 Camberwell Road, Camberwell, Victoria 3124,
Australia (a division of Pearson Australia Group Pty Ltd) • Penguin Books India Pvt Ltd,
11 Community Centre, Panchsheel Park, New Delhi–110 017, India • Penguin Group (NZ),
Cnr Airborne and Rosedale Roads, Albany, Auckland 1310, New Zealand (a division of Pearson
New Zealand Ltd) • Penguin Books (South Africa) (Pty) Ltd, 24 Sturdee Avenue, Rosebank,
Johannesburg 2196, South Africa • Penguin Books Ltd, Registered Offices:
80 Strand, London WC2R 0RL, England

Library of Congress Cataloging-in-Publication Data

Warner, Judith.
Perfect madness : motherhood in the age of anxiety / Judith Warner.
p.   cm.
Includes bibliographical references and index.
ISBN 1-57322-304-2
1. Motherhood—United States.   2. Mothers—United States—Social conditions.
3. Mothers—United States—Psychology.   4. Guilt.   I. Title.
HQ759.W346 2005   2004056615
306.874'3—dc22

Printed in the United States of America
5   7   9   10   8   6   4

This book is printed on acid-free paper. ∞

Book design by Kate Nichols

To my mother—

Who fed me Yodels and Chef Boy-Ar-Dee

Who let me drink coffee (but Gatorade, never)

Who laughed with me until the tears rolled down our faces

And whose love and support never end.

And to Max, Julia, and Emilie—

In gratitude, and with all my love

CONTENTS

PART 1

The Mommy Mystique

"This Mess"

T HIS IS a very personal book.

It is a snapshot of motherhood—of parenthood, really—as I found it in Washington, D.C., and its suburbs from the fall of 2000 to the summer of 2004. And although in writing it I made every effort to take my research further—away from the big cities of the East Coast, back in time to the colonial roots of America's cultural history, then forward again to our day—I know that what I have written here is not an encyclopedic overview of Motherhood, Now and Forever.

It's not a scholarly history.

Neither is it a book of self-help.

It's not a book about the work-family conflict.

Nor is it about "balance," or the problems of working mothers, or the virtues of stay-at-home motherhood.

It does not contain much by way of policy.

It will not tell you how to raise your children.

It is, rather, an exploration of a feeling. That caught-by-the-throat feeling so many mothers have today of *always* doing something wrong.

And it's about a conviction I have that this feeling—this wide-spread, choking cocktail of guilt and anxiety and resentment and regret—is poisoning motherhood for American women today. Lowering our horizons and limiting our minds. Sapping energy that we should have for ourselves and our children. And drowning out thoughts that might lead us, collectively, to formulate solutions.

The feeling has many faces but it doesn't really have a name. It's not depression. It's not oppression. It's a mix of things, a kind of *too-muchness*. An existential discomfort. A "mess," as one woman I interviewed called it, for lack of a better word.

She wasn't a woman who normally lacked for words. She was a newspaper editor. A headline writer. A professional wordsmith. And yet, as she sat with me one night, half-buried in a sofa in a circle of moms, she struggled, and stumbled, as she tried to express what it was that made her life feel like it was always about to come apart.

None of it made much sense, really, she said. She was a person lucky enough to have many choices. In the hope of finding "balance" she'd chosen to scale down her career—working part-time and at night, in order to spend as much time as possible with her nine-year-old daughter.

This is the kind of arrangement that mothers are supposed to dream of. This mom knew she ought to feel blessed. But somehow, nothing had worked out as planned. Working nights meant that she was tired all the time, and cranky, and stressed. And forever annoyed with her husband. And now—her daughter was after her to get a day job. It seemed she was finding that having Mom around most of the time wasn't all it was cracked up to be, particularly if Mom was forever on the edge. So what was she to do?

The woman waved her hands in circles, helplessly. "What I'm trying to figure out—" She paused. "What I'm trying to remember . . . is how I ended up raising this princess . . . how I got into . . . how to get out of . . . this, this, this . . . *this mess.*"

This mess.

The words crackled like lightning in the suburban living room where we'd been sitting since sunset. It was a Tuesday evening in the winter of 2002, the bath-into-bed-time hour was past, and the moms, out for a night without kids, were exhausted. The conversation had been moving laboriously, the big issue, Motherhood, lurching heavily across the coffee table like a big medicine ball full of angst.

Like the newspaper editor, the other moms didn't feel entitled to complain. By any objective measure, they had easy lives—kids in good schools, houses in good neighborhoods, dependable husbands whose incomes allowed them to mostly choose what they wanted to do with their time. Most had chosen to pursue Mommy Track jobs—part-time work, a big cut in ambition and salary. But they didn't mind that; they knew that that was a privilege. Still, there was something that bugged them. It ate away at them. It cast a pall on all the rest. What they couldn't make peace with was the feeling that somehow, more globally, they were living Mommy Track *lives.*

Lives filled with knee pads and bake sales and dentist's appointments and car seats. Lives somehow lesser than those of their full-time working husbands—men who managed, when the kids ran wild in the morning, spilling their Cheerios, and losing their shoes, to lose themselves in the newspaper, fading "into black and white" at the breakfast table, as one mom put it to me, "just like *Father Knows Best.*"

The moms' lives were punctuated by boxer shorts on the floor and quilt-making at school, carpooling and play dates and mother-daughter book clubs, and getting in to see the *right* dentist and worrying about whether they had the *wrong* pediatrician, and, and, and, layer after layer of trivia and absurdity that sometimes made them feel like they were going out of their heads.

Sometimes, a rage seized them that was hard to control. Sometimes, everything just seemed out of control. "Living in past, present, and future all at one time," one mom said, "I get overwhelmed. I get worried about things falling apart."

Every three months, they would blow. Every now and then, their husbands and children knew, they had to leave Mommy alone. It was a standard part of their family lives. The "Zen of the boxer shorts," as one mother called it, could only last for so long.

And the real problem was—the worst of it all was—it wasn't altogether clear that what they were doing with their lives was actually worthwhile. The choices and the compromises—when all was said and done, they didn't seem to add up to all that much. Not to a great sense of achievement. Not to a great sense of pride. There was no gratitude from their families, certainly. Their husbands had started taking a *tone*. It sounded like: "*This* is what I want you to do. . . ." Their children simply wondered what they did with their time.

Their children had almost all of them, and they just wanted more, more, more. And after years of always trying to give more, give their all, they were coming to realize that *more* wasn't necessarily *right*. But what to do, then?

"The children are the center of the household and everything goes around them," said a woman who'd left a prestigious government job working on child-care policy because it allowed her no time with her kids. "You want to do everything and be everything for them because this is your *job* now. You take all the energy and enthusiasm you had in your career and you feel the need to be as successful raising your children as you were in the workplace. And you can make your kids totally crazy in the process."

"And," another stay-at-home mom put in, "the reality is: at the end of the day, you could put your heart in it and it could be all cocked up. For nothing wrong that you did. Your kids could wind up a mess, and there's your life's work."

There was a problem floating in the room, a problem so big and so strange that the women couldn't quite name it. It wasn't exactly guilt. It wasn't exactly stress. It wasn't exactly anger. It was all of that and more.

"*. . . This mess.*"

Those two simple words were like a code-breaker. Everything became clear then, and suddenly, the sentences flew.

"*It's like they keep a tally of the did-nots.*"

"*I am absolutely and scarily consumed by rage.*"

"*I want my kids to think of me not just as doing for them but also as fun.*"

"*I think we're making ourselves crazy.*"

"*Your kids can end up completely messed up.*"

"*Are we neurotic, insecure? What got us to here?*"

I COULDN'T ANSWER those questions back then. I didn't even try. The fact is: I was put off that night by those smartest-of-the-smart, well-off, and powerful women, with their Washington-insider lives.

All women should have problems like yours, I found myself thinking. *We all should be so lucky.*

It was only later, when I stepped back, transcribed the conversation, and read—and read and read—more transcripts and articles and e-mails and books and policy papers, when I stepped back and listened to the cultural conversation on motherhood going on in my home and in theirs and, I believe, *in all of ours,* that I came to see that, indeed, most women did. Have problems like theirs. In varying forms. And to varying degrees, depending on how much money and how much luck and how many real choices they had. I came to believe that all mothers in America, in differing ways and to different degrees, were caught up in The Mess. And that's because the climate in which we now mother is, in many ways, just plain crazy.

It's not the "fault" of the media. Or the Christian Right. Or George W. Bush. Or Phyllis Schlafly. Or Dr. Laura Schlessinger. Or Mrs. Doubtfire. It's *us*—this generation of mothers. And it's the way our culture has groomed and greeted us. Mixing promise with politics, feminism with "family values," science and sound bites and religion and, above all, *fear* into a combustible combination that is nothing less than perfect madness.

1.

Introduction:
The Mommy Mystique

IF YOU HAVE been brought up, all your life, being told you have wonderful choices, you tend, when things go wrong, to assume you made the wrong choices—not to see that the "choices" given you were wrong in the first place.

Similarly, when, for the full course of your motherhood, you live and breathe the overheated smog of The Mess, you tend not to even notice it around you.

It came as a shock to me because, for my first three and a half blessed years of motherhood, I knew something very different.

I didn't realize it then, but I was in paradise.

I WAS LIVING in France, a country that has an astounding array of benefits for families—and for mothers in particular. When my children were born, I stayed in the hospital for five comfortable days. I found a nanny through a free, community-based referral service, then employed her, legally and full-time, for a cost to me of about $10,500 a year, after tax breaks. My elder daughter, from the time she was eighteen months of age, attended excellent part-time preschools where she painted and played with modeling clay and ate cookies and napped for about $150 per month—the top end of the fee scale. She could have started public school at age three, and could have opted to stay until 5 P.M. daily. My friends who were covered by the French social security system (which I did not pay into) had even greater benefits: at least four months of paid maternity leave, the right to stop working for up to three years and have jobs held for them, cash grants, after their second children were born, starting at about $105 per month.

And that was just the beginning. There was more: a culture. An atmosphere. A set of deeply held attitudes toward motherhood—toward adult womanhood—that had the effect of allowing me to have two children, work in an office, work out in a gym, and go out to dinner at night and away for a short vacation with my husband without ever hearing, without ever thinking, the word "guilt."

Guilt just wasn't in the air. It wasn't considered a natural consequence of working motherhood. Neither was the word "selfish" considered the necessary accoutrement of a woman with children who wanted to take time for herself. On the contrary, work was considered a normal part, even a desirable part, of a modern mother's life. It was considered something that broadened her horizons and enhanced her self-esteem—healthy and good things for herself and her children. Taking time for herself was equally considered to be a mother's right—indeed, a mother's responsibility—as was taking time for romance and a social life. The general French conviction that a person should live a "balanced" life was considered especially true for mothers—particularly, I would say, for stay-at-home mothers, who were otherwise considered at risk of falling into excessive child-centeredness.

And that, the French believed, was wrong. Obsessive. Inappropriate. Just plain weird.

I'll always remember the conversation I had with my pediatrician at my elder daughter's five-month checkup. It was time for me to return to work in an office, and I was terrified. I had images in my mind of my baby spending days strapped into her Maxi-Cosi rocking seat, her eyes fixed blankly ahead of her as she sank into a mommy-less emotional void. I told the doctor I was going to start working outside of home and started to cry. "Listen," he said. "You don't just have this child for a couple of months. You'll have her for the rest of your life. You have to have a life of your own. Because if you're happy, she'll be happy. If you're fine, she'll be fine."

I didn't realize what a unique gift these words were until I found myself repeating them, over and over, to friends in America. But back then, I didn't realize how good I had it in France overall. I had no real basis for comparison. True, when I spoke to my friends who'd become mothers back home in the States, I was struck by how grim and strange their lives sounded. One friend warned, as my first pregnancy advanced, "You'd better stop trying to have a career." Another was spending her entire after-tax salary on child care. And another, after eight grueling years of medical school and internships, was feeling guilty about leaving her baby with a part-time sitter to pursue her career as a psychiatrist.

All this sounded crazy to me. I figured my friends had to be bringing their problems upon themselves. The one who wouldn't fire an obviously inadequate nanny? Well, she'd always suffered from liberal guilt. The one who drove herself to a state of nervous exhaustion after a year of sleepless nights in the "family bed"? Well, she had a problem with separation anxiety. This all seemed very foreign. I just couldn't relate.

And then I moved back to America.

I came to Washington, D.C., when my elder daughter was three and a half and my younger daughter was six months old. With "child-care issues" (read: no sitter) keeping me from work, I started spending a lot of time hanging out on the playground and, for the first time, discovered the world of stay-at-home moms. It was an eye-opening experience.

The women around me, for the most part, lived in affluent suburban Washington communities. They had comfortable homes, two or three children, smiling, productive husbands, and a society around them saying they'd made the best possible choices for their lives, yet many of them seemed just miserable. One woman told me she'd lost all interest in sex with her husband. She was just too bored. Another one said that her husband had lost all interest in sex with her. He was just too tired—up at dawn, at work all day, at client dinners in the evenings, and then semiconscious in front of the TV for the hour at night when she saw him. She had become obsessed with organizing a school fund-raiser. Another mom complained of spending her weekends in her car, shuttling between soccer and swim meets and birthday parties. And another had taken up the politics of play dates as an issue in therapy.

The women gathered in groups to let off steam and have a good time. They staged Happy Hours together. They assigned themselves dirty books to read in their book clubs. They had a sense that something was missing from their lives, but that something was elusive—not so easy to name as their semiabsent husbands; not so easy to point to as their lack of work (how, where, why should they work now? they wondered). It wasn't really community that these women lacked; they did, after all, have one another. It was something more. A sense that life should have led up to more than this. A nagging sort of disaffection.

It all reminded me a lot of Betty Friedan's *The Feminine Mystique*. The sense of waste. The diffuse dissatisfaction. The angst, hidden behind all the obsession with trivia, and the push to be perfect. And the tendency—every bit as pronounced among the mothers I met as it had been for the women Friedan interviewed—to blame themselves for their problems.

And yet Friedan had been writing in the prefeminist 1960s. The women she'd interviewed—middle-class housewives, many of whom were college graduates—had real, objective causes for their malaise. Society didn't offer them many choices for self-fulfillment beyond perfect wife-and-motherhood. Their employment options were limited; even more so were their chances for having fulfilling careers. The solution Friedan dreamed of—that they could build their lives as they chose, become self-sufficient, and be fully self-realized human beings—had ostensibly come true for the women of my generation. Yet I saw, looking around, that the form of self-sufficiency we'd come into *wasn't* really a solution.

For the working moms I knew were stressed near the breaking point, looking tired and haggard and old. They shared the same high-level at-home parenting ambitions as the nonworking moms. But they held down out-of-home jobs, too—and if this wasn't enough, they also had to shoulder the burden of Guilt, a media-fed drone that played in their ears every time they sat in traffic at dinnertime: Had they made the right choices? Were their children well taken care of? Should they be working less, differently, not at all? Were they really good enough mothers? Did they really want to be? It seemed to me that although they were to all appearances fully liberated from the "Feminine Mystique" of Friedan's time, they, like the stay-at-home moms, were equally burdened by a new set of life-draining pressures, a new kind of soul-draining perfectionism. I came to think of this as the *Mommy* Mystique.

It was on the airwaves. In the parenting magazines. In the culture all around. It was in the local press, where I was surprised to see laudatory stories of "dedicated" mothers who spent their evenings and weekends driving to and from soccer, attending Girl Scout cookie meetings, über-momming, generally, twenty-four hours a day. I had never once, in almost six years, met a woman in France living her life at this level of stress. Not even my obstetrician—a woman in her forties with four children, who delivered babies at all hours of the day and night—came close.

I had friends in France who were full-time stay-at-home moms with three or four children, but I had never once encountered a woman whose life was overrun by her children's activities. I had never met a mother, working or otherwise, who didn't have the "time" to read a book, or have lunch with a friend, or go out to dinner once in a while. Nor had I ever met a mother who spent what little extra time she had on children's soccer or attending Girl Scout cookie meetings at eight o'clock at night. *Girl Scout cookie meetings? At eight o'clock at night?* The idea would have been absurd. No woman with a family life, the thinking would have run (once the laughter subsided), no woman who wanted to preserve her family life (which, after all, was anchored around her husband) would be out doing children's activities at night. Only an unbalanced person would be doing something like that. A woman insufficiently mindful of herself. A woman who was, perhaps, fearful of adulthood.

I was amazed at the breakdown of boundaries between children and adults and the erosion, for many families, of any notion of adult time and space. In Paris, children ate in the kitchen and played in their rooms. Living rooms and dining rooms were places where grown-ups entertained. In Washington and its suburbs, many houses were being built or had been renovated to eliminate formal living and dining rooms altogether. Instead, the focal point of most houses was the "family room," where a TV and a computer occupied center stage. I saw living rooms reconfigured as alcoves, almost afterthoughts, overrun with plastics or with no furniture at all. And very often, when children came to visit my house (which was too small to have a designated "family" entertainment complex), they jumped on the sofas and threw balls at the lamps.

I was angered by the continued onslaught of press reports about the pernicious effects of day care, and the continual beating-up on working mothers. I found the pressure to breastfeed for at least a year, to endure natural childbirth, and to tolerate the boundary breakdowns of "attachment parenting"—baby-wearing, co-sleeping, long-term breast-feeding and the rest of it—cruelly insensitive to mothers' needs as adult women. And I was amazed by the fact that the women around me didn't seem to find their lives strange. It appeared normal to them that motherhood should be fraught with anxiety and guilt and exhaustion. It didn't seem to dawn on anyone that there could be another way. I was shocked by the degree to which everyone—feminist or not—seemed willing to accept the "choices" given them, even to accept the idea that the narrow paths they'd been forced into living were choices.

The French women I knew did not have to live with the psychological burden of such "choices." They also did not have to do the mathematical calculations practiced by so many American mothers in evaluating whether or not to continue working: Who would come out ahead at the end of the month, mom or babysitter, and by how much? They did not have to buttress themselves against the psychological violence it does to someone who has striven for a goal all her adult life to suddenly discover that her contribution is not "valuable" enough to justify its continuation. They did not have to justify simply being who they were.

Back home in America, I began to think that the problems I'd once attributed to my friends' individual personalities weren't individual, or personal, problems at all. They were, it seemed to me now, symptoms of something much larger. And that something didn't just have to do with the fact that mothers in America didn't have the kind of life-enhancing social benefits I'd enjoyed in France. It had to do with something cultural, not just political, something so all-encompassing that it was all but invisible to the women who'd never had the opportunity to experience motherhood differently.

. . .

I LISTENED to my friends, listened to talk radio, to the mothers on the playground, and to my daughter's nursery school teachers, and I found it all—the general culture of motherhood in America— oppressive. The pressure to perform, to attain levels of perfect self- lessness was insane. And it was, I thought, as I listened to one more anguished friend wringing her hands over the work-family "balance," and another expressing her guilt at not having "succeeded" at breast- feeding, driving American mothers crazy.

Myself along with them.

It took very little time on the ground in America before I found myself becoming unrecognizable. I bought an SUV. I signed my unath- letic elder daughter up for soccer. Other three-year-olds in her class were taking gymnastics, too, and art, and swimming and music. I signed her up for ballet. I bought a small library of pre-K skill books. I went around in a state of quiet panic.

The financial burden of trying to set up a life similar to the one I'd had in France was overwhelming. The calculation was grim: the way things were going, if I wanted to keep on writing, working at home and seeing my children, I would have to take out a home-equity loan to pay my babysitter. Was it worth it? Was I really a good enough writer to justify the sacrifice? Or should I, at long last, just hang it up? The problem was, I wasn't all that good at being a stay-at-home mom.

I started to drink Calvados in the evenings.

At social events, the men and women separated out into two groups, the men discussing sports and stock prices and the women talking about their children. On vacation, the fathers took advantage of "their time" away from work to disappear for whole afternoons of fishing. The mothers continued their daily grind in a new locale.

This reversion to what I would once have termed 1950s-style sex roles wasn't necessarily so different from what I had witnessed among couples with young children in France. Yet there was one significant difference: in America, when couples found themselves sliding back into traditional "masculine" and "feminine" roles, a new power dynamic tended to fall into place as well, with the men distinctly coming out ahead. This was much less true in France—partly, I think, because many more mothers did work full-time and partly because, even in families where the husband was the sole wage earner, the cultural context that was leading American husbands to lord it over their wives was largely missing. Workaholism was frowned upon. Vacation was sacred, as were weekends and holidays. And no matter how hard they worked, no matter how much they tended to distance themselves from the drudgery of diapers and laundry, French men (unless they were the kinds of uncultured boors routinely mocked in movies and TV ads) did not permit themselves to retreat from domestic concerns altogether. They weighed in, as a matter of course, on areas that affected their quality of life: like food and home décor. "We are more 'feminine' than American men," a French diplomat in Washington mused to me. Whether or not that's so, it is true that the "feminine" realm in France is not routinely denigrated, as it is in the United States. And perhaps that's why, for French women my age, inhabiting a traditional "feminine" role as a mother doesn't feel like a tragedy.

Doing so in the States came as a shock to me. Ozzie and Harriet sex roles just weren't what I had expected to find back in America. I was a child of the 1970s, a feminist formed by the 1980s, a product of the girls-can-be-anything school of socialization, which rested on the idea that not only was biology not destiny, it was largely irrelevant. And I had truly believed, gazing back at my country from France, that American feminists had managed to secure for American women a sex-free public space in which they could operate with dignity as people first and women second. I remembered American women as smiling, sympathetic souls, self-possessed and forward-striding. Their prospects, I'd thought, were as unlimited as the blue sky that thrilled my eyes each time I came home and touched down at Kennedy Airport. American women, I'd thought, didn't have to fit into the gray landscape of Old World–style categories like wives or mothers. They were free to be themselves.

Some of this rosy view had been, no doubt, the symptom of a more general nostalgia for home. Some of it was fed by the only images of American women I had access to then: visions derived from CNN, where every woman, from Christiane Amanpour to Janet Reno, looked, from a distance, like an action hero. Women politicians and TV personalities in France all too often were the wives or mistresses of more powerful men, and French movies were filled with sultry consumptives and tooth-baring madwomen. The American movies I saw on the Champs-Élysées in those years were full of virile female stars: Demi Moore as G.I. Jane and a kickboxing Ashley Judd and a blackbelt René Russo breaking heads while pregnant and a whole slew of new women warriors looking fabulous as they ran around with walkie-talkies and guns. I'd leave the theater after watching these American Amazons, see the French women lighting their cigarettes, tugging on their male companions' arms, and pouting their way off into the night, and I'd think: God Bless America. We're doing something right.

Now, back in the United States, I was belatedly realizing that there was a big difference between my memory of young womanhood, my faith in the far-reaching changes wrought by feminism, and the reality of motherhood in America. There was also a big gap between the virility projected by actresses on-screen and the vulnerability felt by the women who watched them. Indeed, I had a new take now on why there had been such a spate of hard-fighting comic book heroines on the American screen during the years I'd been away, the years in which my generation of women had fully come of age professionally and embarked upon motherhood. It wasn't for a sense of identification, not at all. It was to escape—from the feeling of powerlessness brought on by a society that made superhuman demands. To escape the impossible demands of motherhood in particular, just as men had always escaped via superhero movies from impossible demands for power and productivity.

I wondered: How did two generations of feminism bring us here? Why did life feel so difficult? Why, with all our rights and privileges, with all our opportunities and, for some, riches, hadn't we achieved a decent quality of life—that is to say, a life that included time for ourselves and some sense of satisfaction?

In the Spring of 2001, an editor at the *Washington Post*'s "Outlook" section asked me to write a first-person piece comparing ideals of women's equality in France and America. After turning the topic around in my head for a number of weeks, I ended up writing about how my own ideas on the nature of real-life equality had changed: whereas once I'd mocked the French culture of *"différence"* and seduction and had believed that American women were more politically and socially evolved, since moving back to America as a mother I'd come to agree with many European observers that American women, despite their surface equality, lived "dogs' lives." It was time, I suggested, to shift the focus of our political debates away from parochial notions of equality and concentrate more on working to guarantee us all—men, women, and children alike—a decent quality of life.

In the days following the article's publication, I received dozens and dozens of e-mails from readers. Some women wrote me to protest the depiction of their mothering styles as "dogs' lives." But they were surprisingly few. Many more wrote to agree with me—and to ask for more. Why wasn't anybody else writing about this? they asked. Why wasn't anyone else focusing on the issue of quality of life? Could they tell me their stories? Could we keep in touch? Meet for coffee? Did I plan to write a book?

Over and over again, I heard the same refrain: You're right. There's a problem. Life doesn't have to be this way. It's time to take a step back and figure out how to make things better.

Over the course of the next year, I interviewed close to 150 women about their experience of motherhood in America. I talked to equal numbers of working and stay-at-home moms. About half the women were from Washington and its suburbs and the rest were from all around the United States. The majority were white. Many were African-American. Most were American, although a fair number either had grown up overseas or were from families that had only recently settled in the U.S. Almost all were college-educated. Some were well off, others struggled to make ends meet, and most were somewhere in the middle. Their children ranged in age from babies to young teenagers.

I tried not to interview women who were super-superwealthy—the social X-ray types ridiculed in *The Nanny Diaries* or the "New Economy Parents," with their $60,000-a-year nannies, kiddie limo services, and "family chaos consultants" featured in *Business Week*. I also did not interview working-class or poor women—not because I wasn't interested in them, but because I quickly saw that giving sufficient attention and understanding to their experiences was beyond the scope of what I could do with this book.

My goal was to write about the middle class. I soon realized, however, that it is very hard to write about the middle class in America *without* excessively focusing on the upper middle class. (Every other book on "American" motherhood that I have read, from *The Feminine Mystique* to Jessie Bernard's *The Future of Motherhood* to Naomi Wolf's *Misconceptions,* suffers the same fate.) And that is because the influence of the upper middle class is disproportionate in American culture. It is upper-middle-class homes that we see in movies, upper-middle-class lifestyles that are detailed in our magazines, upper-middle-class images of desirability that grace the advertising destined for us all. The upper middle class is our reference point for what the American good life is supposed to look like and contain. This has always been true in America, but became more so in the late 1990s, when the "luxury fever" of the boom years pushed everyone—rich and not-so-rich—to mimic the spending patterns, the ambitions, and the competitive keeping-up-with-the-Joneses of the wealthy. It is because of our overidentification with the upper middle class that so many of us came out of the boom years of the late 1990s so terribly in debt. It is also why so many of us turn ourselves inside out trying to parent to perfection, so that our children will be "winners."

The ways of the upper middle class affect everyone—including, to their detriment, the working class and the poor. And this is because our politicians hail, almost exclusively, from the upper-income reaches of our society. Thus to understand the conflicts and, I would say, the *pathologies* of upper-middle-class thinking is to understand the often perplexing state of family politics in America. As a woman who worked with Hillary Rodham Clinton on child care put it to me, "The whole problem of the upper class making policy is that they have choices and they're conflicted about their choices. The women have the conflict about whether they want to stay home or go to work and the men have the conflict of wanting women to have choices but also wanting their wives to stay home. The people making the policy are not the people enjoying the policy, so they're just conflicted for themselves and making policy for people who don't have the choice."

The middle-class and upper-middle-class women I interviewed for this book were strikingly similar in their attitudes toward motherhood, whatever their race, cultural background, or geographic location in America may have been. On the big issues there were no real differences between working and nonworking mothers, either—a fact that, though it flies in the face of received wisdom about the Mommy Wars—didn't surprise me, given my own experience of having moved between the worlds of working and stay-at-home motherhood.

It wasn't just that the working mothers and stay-at-home moms I interviewed felt similarly about motherhood. It was that they *went about it in much the same ways*. The "stay-at-home" moms very often worked part-time, either from their homes or in an office. Like the working mothers, they were dependent on child care. Indeed, one study I read about actually showed that *one-third* of "nonworking" mothers were *putting their kids in day care for an average of eighteen hours a week by the time they were twelve months old.* And the "working mothers," very often, worked only part-time. Meaning that if their kids were of school age, they saw them for about the same number of hours each day as did the stay-at-home moms.

Many studies have borne these similarities out. At the turn of the millennium, for example, we commonly heard that 64 percent of American mothers worked. In reality, though, just a minority of those mothers were working full-time. Only a third of married mothers with children under six were working full-time year-round, and fully two-thirds of mothers were working less than forty hours a week during their key career years. Indeed, the definition of "working" used to derive the Department of Labor percentages for "working mothers" in America is so all-embracing that it catches many women who would probably consider themselves stay-at-home moms. It includes mothers who work part-time (sometimes as little as one hour a week), mothers who work only seasonally (as little as one week out of the year), mothers who work from home part-time, or mothers who work part-time without pay for a family business.

Clearly, the mothers we see represented in the media replays of the Mommy Wars—the militant stay-at-home moms and the round-the-clock workaholics—are very much the exception to the rule. Yet their images—and their alleged conflicts—tend to dominate our notions of contemporary motherhood. And the pressure to live up to their extreme examples inspires much of the sense of inadequacy that plagues us all. One of my most treasured goals for this book is to put the notion that mothers are profoundly divided—in calling, "values," and style of life—to rest.

. . .

RACE, geographic location, self-identification as a working or stay-at-home mother—none of this made a real difference in the attitudes and mothering styles of the women I interviewed. What did matter, however, was something more intangible: a kind of personal philosophy. The more women bought into the crazy competitiveness of our time, the more they tended to suffer as mothers. Those who, in one way or another, managed to step outside of the parenting pressure cooker tended to have a greater degree of peace of mind and to mother with a greater level of sanity. They did not push themselves or their children to be "winners"—and so seemed to me to be winning out in terms of happiness and quality of life.

I "spoke" with about half of the women I interviewed for this book via the Internet—sending out questionnaires that they answered in essay form. I interviewed the other half in person. We would meet in the evenings, in groups of eight or ten, everyone "playing hooky" from their families, grinning complicitously and chortling pleasantly at the sound of the on-duty dad putting our hostess's kids to bed upstairs. (Meetings in my own home were the exception; my husband worked nights.)

The enthusiasm and excitement were incredible. Total strangers opened their homes to me, invited friends, and put out food for conversations that stretched as late into the night as the next morning's wakeup time allowed. Friends passed the word on to their friends, who spoke to their friends, until, by the end, I had to stop interviewing for sheer lack of time and the mental and physical resources necessary to transcribe and digest all the material.

When our conversations took off, it was exhilarating. It was exhausting. It felt, I imagined, like the consciousness-raising groups of the early days of the second-wave feminist movement (groups that, as a four- or five-year-old, I would not have attended and which took place, in any case, in universes far from my home). The women came to my groups with a sense of mission. They were going to get at the roots of the problems that plague mothers today. (Which some of them called "guilt," some of them called the Mommy Wars, and one of them, a working-mom-turned-stay-at-home, called "feeling like Alice down the rabbit hole.") They were going to find a way out. I always started off the sessions by telling the women about my move from France to America, and about how my shock at how difficult motherhood was here had grown into my book. Sometimes, toward the end of the evening, the tables turned, and they would ask me for some answers. What was the solution? they'd ask. How could we all calm down, feel better, and parent with the relative ease and insouciance that I'd felt as a mother in France?

I heard the questions with a kind of shame. I knew there were some mothers who managed to rise above the excessive nonsense of our times and work out ways to parent with reason and balance. Some of them came to my groups: the successful working mother with the stay-at-home husband, the stay-at-home mother of four who braved universal disdain to put her youngest children (twins) in part-time day care, the mother who stood out on her front lawn with bubbles and toys until the neighborhood kids stopped, and stayed, and enough trust was built among the parents that they started letting their kids run house to house. But I was not one of them.

In fact, as my time back in America lengthened from months into years, I became more and more bound up in all the aspects of motherhood I'd once found strange. The more I reconnected to the world I'd known as a young adult before leaving for France, the more I grew back into the person I'd always been here—a relatively typical, if quirky, would-be overachiever—and the worse I felt about myself as a mother.

In Paris, I'd felt very good about myself just for mothering according to my inclinations. Since I was an American, those inclinations were far more hands-on than those of the women around me, and so I'd easily enjoyed a somewhat smug sense of superiority. Simply by doing things I *enjoyed*—reading to my daughter for hours on end, taking her out to lunch and telling her stories, sitting on the edge of the sandbox in my sneakers, rather than perching peevishly on a park bench and smoking—*just by smiling*—I felt I was earning a perpetual merit badge for Good Motherhood. I had no qualms about eliminating those activities I found needlessly boring or stupid—like the lap-sit story hour at the nearby American Library, with the fish-out-of-water mommies clutching little plastic bags of Cheerios. If it wasn't fun, I figured, what was the point? If my daughter and I were doing some kind of added-value activity together and it wasn't a pleasure, then why bother?

In ever-smiling America, I was learning, it was actually a lot harder to maintain my sense of fun in motherhood. This was in part, for me, because the things I'd considered the simple pleasures of motherhood were harder and harder to come by. Things like pushing the stroller somewhere pretty for a walk—alone or with a friend. There was too much suburban sprawl and our lives were too atomized. Or things like spending lazy weekend days in the park or with another family. Everyone was too busy with "activities." It was hard to spend time just sort of vegetating in the sun because our kids, overstimulated by daily story hours and Gymboree, couldn't just play in the sandbox, or run around the flagpole, or climb without running to us every five minutes. Without our having constantly to explain, interpret, *facilitate* the world for them. (*"What that lady is saying is, she would really prefer you not empty your bucket of sand over her little boy's head. Is that okay with you, honey?"*)

Maybe our children could have run off and played. If we'd let them. But we didn't. There was so much pressure to always be *doing* something with or for them. And doing it right. And I was increasingly feeling that I was doing everything wrong. As a mother. As a woman. As a human being.

A year went by and I could not find a reliable babysitter. I put my elder daughter in a D.C. public school and watched the light in her eyes go dim. (Her kindergarten teacher there told me he'd put all *his* kids in private school.) I did not have a pediatrician available for human contact in an emergency (being given the "opinion of the practice" by one of his nameless nurses when my younger daughter cut her face open just didn't do the trick). I felt like all responsibility for my daughters' care, health, and education resided within our family. Often enough, it seemed to rest on my shoulders alone.

Sometimes now, when I berated myself for any one of my many shortcomings as a mother (I did not do enough ball-playing; I did not have a sufficient variety of arts-and-crafts supplies; I had not [yet] converted my basement into the requisite playroom), I was reminded of the way a friend in Paris—an American married to a Frenchman— had laughed at me when I'd once expressed guilt about sending my toddler daughter off to six hours a week of preschool. "Do you have a mini arts studio in your home?" she'd asked. "Do you have a playhouse and a variety of tricycles? Can you provide new sources of fun and stimulation every day?" The answers were, obviously, no on all counts. The mere idea of having all that equipment at home had seemed absurd. In fact, when she put things that way, it began to seem absurd to keep a child at home when so many wonderful opportunities existed on the outside.

But in Washington, everything was different. The homes around me *were* equipped like mini arts studios. Many people had backyard equipment that rivaled public parks. And there was a sense that whatever was done at home was best. Anything "institutional," as people put it, was far lesser—a sad replacement for the at-home loving care a good mother could provide by herself.

I tried to do it all myself: be mommy and camp counselor and art teacher and prereading specialist (and somehow, in my off-hours, to do my own work). I tried my absolute best. And like so many of the moms around me, I started to go a little crazy.

I spent night after night arranging toys by color and type in the basement and lining up children's books in size order on the bookshelves.

I spent hours on the phone with other mothers, arranging play dates and negotiating birthday party days.

People said I was "organized."

Sometimes, for no apparent reason, I broke out into hives.

Everything was spinning out of control.

THE DAY BEFORE the Iraq war started, with my French au pair fleeing the country like a rat from a sinking ship, this book (officially) due in one week's time, and a surveillance helicopter hovering over my garden, which happens to abut a Jewish preschool, I spent an entire morning frozen before the pages of a mail-order catalogue, unable to decide whether to order the Hello Kitty basic package for my soon-to-be three-year-old's birthday party or to order the deluxe set with Mylar balloon. The Mylar balloon seemed *incredibly important*. When it arrived, it promptly broke.

> A *stay-at-home mom:* "*I don't know how you're going to write a book when you have a birthday party to plan.*"
> A *working mom:* "*I wish I had time to obsess on Hello Kitty.*"

I had not dug my car out from under the eighteen inches of snow that covered it on the day I planned to hand-deliver my daughters' summer-camp applications. As a result, they were placed on a wait list. The letter announcing this came decorated with drawings of happy campers' faces. Without camp, I had no child care.

"It is impossible to live life at this level of pressure!" I screamed at my husband.

He said, "It is fodder for your book."

There was fodder, fodder everywhere (and nothing was getting written).

It was in the toy store, on a Saturday afternoon, when I heard a strange noise coming from the developmentally correct drum aisle and realized that, under a baseball cap, a mommy was crying.

"Don't worry," her friend told her. *"This weekend, we'll get dressed up and go to a bar and feel really sexy."*

"It won't make any difference," the crying mom said.

IT WAS ON THE PHONE as my psychiatrist friend agonized over the fact that her toddler son had needed emergency room treatment. "They held him down! They gave him an IV! I felt I had failed him for letting this happen!"

It was in my living room, night after night, and day after day, as women told me stories of their fears and their failures, their frustrations and their rituals and their bizarre, ever-increasing obsession with mindless trivia.

One woman told of having taken her eighteen-month-old, not-yet-speaking son, to see a team of speech therapists. When, a few weeks—and a few hundred dollars—later, they submitted their report, it read, "He feeds himself with a spoon but he scrapes his teeth. He has trouble gauging fluids from an open cup."

He was speaking by then. The mother threw up her hands in a gesture of absurdity.

"Oh, early intervention," another rushed in. "The stakes are so high. How can you *not* get your child tested? Let's say he had a problem and you missed the opportunity and he'd *never . . .*"

. . .

ONE MOTHER laughed ruefully as she recalled the time she blasted out of work early in order to buy her son some new Yu-Gi-Oh! cards, fell down the escalator in the Metro, cut her knee deeply, and then, as a crowd gathered, sat there dumbly, contemplating her bare bone, and frantically trying to figure out how she'd still make it to the store before it closed.

Another told a group how she spent every Sunday cooking and filling her freezer with nutritious meals for her family. "And then they only eat Weaver chicken nuggets." She laughed.

It was like she'd thrown down a gauntlet.

"I have an *extra* freezer in my basement," another woman asserted.

I heard of a Montessori school that had to cancel a field trip because it had drawn too many parent volunteer chaperones—*not one of whom* was willing to step down and stay home. I heard of a progressive private school that put in place a team of room parent supervisors to keep the regular room parents from feuding. (The supervisors then feuded among themselves.)

Many of the women felt that what they were doing was ridiculous. But they—but we—couldn't stop. Because to stop—to let go—would have been to let things spin out of control even more than they already seemed to be.

I SAW WOMEN trying out all kinds of solutions—ways to create order, assert control, and appease the existential anxiety that ruled their lives. They tried fifteen minutes of floor time and complex activity charts and family meetings to reinforce good behavior and breed good feelings and family dinners where everyone would "connect." But the family dinners never happened, and the meetings were spent explaining the charts, and the good feelings evaporated into rage when the husbands could not—would not!—understand the charts, and the children were begging off the activities anyway, because, they said, it was "just too much."

The anxiety was so palpable. The desire to contain it with magical acts of control was so clear.

And yet it was almost impossible to get at the sources of the fear. ("Stop!" one woman shouted, when I brought up financial anxiety. "You're freaking me out!") Other lines of questioning hit a similar brick wall. Women could rant for hours about their husbands' household uselessness, then avert their eyes and fall silent if I asked if they felt they'd lost power and status in their marriages. Similarly, the very same women who turned themselves inside out trying to create a perfect world for their children greeted suggestions that society might work to create a better world for all families with sharp hostility. *"Do you want the federal government raising your children?"* was the snarl, at the mention of the word "society."

I knew what had worked for me in France. It wasn't just that I had had access to a slew of government-run or -subsidized support services; it was also that I'd had a whole unofficial network of people to help and support me—materially and emotionally—as I navigated the new world of motherhood. There was the midwife who'd appeared as if by magic on day four in the hospital, to offer tissues as I succumbed to the tears of the "baby blues," and who'd said, matter-of-factly, "Everything is coming out now. Blood, milk, tears. You have to let it flow."

There was my local pharmacist who, unasked, filled my shopping bag with breast pads. The pediatrician who answered his own phone. The network of on-call doctors who made house calls at any time of day or night. The public elementary school principal who gave us a personal tour of her school and encouraged us to call her if we had any questions. In short, an extended community of people who'd guaranteed that I was never, from the moment I became a mother onward, left to fend for myself alone.

I was not naïve enough to think that, economically or politically, we could adapt the French system here, but I did believe that we could learn much from its psychology: that if you support mothers materially, you support them emotionally, and this support translates into a much lower level of anxiety, and a much greater level of mental freedom. I knew that there was a kind of existential safety to be derived from a world in which there were structures in place to help you take care of your children: Day-care centers that had guaranteed standards of quality. Public schools whose early-education programs were a source of national pride. Small things, independent of government support: reasonably priced agencies that could be counted on to provide quality babysitters, a community center that made referrals to child-care services. And there was much inspiration to be gleaned from a culture in which the needs of the mother were considered every bit as central to family happiness as the needs of the child. This was a mindset that translated into a much more humane approach to motherhood than the hubristic perfectionism we practiced here: friends who, instead of trading tips on how to pump breast milk in the office, would acknowledge that, after a few months, it was acceptable to stop breastfeeding in order to start feeling like yourself again. Pediatricians who prescribed taking care of yourself as a precondition to taking good care of your children. A general message that it was a bad thing to go it alone. And that all-or-nothing situations were bound to be disasters.

I realized, listening to the silences that fell sometimes in my interview groups, that there are things that are sayable and unsayable about motherhood today. It is permissible, for example, to talk a lot about guilt, but not a lot about ambition. You can talk a lot about sex (or its lack), but not about the feelings that are keeping women from sleeping with their husbands. You can talk about society's lack of "appreciation" of mothers and the need for more social validation—but not about policy solutions that might actually make life better.

You cannot really challenge the American culture of rugged individualism. Because beyond the pretty words we have about "caring" or "community" (words that tend to get the government off the hook), we lack the most basic notions now of what a different kind of culture might look or feel like.

It began to seem to me that, like the inane trivia that blocks so many mothers' minds when life becomes too much, there is a kind of fog surrounding the issue of motherhood today, a mess of diversionary thought keeping women from thinking clearly about what is happening in their lives and what they can do to change it.

There is a web of beliefs, so close to the bone as to be indiscernible, that blocks women from thinking their way out of the culture of motherhood that so fatigues them. These beliefs form the psychological weight that makes motherhood in America so arduous. I call this web of belief the Mommy Mystique because I think that, like Friedan's Feminine Mystique, it is, above all, a form of self-blinding. It rests on an almost religious adherence to ideas about child-rearing, about marriage and sex roles and society that supports the status quo even as mothers denounce it, even as children complain about it, even as "the experts" warn that our way of doing things is stressing children to the core.

THE MOMMY MYSTIQUE tells us that we are the luckiest women in the world—the freest, with the most choices, the broadest horizons, the best luck, and the most wealth. It says we have the knowledge and know-how to make "informed decisions" that will guarantee the successful course of our children's lives. It tells us that if we choose badly our children will fall prey to countless dangers—from insecure attachment to drugs to kidnapping to a third-rate college. And if this happens, if our children stray from the path toward happiness and success, we will have no one but ourselves to blame. Because to point fingers out at society, to look beyond ourselves, is to shirk "personal responsibility." To admit that we cannot do everything ourselves, that indeed we need help—and help on a large, systematic scale—is tantamount to admitting personal failure.

Comforted by the Mommy Mystique, we are convinced that every decision we make, every detail we control, is *incredibly important.*

Entire towns turn themselves inside out for a spot in the right ballet class. Parents prostitute their souls for spots in private schools. We read about how our children can't get into good colleges unless they are superhuman. We know that our public school systems can't provide an education in superhumanness (much less basic well-roundedness, in many places). Without a good college education our children won't be able to get jobs, won't be able to pay back their college loans (tuition having become unaffordable for so many of us), won't be able to buy a house or have the middle-class existence our parents seemed to find easy but that we can barely sustain. Ergo: soccer and violin and public service and weekends of baseball practice become *vitally important* because if we don't do everything right for our children, they may be consigned, down the line, to failure. To loserdom.

We are consumed with doing for our children in mind and soul and body—and the result is we are so depleted that we have little of ourselves left for ourselves. And whatever anger we might otherwise feel—at society, at our husbands, at the experts that led us to this pass—is directed, also, just at ourselves.

Or at the one permissible target: other mothers.

2.

The *New* Problem That
Has No Name

LIFE'S WORK

The old illusions of what life was supposed to hold, the restless re-
mains, the undefined dreams do not die as they were supposed to.
Probably every educated wife has found herself staring at a moun-
tain of dirty diapers and asking herself desperately, "Is this all
there is?" And at the same time she is embarrassed by her dissatis-
faction; she, of all people, with her intelligence and realistic view of
life, should be able to rise above it. But the paradox is that it is she
who is least able to. She lives for a better day. Things will be eas-
ier when this baby is born, or that one toilet-trained, or the children
are all in school; and she will have time to be pretty and intelligent
and young again.

NORA JOHNSON, *THE CAPTIVITY OF MARRIAGE*, 1961

FORTY YEARS AGO, there began to be much serious talk about a
creepy not-wellness afflicting the most fortunate American wives and
mothers.

Smart women, loaded with energy, and relieved, thanks to labor-saving devices, of much of the time-consuming household work that had taken up their mothers' lives, were losing themselves in make-work and trivia. "What has modern woman done with the four or five hours she used to spend at the wash line? Chances are she has let herself be dragooned into doing something that is just as tiring and time-consuming," said *Redbook*. "She is working on one more committee, helping out at a pre-kindergarten art group or collecting furniture or clothing for the town swap shop . . . permit[ting] the time saved by [the] mechanical devices to be wiped out by increased standards of performance." One woman who described her typical day of high-intensity homemaking and child-rearing complained, "By noon I'm ready for a padded cell."

A recent revolution in the social sciences had rejected the view that children were born with an innate set of traits that would evolve into their adult personalities in favor of a belief in the power of the environment. Starting in the early 1960s, greater awareness of the work of Jean Piaget and other, more recent advances in cognitive psychology shed new light on early learning and the potential for parents to enhance their young children's intellectual abilities. As the decade advanced, best-selling authors of child-care guides like R. Fitzhugh Dodson and Dr. Spock became influential popularizers of the new science of the mind. Children were not just born bright and successful, they taught; they could be made that way. Provided, of course, they had a mother (it was always a mother then) with the necessary degree of devotion and enlightenment to bring their gifts to light. "Armed with the accumulated knowledge of science about what goes on inside the mind of a child, a loving and concerned mother can learn how to raise that child to become a happy and intelligent adult," said Dodson in his 1970 best-seller *How to Parent*. Spock explained, "We have learned from psychoanalytic studies that the influence that makes a very few individuals become extraordinarily productive or creative in their fields is, most often, the inspiration they received from a particularly strong relationship with a mother who had especially high aspirations for her children."

This, of course, created a huge new responsibility for mothers. They not only had to feed, clothe, and provide for their children correctly, they also had to create the conditions that would allow their inner potential to be maximized. The sociologist Philip Slater, observing Spockian parenting in his trenchant book *The Pursuit of Loneliness,* put it thus: "The parents under the old method felt they had done their job well if the child was obedient, even if he turned out dull, unimaginative, surly, sadistic and sexually incapacitated. Spockian parents feel that it is their responsibility to make their child into the most all-around perfect adult possible, which means paying a great deal of attention to his inner states and latent characteristics. . . . Most middle class, Spock-oriented mothers believe, deep in their hearts, that if they did their job well enough all of their children would be creative, intelligent, kind, generous, happy, grave, spontaneous and good—each, of course, in his or her own special way."

Mothers felt overwhelmed by their new responsibility for not only the health and welfare but the psychological well-being and potential of their children. "This was to be our life's work," was how writer Anne Roiphe remembered early 1960s motherhood, forty years later. "I knew that my baby was my destiny, and my worth would be judged by how well she thrived. Each mother knew that if her child developed a tick, a stammer, a fear of vacuum cleaners, or excessive shyness, she would be blamed."

Many women reported suffering from identity crises. They felt isolated in the suburbs, far from friends and their families, and the traditional support systems of other female relatives that their mothers had enjoyed. They felt tied down to their homes, as though they had no time for themselves. They lost their tempers and "hollered" at their children. They relieved some of their tension and boredom and loneliness through activities. There was PTA membership and library volunteering and, of course, the endless rounds of chauffeuring that their children demanded.

The problems were particularly acute, the experts said, for college-educated women, who'd embarked upon adulthood expecting to have egalitarian relations with men. They too, after all, like the men in their lives, had been trained in logical thinking. To be task-oriented and rational. To solve problems and find solutions. And they'd also been led to expect that a "companionable marriage" (as the women's magazines put it) would be the next step. The experts told them they would have the most progressive marriages the world had ever seen. All the talk was of "sharing" and romantic love and communication and great sex, and a break with the dutiful, hierarchic marriages of an earlier generation. All these expectations ran aground when they married and became mothers. Motherhood, for one thing, was not a task-oriented activity. It could be mentally stultifying for a woman used to abstract thinking: "She vaguely feels that she is frittering away her days and that a half-defined but important part of her ability is lying around unused," wrote Nora Johnson, who anticipated Betty Friedan's watershed book *The Feminine Mystique* by two years with her June 1961 *Atlantic Monthly* article, "The Captivity of Marriage."

Educated women were *"'touched with a sense of grievance too vivid to put them at rest,'"* said Bruno Bettelheim in *Harper's Magazine* in 1962. "The ways in which we bring up many girls in America, and the goals we set for them are so strangely—and often painfully—contradictory that it is only too predictable that their expectations of love and work and marriage should frequently be confused, and that deep satisfaction should elude them. . . . After marriage, her schooling is for naught: the training of her youth is seemingly intended to fall away like an afterbirth. After years of apparent equality, it is made clear that males are *more* equal."

Most husbands, it appeared, had not read up on the new egalitarian marriages that the sociologists deemed the order of the day. They still wanted wives who were "a combination of Fannie Farmer and Marilyn Monroe," as one young wife complained. And, above all, they didn't want to hear that their wives were unhappy. "Problems? What kind of problems? My wife is well educated and in perfect health. We have three fine children and she doesn't have to have any more unless she wants to. She has the face and figure of a teenager and a closetful of clothes. She has a home of her own and sixteen different kinds of push-button machinery to do her housework for her. She has a car to drive. I take her out to dinner. . . . I am getting sick and tired of hearing about the problems of today's married woman!" a husband complained to *Redbook*.

Women were afraid of being called neurotic. So they put a little lipstick on and kept busy. They started doing their children's homework for them. They pushed their children into meaningless activities, whipped up competition within their communities—battled among friends—for the best birthday party, the best barbecue. They let their kids' social lives take over theirs, let their kids' lives consume them altogether, to give themselves, in the psychological parlance of the day, a "sense of significance." There was a sense, among many psychologists, that the pressures on women were cracking them apart. Tranquilizer use was on the rise; one such pill, Pacatal, was advertised as a way to "release the housewife from the grip of neurosis."

And at the fringes of the mainstream, some voices were emerging to suggest that the goal of therapy presented to women—"adjustment" to the "realities" of their lives—maybe was doing them more harm than good. Betty Friedan, for one, saw an epidemic of depression and anxiety and rage around her. She called it "The Problem That Has No Name." And she wrote, in *The Feminine Mystique,* that a culture-wide "mystique of feminine fulfillment" was driving women quietly insane.

Today, of course, we no longer worship women who, like the "happy housewife heroine" of Friedan's time, can find fulfillment in making their floors shine. The world has changed immeasurably for women since the early 1960s, when many of us would not have been able to get a credit card in our own names, would have needed our husband's permission to get a job, and would, when we graduated from college, have been given typing tests as a career counseling service.

We do have so many more options than did the women of Friedan's generation, who, if they didn't leave college altogether to get married, were herded, afterward, into the main female professions of teaching, secretarial work, and nursing and were subject to condescension and ridicule if they tried to branch out further into the typically "male" professions. We do not have to leave work now when our pregnancies start showing. Day care *does* exist—which it did not, for all intents and purposes, in the 1960s. We have antidiscrimination laws, access to contraception. The ideal that Betty Friedan dreamed of for women, that we'd be able to reach our "full human potential—by participating in the mainstream of society," is possible for us. It is inconceivable today that we might read, in a publication as mainstream as *Look* magazine once was, an exhortation to would-be working mothers as extreme as this 1966 "Memo to the American Woman": "Your husband cannot habitually cope with laundry, supper, blowing the children's noses—and keep his masculinity. . . . On the whole, women have less intellectual acumen than men . . . what woman has ever achieved the greatness of Einstein, Dostoevski, Beethoven or Buddha? . . . If you are determined to take on the responsibilities of an executive position, you must be just as willing to help your child with his homework and cook (or plan) your husband's dinner, or you will be a failure as a woman, and therefore, as a human being."

Yet, bizarrely, it is impossible to read the depictions of motherhood in Friedan's time without a shock of recognition. When the women's magazines captured the malaise of middle-class wives and mothers then, they *could have been describing us.* No matter how much the external conditions of our lives have changed, the private monologues that narrate our inner lives have remained to a large degree the same.

>*"I want status, I want self-respect. I want people to think that what I'm doing is important."*
>
>*"I am constantly worried about whether or not I'm doing or saying the right thing. . . . I feel pushed and pulled. Most of the time I'm under terrible pressure."*
>
>*"I have no time for myself, no life of my own. Every minute belongs to my family. . . . I feel like a pie cut up in six pieces being served to a dinner party of ten."*

So said the emblematic young housewife, circa 1960, quoted by *Redbook* to explain "Why Young Mothers Feel Trapped."

>*"I fear I cannot love enough or in the right way or in the right amounts . . . that I am not able to relax or feel comfortable in my role as a mother . . . that I am not sure I know how to be what my kids and husband need me to be. That I am not providing the home life I wanted to have when I was growing up."*
>
>*"There are crumbs under my toaster. . . . I want to weigh 125 pounds. . . . I want my baby to be very happy. . . . I want to spend enough time with my husband . . . have time to myself . . . read, tend to my nails . . . maybe a stroll in the park? . . . Do I give my husband enough attention? Does my baby love her nanny more than me?"*
>
>*"I put all my inadequacies in a row in the morning. All the things in my life that I'm not doing perfectly. My house isn't decorated enough for Halloween. I didn't really celebrate enough this big promotion my husband had at work. I have all these baby presents I haven't sent out. I should be making napkin rings with my kids."*

This is how three thirty- and forty-something mothers, working and not, explained to me in 2002 why they felt trapped by The Mess. Despite the fact that we could now ostensibly choose loftier and less self-immolating goals, we still strive for a kind of Donna Reed–inspired perfection in everything we do for our children.

One of the most widely quoted literary images of recent years was the opening scene from British journalist Allison Pearson's 2002 novel *I Don't Know How She Does It,* where frenetic working mom Kate Reddy stays up until 2 A.M. pounding mince pies she'd bought for a school bake sale to give them a homemade look. She doesn't have to do this, of course. No one expects it of her. But she has to. She just *has to.* There is another imperative at work, and it is stronger than whatever critical faculties may still exist in her mind, reminding her of what her life really is about. It is a kind of magical thinking in which compulsive, trivial acts will bring all the unruliness of life under control.

Here is how Kate Reddy's mind races when she relaxes at the end of a day at work at the bank: "Fruit jellies Uncle Alf. Travel sick sweets? Ask Paula collect dry cleaning. Personal shopper how much? Pelvic floor *squeeze.*"

And here is how a transportation consultant, a graduate of the Kennedy School, described to me the "immense stress" of her son's fourth birthday party:

> *First, there was the whole debate about whether to have the whole class or just a few friends. Then there was the whole debate about whether to do the party at home or whether to go to some place that does package deals. If we stayed at home, would we have the magician, the clown, the musician, the Moon Bounce? . . . I felt great angst about whether this measured up. How would the other mothers judge me for the decisions I made and would I be labeled in some neg-*

ative way? What does my decision indicate about our financial sta-tus, my organizational talents or lack of them, or our willingness to indulge our child? On the morning of the party, my stress was all about how our deck needed to be refinished, the flower beds needed to be edged and weeded, and I didn't have the perfect "mother of the birth-day boy" sweater to throw on over my jeans so that I looked chic yet casual.

How can we be so foolish? So caught up in trivialities? So small in our scope and in our concerns—so distant from the big issues? The questions just add another layer of guilt to the chorus of self-criticism already coursing through our minds.

I think we should give ourselves a break.

Because our trivia isn't really, at base, so very trivial. It is a screen for bigger, more unsayable thoughts: *Am I good enough? Do I matter? Are we rich enough? Can we compete?* It is symptomatic. A symptom of The Mess that we're in.

The Mess is a kind of black cloud in today's mothers' lives. It col-onizes our minds. Limits our thoughts. Pulls us away from our hus-bands and kills our sexuality. "When all the minutiae fill your brain, the stuff you carry around, and that to-do list, intimacy with your hus-band, sex, or just intimate conversation becomes another to-do-list item," says a former lawyer, now staying at home with her daughter. "Having that big to-do list desexualizes me. And it's really hard to get back into that feeling."

The Mess buzzes noisily, accusingly:

"Are the girls falling behind in their ice-skating skills?"

"Am I doing enough? Am I productive?"

"I should not have said 'Bad boy.'"

It is a wall of inner noise that blocks out other thoughts, thoughts that are really much more challenging than the daily contests of per-fection that we impose on ourselves, thoughts that lead places that we really don't want to go, toward problems that we really don't want to face. It blocks out problems that strike at the heart of our marriages, at our sense of ourselves as in-control women, and at our society's priorities and values.

These problems are really not so trivial, despite the trivializing forms we give them in our minds. They speak to serious issues: If you don't obsessively campaign to get your child into the ideal preschool, there is no adequate day care in your area; if your toddler doesn't go to Baby Music Class and pre-pre-Olympic tumbling and Mommy & Me, you will go insane because you are at home all the time and your husband works until 8:30 at night. . . . If you don't read every baby book cover to cover, scour the Internet for information, obsess on food labels, and put a *cordon sanitaire* around your child, you will wallow in ignorance and potentially allow your child to come to harm, since your pediatrician doesn't take phone calls and won't waste your ten minutes of appointment time on answering questions. Because you have no family nearby . . . because you want to do things better than your family did, anyway . . . because the responsibility for absolutely *everything* is resting on your shoulders, and this responsibility is so overwhelming that you have to shut the awareness of it down . . . The Mess steps in. And, when you think about it long and hard enough, take it apart, and question why it exists, The Mess stops seeming so trivial. It starts to seem something like a necessary way of life.

The upshot of all this is that, for all our progress, for all the advantages and opportunities we've had in our lives, many of us live motherhood as though we were back in the days of the Feminine Mystique. We have revived housework and handicrafts, taking them, via Martha Stewart and *Family Fun* magazine, to a level of fetishistic obsession. We have resurrected the idea of making our children our "life's work." And even more bizarrely, in many of our marriages we are reliving many of the patterns of sex roles and power that we thought would retire with our parents' generation.

Things like carrying the burden of family life almost single-handedly.

Things like using sex to get household money.

Things like settling—with age, anger, and not-caring—into living parallel lives.

A GENERATION OF CONTROL FREAKS

How could this have happened? Why is it that the most liberated and privileged generation of women America has ever seen has enslaved itself to such a restrictive, mentally binding image of motherhood?

The answer isn't simple. The Mommy Mystique isn't the work of any kind of "right-wing conspiracy." It isn't even, exclusively, a matter of our trying to fit into unrealistic, unnatural ideals imposed on us by the media or by that nebulous thing, "society." After all, like men, we now shape the media. We are fully part of society, not marginal to it. The demon images of perfect motherhood that haunt us are very largely of our own creation. They are not just a matter of what we think and what we do. They are part and parcel of *who we are.* And of how we were brought up—in a certain time, a certain place, and under the sway of a certain kind of politics.

I think of "us" as the first post–baby boom generation, girls of the 1960s and 1970s who came of age politically in the Carter, Reagan, and Bush I years. This roughly translates into women born from 1958 (the tail end of the baby boom, if you define the end of the baby boom as the first postwar drop in birth rate, which came by the end of 1957) through the early 1970s—a range of years that corresponds to the ages of the vast majority of women I interviewed for this book.

We are, in many ways, a blessed group. Most of the major battles of the women's movement were fought in our early childhood—or even before we were born. By the time we entered school, we were reaping the rewards of the women's movement as our natural due. More important, perhaps, as we grew up, we believed that we'd inherited a basically egalitarian world. Many of us did not think we had to be politicized as women or to think in terms larger than the minutiae of our daily strivings. Overall, we did not intend to change the world. Partly, this was because we did not generally believe that the world needed changing. And partly it was because disdaining a change-the-world attitude was part of our political culture. We had the privilege of being complacent, and developed the habit of looking down on our over-the-top, "bra-burning" feminist elders.

But there was a gap between the story we told ourselves—that our society told itself—about our generation's place in American women's history and where we really were. The seamless story of women's progress that underlay our self-image hid a number of contradictions. Chief among them: while the period of our childhood and coming of age were years of significant gains for women in the areas of reproductive freedom, the number of women in the professions, tougher job-discrimination laws, sexual-harassment laws, and guarantees of equal treatment in school and sports, they were also marked by some very significant failures. The Equal Rights Amendment, which would have greatly broadened the reach of existing antidiscrimination legislation, failed—largely because of fear-mongering by a small number of archconservatives. *Roe v. Wade*, which abortion rights proponents had hoped would establish a basic principle of female bodily integrity, did precisely the opposite. It opened our bodies to constant—and chronic—political warfare and regulation.

The *Roe v. Wade* decision and its often violent aftermath also forced the feminist movement, from the backlash years of the late 1970s onward, to largely telescope its political efforts from a wider range of women's and family issues to the abortion battlefield. The result was that the discourse of feminism narrowed and mutated as well. Control of the body—"choice"—became the focus of feminist politics. It also became the focus of right-wing politics. And it was, from the 1970s onward, increasingly the focus of wider American trends—the health food craze, the diet boom, the exercise obsession. Self-control, self-definition, independence, freedom of choice as consumerism—they all collapsed together in the "yuppie" era of the 1980s. And feminism, filtered down and diluted by the mass media, came to be, not about a redefinition of womanhood or a reorganization of family life and society, but about questions of performance and control. The American secular religion of self-controlling individualism, coupled with this newly narrowed form of feminism, shut down the prospect of finding collective solutions. "Keep your laws off my body" became the rallying cry, not "Let's change the body of law." This would prove to be a time bomb. For the emphasis on control of the body hid the fact that a larger politics that would have given women more permanent and far-reaching control of their lives—with real choices to carry them through all the phases of their lives, including motherhood—was nonexistent.

Most of us in the post–baby boom generation did not learn our feminism—that is to say, a sense of ourselves as women in an era saturated by feminism—through consciousness-raising sessions or marches. We learned it by going to school and through the popular media. The watered-down, power-through-control vision of female selfhood we imbibed became the backbone of our identity.

This vision had a very perverse effect on our sense of ourselves and of our place in society. Because, as both feminist and antifeminist forces made clear, our selfhood was wrapped up in our sexuality, which rested, largely, upon control of our bodies. Control—not empowerment. And control through what means? The only ones available to us then in the political landscape of the deeply reactionary Reagan and Bush years: self-control, personal achievement, self-perfection. This felt like empowerment, but it wasn't—not in the long term. For instead of using whatever tools of self-empowerment we had to gain control of our surroundings and change our world, we turned them inward and used them to police ourselves. Rather than becoming rebels or pioneers like our baby boomer predecessors, we became a generation of control freaks.

The signs were everywhere. Eating disorders. Lactose intolerance. The general popularity of one-size-fits-all food allergies. It was like an outbreak of modern-day hysteria: "epidemic" numbers of young women (these things were always called "epidemic" back then) couldn't eat, couldn't drink, couldn't exist in the world as they found it. But they could—and they did—make every effort to control their environment. Regulating, with astounding amounts of physical and mental energy, the intake and output from their bodies. This became so widespread that by the mid-1990s a chorus of experts had emerged to say that control-freakishness was the *normative* way for young women to deal with food and their bodies. I would say that, for our generation, it was the normative way of dealing with adult life generally.

How surprising is it, then, that when we became mothers, we took to purifying and regulating our children's environments—cheered on by parenting magazines and their advertisers, and reinforced in the sense of our rightness by the increasingly anxiety-filled world we saw around us?

Motherhood could, after all, have been profoundly destabilizing. Pregnancy, childbirth, lactation, they all meant a temporary loss of control—of our bodies and of our careers. In response to this lack of control, we adopted a whole new range of controlling behaviors. We approached the enormous upheavals of pregnancy and childbirth as though they were normal life events we could in some way control. We sought to prove our mastery of them, our self-sufficiency, through natural childbirth, "birthing plans," and Olympic-level breastfeeding. We became mothering perfectionists.

Fans of attachment parenting—the practice that dominates, in watered-down form, among the middle class and upper middle class today—we tried never to leave our babies alone. When we socialized, we brought the folding cribs. We allowed our friends to organize our social lives around *their* babies' sleep and eating schedules. We cooked our own baby food. If we had to leave our babies, we pumped milk. In our nonworking moments, we filled our babies' lives with enriching, entrancing, eyes-entwined-with-Mommy activities.

And as our babies grow up into children, we have to be there, too, all the time: on constant play dates, school committees, and field trips, braving the rush-hour traffic to shuttle back and forth to activities. Ever vigilant. Ever devoted. Ever in control.

And as life in post-9/11 America grows more and more fragile-seeming and fearful, as more and more people feel more disempowered, as the bills pile up and good jobs in many fields grow scarce, and talk of emergency evacuation plans makes us loath to open the envelopes sent home from school, we run faster and faster. We are vigilant, dutiful, and, above all, organized. And most of us do not stop and ask ourselves why life feels so crummy. We do not realize that we are digging ourselves deeper and deeper into a mess. We take for granted that life has to be the way it is because, in the larger context of our society and our collective psychology, it feels normal. But what we don't see is that, in fact, we have normalized a way of being that is not normal, or natural, or necessary.

It is a situation ripe for correction.

THE CHOICE MYTH

Over the course of the past few years, when I met with women to talk about their experiences of motherhood, the conversation very often began like this:

We are so lucky.

Everything is great.

We have choices.

We have freedoms.

We wouldn't have it any other way.

But then somebody would begin to tell her story. And it would sound something like this:

I'm somebody who was very career-driven. {But} I felt from the very beginning that I was being asked to make impossible choices and it didn't matter what you chose, that there was some large segment of society that would condemn you for it. And there was no support system to make any of those choices.

While (in my twenties) my career was very important to me, I also knew that having kids was really important, so I spent a couple of years trying to establish myself and then trying to get pregnant. I was a policy analyst and manager at {a government agency}. I chose to take six months off with each of my kids, which was entirely pay-free. I was lucky enough to negotiate that with my bosses—that's what you have to say: lucky enough. But to be sure that I would get back to things I was doing that were important to me I kept working all that time from home without pay. And when I came back, they'd given most of my work to young unmarried guys and I had to fight tooth and nail to get it back.

I never really got back my high-profile stuff. I had to change jobs, despite all my unpaid work. And then, on the first day back from my maternity leave after my second child was born, I was waiting for medical results—my daughter had had a tumor removed just a few days before, she was six months old and we didn't know whether she had cancer or not—my boss said, "What are you going to do?" And I said, "Well, I'm waiting to get my projects back. And he said, "Well, with one kid I could see it, but with two . . . maybe you should take on some other stuff." He said, "You seem very distracted today." I said, "It's my first day back and my baby may have cancer."

He said, "I have these two guys, they just came out of the Kennedy School at Harvard and they're willing to work twelve hours a day. They really want your stuff. What do you want to do? You have to decide if you're a mom or an analyst." I said, "I could sue you for what you just said." And he said, "Yeah, but you'd ruin your husband's career." My husband also worked at {the agency}. That was my choice. And over the next six months they just tortured me until I left.

Now {after a work-related car accident left her in chronic pain} I'm home on disability and everybody's like, "Isn't that a hidden blessing, now you're home with your kids?" And I think, No! It's horrible. I don't want to be home with my kids! I'm not good at this! This is not what I should be doing! But people don't want to hear that.

That would change the mood.

And then there would be other stories, like this:

I always imagined that I would earn a graduate degree in early childhood education and begin teaching college or open my own day care after having my own family. In reality, I quit working a few months before my daughter was born. And I have never reentered the workforce on a full-time basis since that time. I found that earning enough to pay for day care was impossible.

Or this:

I was very ambitious when I was in my twenties. I had hoped to be a high-powered finance executive. I didn't give much thought to the gender issue and figured since I was smart I could overcome any obstacles. Having kids has changed my perspective. . . . My husband is an attorney and wouldn't cope well on the Daddy Track, so we made the conscious decision to let him be the primary breadwinner.

Or this:

I found being a physician and a mother incompatible. Many other women seemed able to manage but I couldn't. . . . I found that society was up against me. Schools had no obligation to help working mothers. Day care ate up my salary. . . . I felt like I was living in hell. I felt betrayed by the promises of feminism. . . . With children it all seemed theoretical with no basis in reality. I was furious at the outside world and furious that women and men both conspired to keep the status quo. The solution was simple: I decided to switch {from being a psychiatrist} to a less demanding career, one that could easily be dropped temporarily so I could be "on call" for my family. But you can imagine the emotional toll in terms of identity, guilt over taking someone's place in medical school who would have gone longer, and guilt over not serving a vulnerable and needy population.

And before you knew it, we were back to The Mess.

(I found a similar pattern with the topic of marriage. Nearly every single woman I interviewed for this book said she was married to a "wonderful husband." But more on that later.)

Like the women of the early 1960s, the women I spoke with from 2001 to 2003 were suffering from a clash of expectations, popular rhetoric, and reality. That earlier group of women, members of the "Eisenhower generation," had attended college in far greater numbers than women ever had before and grew up believing they were the most "emancipated" women in the world. They entered the workforce in unprecedented numbers. For the most part, they did not perceive their lives as a story of oppression. They were told—they believed—that they had choices. "Nowadays, women have as many occupations open to them as men and can be selective in embracing them," wrote Phyllis McGinley, a popular magazine writer of the early 1960s, whose views were considerably more mainstream than Betty Friedan's. "We

can be physicians or ambassadors, advertising experts or golf professionals. Doctor, lawyer, merchant, chief—name a career and it is within
our reach. So when we choose to be housewives, we are only exercising free will, we enter that field with heads high and eyes open."

As young women, we had choices—endless choices. But motherhood made it often impossible to act on our choices. Or gave us
choices on the order of: You can continue to pursue your dreams at the
cost of abandoning your children to long hours of inadequate child
care. These were choices that didn't feel like choices at all. And they
came at the cost of our "full human potential." That is to say, at the
cost of keeping alive the various parts of ourselves—the ambitious
part, the nurturing part, the sexual part, the active part, the intellectual part, the domestic part—that combine to make us human.

Many women of the post–baby boom generation simply weren't
prepared to contemplate these kinds of choices. They didn't realize just
how bad the incompatibility would be between the total freedom of
their youth and the culture of total motherhood they'd encounter
once they had children. "I'm still feeling robbed that I have to make
a choice because I don't want to be choosing at all," a woman who formerly worked fifteen hours a day in the White House told me, describing her current, fumbling attempts to balance some semblance
of her old career ambitions against the demands of motherhood.

Many women tried, and continue to try, to make their our own
paths. They chip away at their freedom, tone down their careers. A
few brave souls even try to turn down the volume of their motherhood.
And yet, often enough, it just doesn't work. Their "choices" come back
to haunt them. Life doesn't *quite* work out. They believe then that
they have chosen poorly. They blame themselves, just as the women
of the early 1960s did. "Locked as we all were then in that mystique,
which kept us passive and apart, and kept us even from seeing our
real problems and possibilities, I, like other women, thought there was

something wrong with *me* because I didn't have an orgasm waxing the kitchen floor," wrote Betty Friedan, in 1973, of her Feminine Mystique years. Like the women of the pre-feminist 1960s, most women today almost never stop to think that perhaps the choices they've been offered aren't really choices to begin with.

What kind of choice is it really, after all, when motherhood forces you into a delicate balancing act—not just between work and family, as the equation is typically phrased, but between your premotherhood and postmotherhood identities? What kind of life is it when you have to choose between becoming a mother and remaining yourself?

No wonder so many women today—like their predecessors forty years ago—have the gnawing sense that something has gone wrong. No wonder so many of us are drowning in the mental sludge of The Mess. Something is missing, and it's something not so easy to name as semiabsent husbands, not so easy to point to as a lack of work, or too much work, or a lack of adequate child care. It's the sense that life should have led up to more than it has. A sense that after all the hard work, for all our achievements as individuals and as a "postfeminist" generation, life should be better than this. Because, for all our heroic efforts, we are playing a losing game. We have bought into a vision of motherhood that is leaving us completely burned out. And, like its predecessor, this *New* Problem That Has No Name is making women sick at heart.

ONE OF THE MOST SURPRISING THINGS about our current culture of motherhood is that while it inspires widespread complaint, it has not led to any kind of organized movement for change. As Ann Crittenden notes, in *The Price of Motherhood,* women not only haven't united to fight for change, they have tended to fight one another instead—namely, by buying into the media-stoked Mommy Wars. The feminist movement these days is all but silent on the issue of child care and truly silent on the question of middle-class mothers' general quality of life. (Happiness has never ranked high as a feminist political goal.) The media tend to give notice to studies showing the negative effects of day care and to every nanny horror story that comes their way, but don't report much on positive child-care alternatives. The political thinking that has held sway for decades is that family issues are primarily private concerns—amenable to, at best, private workplace solutions. (Never mind that the largest, most innovative, and highly rated child-care system in America is operated by the military.) As a result, American women tend to believe that what we've got is, for better or worse, as good as it can get. Whatever doesn't work is *our* problem, and it's up to us to find solutions.

This, I think, is the key to the Mommy Mystique. It is the essence of The Mess. It is the basic reason why our generation has turned all the energy that we might be directing outward—to, say, making the world a better place—inward instead, where it has been put to the questionable purpose of our own self-perfection.

Our baby boomer elders often call us selfish, but in doing so they miss a larger point: that what our obsessive looking-inward hides is at base a kind of despair. A lack of faith that change can come to the outside world. A lack of belief in our political culture or our institutions. Our outlook is something very much akin to what cognitive behavioralists call "learned helplessness"—the kind of instinctive giving-up in the face of difficulty that people do when they've come to think they have no real power.

The desperate, grasping, and controlling way so many women go about the job of motherhood, turning energy that could be used to demand social change inward into control-freakishness, is our hallmark as a generation. We have taken it upon ourselves as supermothers to be everything to our children that society refuses to be: not just loving nurturers but educators, entertainers, guardians of environmental purity, protectors of a stable and prosperous future. This ultimately impotent control-freakishness is the form of learned helplessness acquired by a generation of women confronted by a world in which finding real solutions to improve family life seems impossible. And it really needs to change.

For too many women in America are becoming sick with exhaustion and stress as they try to do things that can't be—shouldn't be—done. Too many are eaten up by resentment toward their husbands, who are not subject to the same heartless pressures. Too many are becoming anxious and depressed because they are overwhelmed and disappointed. Too many are letting their lives be poisoned by guilt because their expectations can't be met, and because there is an enormous cognitive dissonance between what they know to be right for themselves and what they're told is right for their children. Too many feel out of control.

Too many of us now allow ourselves to be defined by motherhood and direct every ounce of our energy into our children. This sounds noble on the surface but in fact it's doing no one—not ourselves, or our children—any good. Because when we lose ourselves in our mommy selves, we experience this loss as depression. When we disempower ourselves in our mommy selves, we experience this weakness as anxiety. When we desexualize ourselves in our mommy selves, it leads us to feel dead in our skin. All this places an undue burden upon our children. By making them the be-all-and-end-all of our lives, by breaking down the boundaries between ourselves and them so thoroughly, by giving them so much power within the family when they're very small, we risk overwhelming them psychologically and ill-preparing them, socially, for the world of other children and, eventually, other adults. Nursery school and kindergarten teachers are already complaining that our children are so indulged, made so royal at home, that they come to school lacking compassion for others and with real problems functioning socially.

In the way we go about mothering today, we communicate to our kids all our anxiety, our competitiveness, and our narcissism. And as everyone knows, children pick up on everything.

IN EARLY 2003, I spent a Sunday afternoon in the home of a friend, who writes for the *Washington Post.* While our daughters played with Barbies upstairs, we got out a map and plotted an escape route from Washington in the case of a terrorist attack. She used that anecdote later in the lead paragraph to a column about the anxieties of life under the threat of terrorism, called "Life in the Orange Zone." Almost immediately after the column ran, a reader called her to say, "The real reason you have to be anxious is that you let your girls play with Barbies."

This story, however ridiculous, is typical of an insidious trend in American thinking these days. There seems to be a society-wide refusal to think about the problems of motherhood in big-issue terms. There is a kind of mental allergy to talking about external causes for our woes. The mind rebels against external threats and fixates instead on controllable private nonsense. This is really too bad. For had women not been able to rise beyond what were termed their own "neurotic concerns" to see the bigger picture of their systematic inequality forty-odd years ago, we would not be living in the more egalitarian world we inhabit today.

The mess of the Mommy Mystique—the belief that we can and should control every aspect of our children's lives, that our lives are the sum total of our personal choices, that our limitations stem from choosing poorly and that our problems are chiefly private, rather than public, in nature—is *not* an individual problem that individual women should have to scramble to deal with. It is a social malady—a perverse form of individualism, based on a self-defeating allegiance to a punitive notion of choice; a way of privatizing problems that are social in scope and rendering them, in the absence of real solutions, amenable to one's private powers of control. It demands a collective coming-into-awareness, at the very least. And, I believe, once that awareness is reached, it cannot be cured without some collective, structural solutions.

But first we have to dig our way out of the mess. And replace the motherhood religion that reigns in our time with some real-life rationality.

PART 2

The Motherhood Religion

3.

The Sacrificial Mother

REMEMBER Shel Silverstein's classic children's book *The Giving Tree?* In it, a tree loves a little boy and he loves her back. He takes her leaves, climbs her trunk, swings from her branches, eats her apples, and sleeps in her shade. When he grows up, he sells her apples for money, cuts off her branches to build a house, and cuts down her trunk to make a boat. And then, when he's old and too tired to move, and she's nothing more than a stump, he sits down on her and rests.

Many people have read that story as a metaphor for motherhood. Martha Spice lived it.

Spice, a middle-aged mother of four, was the subject of a recent Mother's Day profile in the *Baltimore Sun*. A "thin, thin woman with chestnut eyes and a Joan-of-Arc haircut," she was presented as a paragon of self-sacrifice, a woman who "drives the kids to school, tends house, teaches, cooks, eats and breathes the mystically selfless process of motherhood."

Martha devoted herself—body, mind, and soul—to the education of her children, producing, home-schooling, three genius sons along the way. She protected them from their many food allergies ("typical of exceptional children") and starved herself in the process: "By the time infant Adam came along, Martha subsisted on a diet of chicken, bananas and water so she could breast-feed and not pass anything along to aggravate their illnesses. At 5-foot-8 she weighed less than 90 pounds. She went long stretches with three hours of sleep at night, if she slept at all."

She spent hours in her car. As she drove, her sons berated her for not going faster. She could not go faster, however (we learned), because she was blind in one eye. She could not even answer back to her hectoring sons, because she was in too much pain. Merely turning the steering wheel was causing her agony, because there was a catheter in her chest, and the catheter was slipping. There was a catheter in her chest because—and here was where the story veered to the irredeemably sinister—Martha had end-stage renal disease. She was being kept alive by peritoneal dialysis.

Fortunately for her, this had the advantage of being a do-it-yourself, at-home treatment. "A busy mother can stagger four fluid exchanges through the day and still keep up the family's routine—like shopping for groceries, taking the 15-year-old to get his hair cut or driving a 13-year-old to college," the *Sun* raved.

Martha had, of course, been told to slow down. (*"But with four children and a husband that travels, how do you slow down?"*) And so now, navigating the suburbs in her minivan, with her slipping catheter and her martyr's do, she was literally driving herself to death. She was, said the *Sun,* like a dirty bedroom slipper: "weary and old, just plain worn out." But that was okay, we read. Because Martha knew that she had fulfilled "her vocation . . . her life's true mission." She had made her "sacrifice," seen her last boy off to college, and now she was "done." Like a human giving tree about to be mulched, Martha was sapped, tapped of every iota of strength and spirit. She was ready to meet her Maker.

"Now," the *Sun* sighed, "it's just a matter of letting go."

AT ANOTHER TIME, in another place, this story of sacrificial motherhood would have read like an exercise in suicidal mania. But these days, it can pass for an inspirational parable. Giving Tree Motherhood (as American University law professor Joan Williams has called it) is *in*. And for many women, it is not just a lifestyle choice, it is a spiritual calling.

> *"For as long as I can remember I have been wrestling to find something that would give meaning to my life, something to feed my spiritual hunger, soothe my churning psyche, to ground me in the Now."*
> IRIS KRASNOW, *SURRENDERING TO MOTHERHOOD*, 1997

In this postfeminist era, with motherhood at last something chosen, not imposed; with assisted reproduction having made conception itself less a matter of miracles than of mechanics, it might seem surprising that all the old words so closely linked to religion—words like "vocation" and "mission" and "calling" and "sacrifice"—cling so tenaciously to the subject of maternity. But it really shouldn't come as a surprise.

After all, Americans make a religion of everything. It isn't just that we are an extremely religiously observant people. It's that our faith, our inspirational bent, leads us to constantly elevate *everything*—our ideas, our opinions, our tax policies, our diet crazes and stroller choices—to the level of theological doctrine.

"An air of Messianic expectation pervades the culture," the sociologist John R. Seeley wrote in 1967:

If devotion to an Idea, if ardor in its affectionate development, if the rendering of the idea immanent in the body of thought of the time, and if the pervasive embodiment of the idea in behavior are, as I believe, the hallmarks of a "religious" attitude toward it, then ideas are religiously treated in America. It is true that one religion readily succeeds another, but this is rather from the devotion to the general religious quest than from disloyalty to the particular religion abandoned. . . . Lastly, contradictory but coexistent . . . everything that is anything tends to become an industry. . . . Whether the matter is child-raising or "higher education" or "entertainment"—or even religion in the narrower sense—almost inevitably it is so organized and so put into "production."

It is no less with motherhood.

From the late eighteenth century, when evangelical Protestantism and Enlightenment rationalism combined to invest motherhood with world-making purpose, to today, when the decision to breastfeed or not carries heaven-or-hell urgency, motherhood has been made into a "production" of the highest consequence.

In the eighteenth and nineteenth centuries, the purpose of motherhood was overtly religious. Children were potentially evil creatures whose wills had to be broken in order to guarantee them a future on the track to salvation. Mothers were responsible not only for their individual children's souls but, collectively, for the very soul of the nation. Susannah Wesley, mother of John Wesley, the founder of Methodism, put it thus:

As self-will is the root of all sin and misery, so whatever cherishes this in children knows their after-wretchedness and irreligion; whatever checks and mortifies it promotes their future happiness and piety. This is still more evident, if we further consider, that . . . the one grand impediment to our temporal and eternal happiness being this self-will, no indulgences of it can be trivial, no denial unprofitable. Heaven or hell depends on this alone.

Heaven or hell . . .

Puritan ministers railed against the practice of using wet nurses as an example of "sinful sloth, vanity and selfishness." In the late eighteenth century, Protestant evangelicals said that mothers who used wet nurses were going against the will of God. A century later, guardians of maternal virtue blasted the new practice of bottle feeding and any mother who would do it; she was depicted, as Daniel R. Miller and Guy E. Swanson put it, in *The Changing American Parent,* as "an unnatural degenerate who preferred books and a gay social whirl to the true and inborn responsibilities of motherhood."

By the early twentieth century, the explicitly Christian religion of motherhood had been overtaken by the new secular religion of science. The ministers who had once called upon mothers to save their children's souls were supplanted by a new lay clergy of experts who instructed them, instead, in how to use the techniques of "scientific parenting" to protect their children's bodies from disease. The desacralization of the motherhood religion did not, however, make motherhood's purpose any less important or the exhortations from motherhood experts any less doctrinaire. Instead, the Calvinist harshness of the early American cult of motherhood survived in the punitive tone in the writing for and about mothers, and in an overdetermination of all maternal acts as ultimate expressions of good and evil.

It was undoubtedly not accidental that Luther E. Holt Jr.'s 1894 book, *The Care and Feeding of Children,* which survived for decades as *the* standard child-care guide of the scientific parenting movement, was subtitled "A Catechism for the Use of Mothers and Children's Nurses." For as Ellen Key, a turn-of-the-century reformer who wrote and lectured widely on the subject of motherhood made clear, "scientific parenting" was meant to be no less spiritual or totalizing a quest for the devoted mother than was the Protestant goal of salvation. "Our soul is to be filled by the child," she wrote in her 1909 book *The Century of the Child.* ". . . The child should be in one's thoughts when one is sitting at home or walking along the road, when one is lying down or when one is standing up. This devotion, much more than the hours immediately given to one's children, is the absorbing thing; the occupation which makes an earnest mother always go to any external activity with divided soul and dissipated energy."

And in a passage whose echoes can still be heard today in the writings of some child-rearing experts and the mothers who follow them, she equated supermotherhood with the total breakdown of boundaries between mother and child. The forward-thinking, health-oriented mother, she wrote, must "be as entirely and simply taken up with the child as the child himself is absorbed by his life."

OVER THE COURSE of the twentieth century a succession of new religions—Freudianism, feminism, individualism, success—lent their spirit and iconography to the motherhood religion. The icons of ideal motherhood—the "motherly" mother of the Freudians, the tuned-in mother prescribed by Spock, the liberated mother of the 1970s, the self-actualizing mother of the 1980s—evolved in a generally forward-looking arc, liberating the mother's "soul" from total possession by her child, and reflecting the changing social realities of the times. Then this changed, at the very end of the twentieth century, when all of a sudden the progress stopped, and reaction set in. The Sacrificial Mother—epitomized by the unbelievable Martha Spice—emerged as the icon of the motherhood religion in our time. It hardly mattered that our society had turned itself inside out in the course of the century, and that the very fiber of women's identity had changed along with it. Ellen Key's exhortation—that a woman give her whole self, her entire "soul," to her child—lived on.

In our time, however, it wouldn't be enough for a woman to give her "soul" to motherhood. She'd have to give her body, mind, and marriage, too. She'd be expected to lose herself within motherhood, first in a fusionlike bonding with her baby and later in the rounds of kid activities that would devour her life. And for the millennial mother, this loss of self, this self-sacrifice, wouldn't even be mourned as a loss. It would be embraced, with open arms, and celebrated—as though it were the highest evolution of all the forms of motherhood that had come before.

So that, by 2002, it would be common to hear a thirty-something mother say something like this: "Feminism was fought so that we could have choices. And my choice is to stay home with my kids."

Or this: "All other interests are simply subordinate to my children. There is not a thing in this world that can distract me from my kids."

Or this: "They are my reality."

It was the age of total-reality motherhood.

TOTAL-REALITY MOTHERHOOD

That remotely familiar stranger that I used to define as myself could not have imagined the pleasure of being cocooned in the house, couldn't have imagined the desire, the passionate obsession, to enslave myself to another. Totally absorbed, I lost myself within the tiny coil, the perfect comma, of her body.

In 1999, author Nora Okja Keller perfectly captured the emotional tenor of total-reality motherhood in an essay published in Salon magazine's *Mothers Who Think* collection. "My world shrunk to the size of her body," she wrote, of her feelings after the birth of her baby daughter. "Immersed in her smell, her feedings, her needs, I couldn't imagine doing anything without her, that didn't involve her. I remembered my life before she was born as if it were a dream, as if it belonged to some other person I knew only vaguely."

An attempt at leaving her baby with a sitter went badly, Keller wrote. Preschool went worse. At drop-off time in the mornings, her daughter cried; Keller sobbed, and later viewed the teacher's reassurances that her daughter had stopped crying ten minutes later as a lie, "a preschool conspiracy." Soon after, she decided to keep her daughter home from preschool altogether.

WHEREAS AT ANOTHER TIME, in another place, Keller's desperate attachment to her daughter would have been viewed as something that a good mother would get over and control, at the turn of the millennium it was something that could be expressed without regret. It was a feeling to revel in, as something honest and "real," and slightly subversive—an in-your-face response to the emotional efficiency of the Nursery School Establishment. It was, in short, a noble sentiment. A *normal* sentiment.

And if you read through the most popular parenting guides and magazines of the era, and listened in on conversations in our playgrounds and preschools, its echo could be heard everywhere. The icon of ideal motherhood at the dawn of the twenty-first century was a woman so bound up in her child, so tightly bonded and fused, that she herself—soul, mind, and body—all but disappeared.

The ideal Mom, as glimpsed in *Parents,* in Brazelton, and at Gymboree, had no boundaries. She wore kids' clothes—overall shorts, and sneakers, and jumpers or smocks. She decorated her home in bright-colored plastics. She embraced boredom and repetition, and eschewed speedy action (and critical thinking) in order to run, more smoothly, on baby time.

Parenting magazine called this accepting the "Zen of motherhood . . . changing the dirty diaper and actually reveling in itself, not its resolution."

The ideal mother was Zen. She learned to exist in an eternal present. She accepted that she might well never realize her dreams for her life. She relinquished desire.

She gave up on feeling sexy for what *The New Yorker* called the "Eros of parenthood"—the squeezy feel of a chubby bottom, the silky softness of a baby's head. Her body was her child's, so were her possessions. Pillows, pots, plates, jewelry, and clothes—all got thrown on the floor, dribbled with juice, coated in scum. So did she.

She accepted that she would never again enjoy the romantic relationship she once had with her husband.

She accepted that he would never really split domestic tasks with her—do the mental work, for example, of figuring out how to remove apple juice scum from upholstery—not because he *couldn't,* exactly, or because he *wouldn't,* exactly, but because . . . just because . . . men and women were *different* that way. And that was okay. Because she was Zen. (Though her pre-mom self had been brought up to think and be just the opposite.)

The ideal mom did not need anymore to be deeply bonded with her husband. For she had "affective synchrony" with her child. She met him "at his level," spending hour after hour on the floor, "facilitating" his exploration of his environment. On rainy days, she made herself into a Mommy Gym and let him climb all over her. Or she used herself as a learning tool—holding small picture cards in front of her baby's face, watching the poor creature's eyes flicker back and forth to find similarities and differences between them. (This "set the stage" for letter recognition later on, *Parents* taught.)

She never let her child out of her sight. She never turned off the stream of Mommy-as-Entertainment. In the car, she looked out the window and pointed out new and vocabulary-enriching things. If her baby could not speak, she took him to sign-language class, to get a leg up on nonverbal communication skills. She never used the TV "as a babysitter," but if she had to turn it on, then she "co-watched" Baby Einstein, narrating for her child in the silences.

She relinquished all claim to an inner life.

Maybe she "wore" her baby; maybe she didn't. Maybe she slept with her child (she read that it extended "quality time," allowing parents to "interact" with their baby even in their sleep); maybe she didn't. If she did, beyond her back pain and sleep-deprivation-induced delirium, she felt the sweet glow of virtue. If she didn't, she compensated otherwise. She played "synchrony games." She bought the Phonics bus. She read *Spot's Big Book of Colors, Shapes and Numbers* for the ten thousandth time, with gusto, because, if she didn't, her child might "mirror" her lassitude.

She maintained eye contact. She engaged in positive mirroring.

If she didn't, her child risked having "abandonment issues."

If she didn't, she risked finding her child one day staring out from his or her crib like the babies in her old psychology textbook, their faces frozen in a rictus of grief, some of whom *died of despair* over their separation from their mothers.

She would not let her child feel loneliness or pain. She would keep the connection going at all times.

She would breastfeed for *at least* a year. If she worked, she would pump milk, seated on the lid of a toilet, humiliating noises rising from her stall while her friends ate lunch or read the paper or worked out at the gym. She dared not stop—studies showed that denying her baby her milk could cost him six IQ points: "the difference between normal and bright-normal, or bright-normal and superior." Breastfeeding was not just a superior way to provide nourishment for her baby, it was part and parcel of a kind of superior motherhood. ("The needs of their babies are not only for mother's milk, or mother's breast, but for all of her," La Leche League founder Mary White had written.)

She relinquished all thoughts that were "selfish." Everything, every moment in her child's life, was so important, so *determinative,* that it required that she constantly give her all.

She allowed herself two basic states of mind: kid consumption and guilt. She suffered hair loss and memory loss and headaches. And yet no matter what she did, no matter how much sacrifice she made, it was never enough.

The experts wouldn't give her a break. Penelope Leach said she could never really hope to delegate anything of great importance to her husband because, as we all know, men and women are *different.* Stanley Greenspan said she could not let her preschool child play on his or her own for longer than fifteen minutes and that *most* of her child's waking time had to be spent in "face-to-face" interaction. T. Berry Brazelton said to take inspiration from the women in the highlands of Mexico, who, he wrote, breastfeed *up to 70 to 90 times a day:* "That's being 'there' for the baby!" And, above all, they agreed on one thing: that none of this—none of the gooing and cooing and crawling and bonding and talking and singing and Popsicle-stick-gluing—would work, would mean a thing, if it was not done with absolute joy, with "great delight and pleasure," *at each and every moment in the day.*

Is it any wonder that 70 percent of mothers surveyed in 2000 said they found motherhood "incredibly stressful"?

IT WASN'T ALWAYS like this. In fact, never before in America— not even in the much-maligned 1950s—has motherhood been conceived in this totalizing, self-annihilating, utterly ridiculous way.

Our mothers did things very differently. Many of them, by the mid- to late 1960s, were already starting to rebel against the cult of perfect wifehood of the postwar years, and especially against the high-maintenance domesticity of their pre-washing-machine mothers. They loved convenience foods. "Cow's milk—straight out of the refrigerator," as one woman laughingly recalled her mother's "shortcuts" in her infancy to me. They bought the *I Hate to Cook Book*. They opted for ease, for practicality. This was their "liberation." Those who came from immigrant backgrounds, in particular, didn't want anything to do with the labor-intensive and emotionally overbearing parenting that they'd seen in their families. No one wanted to be like that awful bugaboo, Mrs. Portnoy—the guilt-producing "Jewish mother." (Who, the experts warned, didn't necessarily have to be Jewish.) They adopted a kind of cool and detached emotional posture, showing that they weren't going to be sucked in by *all that*. They wanted no part of Old World emotionality. They kept their feelings in check.

While we would come to fear harming our children by not *being there* enough for them, our mothers' collective psyches bore the traces of expert injunctions against being *overmuch*. This was because, for decades and decades before they'd become mothers, the experts had been warning that too much "smother-love" was a poison.

The behaviorists of the 1920s, whose psychological teachings on parenthood extended the principles of scientific parenting from the child's body to his mind, were categorical in their belief that it was a mother's moral duty to keep her self separate from her offspring's. John Watson, popularly known as the father of behaviorism, believed that coddling children was psychologically harmful to them. "Never hug and kiss them, never let them sit in your lap," he had warned in his 1928 book, *Psychological Care of Infant and Child*. "Let your behavior always be objective and kindly firm."

Once behaviorism became doctrine, the general consensus emerged in the expert community that mothers actually posed a threat to their children and to society at large. The popular book *Parents and Children*, published in 1928, by Ernest R. Groves and Gladys Hoagland Groves, had a chapter called "The Dangerous Mother." Watson himself said such things as "It is a serious question in my mind whether there should be individual homes for children—or even whether children should know their own parents. There are undoubtedly much more scientific ways of bringing up children which will probably mean finer and happier children."

The writings of Sigmund Freud reached America in about 1909. Freud did not write extensively about mothers per se, except as they figured as love objects for their children. But his followers, popularizing his ideas from the 1930s and 1940s onward, did, extensively. Helene Deutsch, in particular, elaborated a notion of ideal motherhood from her understanding of the particular psychology of women, which, she said, was based upon a kind of primary masochism. Her maternal ideal, which she called "complete motherliness," depended on a woman's having renounced all "masculine wishes" and fully accepted her passive, "feminine role." If a mother did not do this, if her active, aggressive, masculine wishes lived on, either in the way she lived her life *or* in her unconscious desires, her children would be marked with pathologies. And one way to produce pathology was to be too attached to her child. "The masochistic components of motherliness manifest themselves in the mother's readiness for self-sacrifice, but . . . without demand for any obvious return on the part of the object, i.e., the child, and also in her willingness to undergo pain for the sake of her child as well as to renounce the child's dependence upon her when his hour of liberation comes," wrote Deutsch, of her "motherly type par excellence."

World War II provided psychologists for the first time with the opportunity to acquire wide-ranging statistics on the incidence of psychological disorders among the nation's men, thanks to testing done by the Selective Service Administration and by Army psychologists. What they found provoked widespread anxiety on the part of the mental health establishment: nearly one-fifth of all the men called up to serve in the war were either rejected or unable to complete their service for "neuropsychiatric reasons." The cause of all this neurosis, said Edward A. Strecker, a consultant to the surgeons general of the Army and Navy and an adviser to the secretary of war, was that these men were "their mothers' sons." In a despairing book of this title, in which he shared his experience of having encountered too many mama's boys at military induction centers during the war, Strecker blasted the kind of doting mother he called a "mom"—"a woman whose maternal behavior is motivated by the seeking of emotional recompense for the buffets which life has dealt her own ego." She was, he said, a woman who had "failed in the elementary mother function of weaning her offspring emotionally as well as physically."

The influential author Philip Wylie had warned, in 1942, about a "Generation of Vipers" unmanning their sons with excess affection. Now, in the wake of Strecker's findings, warnings about the menace of "momism" abounded. In 1945, *Ladies' Home Journal* published an article, "Are American Moms a Menace?," which stated that "'mom' is often a dangerous influence on her sons and a threat to our national existence." Author Amram Sheinfeld noted that Adolf Hitler was the "only son and spoiled darling of his not-too-bright mother," who encouraged his ambition to be an artist even though he had no talent. Sheinfeld suggested that one antidote to the problem of maternal overattachment was to breastfeed only as long as is "absolutely necessary."

In their widely cited 1947 book, *Modern Woman: The Lost Sex,* Ferdinand Lundberg and Marynia F. Farnham warned of a "ghostly epidemic" of neurosis in America, and ranked the "neurotic" mother as someone just short of a criminal. "We may casually remark," the authors wrote, "that Hitler was not a woman, nor was Mussolini," but "biographers will, one day, we hope come to understand that their true subject is hardly the man (or woman) they have chosen to scrutinize . . . but the mother or her substitute. Men, standing before the bar of historical judgment, might often well begin their defense with the words: 'I had a mother . . .'" And as late as 1965, psychoanalyst René Spitz warned that a mother's personality was a "psychological toxin," its poison extending right down to her *unconscious* feelings, which, unavowed and unexpressed, could cause her children to fall ill. Her "anxious overconcern," he said, would lead to colic, and her "hostility in the guise of manifest anxiety" to infantile eczema. (This belief in the overdetermination of childhood illness would continue through the 1970s, with, in perhaps the most outrageous example, Bruno Bettelheim arguing that cold, rejecting mothers could produce autistic children, whom he likened to prisoners in concentration camps.)

The awful thing about the Freudian pathologizing of maternal attachment was that many of the psychoanalysts' depictions of good motherhood sounded, to the untrained ear, at least, just like their depictions of bad motherhood. That is to say, they made good motherhood sound like an extreme, even fused, form of bonded attachment. Lundberg and Farnham—who lambasted the "overattached mother" as one who "by swamping the child with demonstrations of love and solicitude . . . undermines the ego until it has in it little feelings of strength"—described the ideal mother as one who was fused in such a profound state of "sympathy" with her child that she was "constitutionally unable" to frustrate his needs. D. W. Winnicott defined his "good-enough mother" as one similarly at one with her child, "able to meet the needs of her infant at the beginning and to meet these needs so well that the infant, as emergence from the matrix of the infant-mother relationship takes place, is able to have a brief *experience of omnipotence*" (italics in original).

What distinguished this good kind of fusion from the bad kind of fusion shown by the overattached mother? In the experts' eyes it had to do with needs: whether the mother's needs or the children's needs were being met by the interaction. (And these were needs defined *in the abstract,* since psychoanalysts, generally, did not look at concrete interactions between mother and child.) There may have been much truth to this idea, but sorting it all out was beyond the ken of most moms, who would, in the end, simply glean from the scolding tone of expert opinion that whatever they did was basically wrong.

Jessie Bernard, whose important 1974 book, *The Future of Motherhood,* provided a final snapshot of mid-century motherhood just before it faded forever into feminist prehistory, described the quagmire of the post-war mother thus:

> On the one hand, infinite amounts of attention were due her children; on the other, too much of an emotional investment in her children was to be avoided. If she tried to integrate her productive and maternal roles, she was overcome with guilt feelings for somehow or other neglecting her children. If she sacrificed her worker role she was accused by some of being overcommitted to her school-age children, or of interfering too much in the lives of older children. She was to invest most of her time in the care of her babies until they were, let us say, five or six; but she was not to have too much influence over them. She was not to permit them, especially the boys, to become too attached to her or dependent on her.

The legacy of this campaign against maternal overinvolvement lived on strongly among the women of our mothers' generation. Helena Znaniecka Lopata, who studied the "young and modern" residents of twelve Midwestern suburbs and gathered her research in the 1971 book *Occupation: Housewife,* said that mothers in the mid-1960s who tried to enrich their otherwise isolated lives by getting involved with children's activities "often met with derogatory comments which attempt to make women feel they are truly the 'generation of Vipers' and 'overprotective mothers.'" She noted that the women who took their children around for activities often felt *guilty* about doing so. "Chauffeuring children is seen as only a means of meeting the exploitive or other neurotic needs of mothers, while a child's interest in some competency-building activity is sarcastically explained as a consequence of the prodding of a domineering matriarch."

At any rate, even if they had had the inclination or the encouragement to do so, there wasn't time for our mothers to raise us with the exclusive intensity we put into our mothering efforts today. Families were larger. Children didn't necessarily attend school before first grade. Indeed, in the late 1960s, only 10 percent of children under age five went to school. Mothers did more housework. They didn't have time to religiously get in their sessions of "floor time" with each child. They stuck their little ones in playpens and did the ironing. And as children grew beyond the preschool years and became more independent, there wasn't any need for high-maintenance mothering. Kids ran around their neighborhoods or rode off on their bikes, disappearing for whole mornings and afternoons, returning only when their mothers rang the dinner bell or darkness fell. And that was considered just fine.

"We have changed the standards of what constitutes good mothering," is the conclusion of Suzanne Bianchi, a University of Maryland sociologist, who has conducted extensive studies to compare how American mothers, from the 1920s to the present, make use of their time. She has found that mothers today—*whether or not they work*—spend more time per child than did mothers in the "'family-oriented 1960s'" because they have "shifted load" away from housework and other non–child-centered tasks.

"My mom had three kids under twenty-two months. She didn't get a lot of help from my dad. She didn't drive a car. She did what she had to do to survive," a stay-at-home mother of four told me. She laughed out loud, without bitterness, at the memory of her mother's far-from-attachment parenting style. *"I remember her being on the phone, talking for hours. Once I held up a piece of paper and said, 'Do you like my artwork?' and she said, 'Yes, it's lovely.' And it was a blank sheet of paper."*

Survival, for our mothers, meant sometimes tuning out the kids. It meant less coddling, fewer at-home self-esteem workshops (how many of us grew up hearing "Good job!" all the time?), and more religiously observed "date nights" (as we, in our preciosity, call them) with their husbands. And that, too, was considered just fine.

Parenting manuals in the 1960s continued to warn mothers against overbearing involvement with their children. Yet, like Dr. Spock, whose *Baby and Child Care* was by then the unrivaled best-seller among parenting guides (my mother called it her bible), experts in our mothers' era expressed concern less with the formation of "neuroses" in children than with motherly impediments to a child's naturally developing skills, traits, and feelings of mastery.

Psychiatrist Walter Kempler, in *Today's Health,* warned that constant attention and excessive chatter from Mother and too much direction from her in play ("look at this, look at that") would result in "an irreparable loss, in which a child's natural curiosity for the world becomes obscured by a dependence upon his parents for suggestions and direction." He argued against smothering and in favor of "attentive neglect," saying "be with your child and do things with him while, in a sense, ignoring him."

The sociologist Alice Rossi in 1964 denounced the "fire-department ideology of child rearing," which she characterized as the view that "a mother should be available to her children ten hours a day, on the chance that the child may need or want her help for one of the ten hours." She wrote, "The result is not good mothering, but a kind of smothering that can develop excessive dependency between mother and child. . . . If we consider self-assertion, independence, and responsibility to be desirable traits in adults, then children should be reared to facilitate the development of these qualities. One of the best ways of doing this is for the mother to be a living model of these qualities herself. . . . As 'fire-department mothering' is curtailed, the child's opportunities for privacy and experience in doing, thinking, and worrying through things for himself will increase."

Best-selling authors like R. Fitzhugh Dodson and Dr. Spock told mothers that they should, above all, *enjoy* their children. René Spitz said the ideal was that "the parents enjoy their child and that the child enjoys his parents." Dodson, though a major advocate of intellectual stimulation in early childhood, also warned against making a fetish of it. Seeing, perhaps, the potential for hyperparenting in the future, he warned, "Please do not . . . conclude that you must spend most of your baby's waking moments playing with him. Even if you had a housekeeper to do all of your housework and no other children to occupy you, you still wouldn't feel like playing with your baby all of his waking moments. Don't let playing with him become an obligation; keep it fun. Talk to him when you feel like talking to him. Play with him when you feel like playing with him. Cuddle him when you feel like it. That way you will enjoy him, and he will enjoy you."

The experts of the 1960s held that mothers should set limits. Limits on their children's behavior and on their own level of maternal enmeshment. For the former, they encouraged reasonable discipline, including spankings. Dr. Spock believed that parents, while doing all they could to empathize with their children, also had to hold on to their boundaries, establish rules of acceptable behavior, and *not* accept every annoying childhood act as a necessary expression of their children's inner beings. In a 1960 article, "Russian Children Don't Whine, Squabble or Break Things—Why?," he worried that a "considerable misinterpretation and misapplication" of Freudian parenting practices had allowed American children to start to run amok. "Parents who lacked confidence in their own common sense became anxious about the possible harm they might do their children if they inhibited them or made them resentful through discipline," he wrote of the postwar period. "They decided when in doubt it was better not to interfere. . . . Their children have felt a lack of direction, and often acted up. The parents have tried hard to suppress their irritation at the misbehavior. But each time their patience has broken they have felt guilty and tried harder to suppress the irritation. I think that this kind of conflict in parents—between irritation and guilt—is what has allowed a lot— not all—of the minor squabbling, whining, inconsiderateness, abuse of toys and furnishings which are so common in American children."

The experts urged mothers to guard against becoming excessively involved, and to remember that their duties to their families extended not just to their children but to their husbands. Marriage—sustaining it, stoking its romance—was considered part of a mother's work. It was considered unhealthy—indeed, dangerous—in an age when the rising divorce rate struck fear into many mothers' hearts, to get so caught up in your children that you neglected your husband.

This meant keeping yourself sexually attractive. It meant knowing how to create a mood conducive to romance. It meant letting a man feel, when he came home in the evening, that he wasn't in for a second shift, after work, as a "mom."

> When father returns home in the evening, he needs a quiet transition period between the demands of the world and the demands of his family. Father should not be met at the door with a bombardment of complaints and requests. A ready drink, a hot shower, the daily mail, the weekly magazine, and the "no questions" period help create an oasis of tranquility that adds greatly to the quality of family life. From early childhood, children learn that when daddy comes home, he needs a short period of calm and comfort.

That is how Haim Ginott, author of the 1965 best-seller *Between Parent and Child,* put it. (I personally can never read this without a giggle of mild hysteria.)

Doing all this was essential, the experts said, not just for the health of your marriage but also for the psychological well-being of your children. For children, it was believed, needed to learn their future sex roles from their mothers and fathers. If they didn't grow up seeing a womanly woman and a manly man, they would have problems "adjusting" in later life. And Ginott, for one, believed that propping up the romantic role of the father had another important purpose as well: it would secure a necessary wedge between mother and child.

. . .

THIS 1960S–ERA VISION of how to correctly go about motherhood has come in for a right round of abuse in our era. Not just because of its sexist underpinnings (attacking them, of course, is like shooting fish in a barrel), but because a fair number of mothers today view our mothers' setting limits as little less than an exercise in expert-sanctioned psychological abandonment. Dr. Spock, in particular, whose *Baby and Child Care,* by the late 1990s, had outsold all other books in the history of publishing except for the Bible, has been singularly reviled as an unfeeling Patriarch. (And this after decades of bashing by conservatives, who blamed him, and his so-called "permissive" parenting theories, for having caused the social disruptions of the late 1960s.)

Today's mothers, "as compared with the housewives of post-war suburbia . . . may suffer a little bit less at their inability to show off cheerfully unattached offspring to the world, but benefit a little bit more from long, peaceful moments when the touch of their children goes all through them," is how author Elizabeth Bernstein, a lawyer turned "full-time" mother, put it, in a relatively typical critique of Spockian parenting published in 2000. She issued contempt for our mothers, "who let the baby cry while they got house and supper ready for their husbands," who banished "any degree of mother-child attachment which got in the way of marital togetherness once Daddy had come home," and who were willing, egged on by Dr. Spock, "to go to extremes . . . to get the child to shut up and stay away from the parental bed at night. With remarkable regularity, women who couldn't bear to listen to their children's cries any longer were advised to turn to solutions which increased their sexual attractiveness or availability— go to the beauty parlor, buy a new dress, take two weeks in Florida with your husband."

Attachment parenting—the parenting practice that has come to dominate, in watered-down form, in our era—has been understood by many of its practitioners as a way to undo the psychological damage visited upon us by our coiffed and husband-pleasing Spockian mothers. Whether our mothers did, actually, damage us by preserving some space and time to themselves is, of course, debatable. And whether this new parenting practice will actually do a new generation of children any good remains to be seen.

Who, after all, could have predicted in advance what the effect would be when the fatherly control of the family physician would be superseded by the control-freakishness of the generation of girls who Could Have Done Anything? Or how perverted the lessons of early-childhood cognitive development could become when passed through the filter of *Parents* magazine? Or how atrocious efforts to "empathize" could become, at the turn of the millennium, as children tromped around on furniture or threw sand in each other's eyes, and their mothers, laying aside their cell phones, knelt, made eye contact, and asked them if they had "something to say"? The long-term effects of this touchy-feely form of mothering will undoubtedly become clear when our children become old enough to make their mark on society—and to tell us all about how we have wronged them.

What is already clear, however, is that this effort to heal our narcissistic wounds has, in many ways, undone the progress toward securing a place for *self* within motherhood that began at the end of our mothers' era.

MOTHERS' LIB

In the early 1970s, expert urgings that mothers should keep themselves whole and not become excessively bound up with their children took on a radical new spin. Motherhood was said, by those looking for freer and more "authentic" ways of being, to be bad for adult relationships, bad for self-worth, and bad for the planet. "Children cause divorces," said psychologist Arnold Silverman, coauthor of *The Case*

Against Having Children. "The woman who loves children need not become a mother, any more than the woman who loves sex need become a prostitute," opined James McCawley, of the Population Institute in Washington. The notion of "maternal instinct" came under fire. Maternity *itself* was viewed as suspect by radical feminists like Shulamith Firestone, who wrote in her 1970 book, *The Dialectic of Sex:* "The heart of women's oppression is her childbearing and child-rearing roles."

Securing time and space and identity for one's self was one of the first and most basic demands of early-second-wave feminism. Women who "are forced to live through their children and husbands," wrote Lucy Komisar, an early organizer of consciousness-raising groups, "feel cheated and resentful when they realize that is not enough. . . . Middle-aged women who feel empty and useless are the mainstay of America's psychiatrists." Books like Ellen Peck's *The Baby Trap* argued against giving up the pleasures of companionable adult married life for parenthood. Jane Lazarre, in *The Mother Knot,* took apart the image of the "good mother"—a "tyrannical goddess of stupefying love and murderous masochism . . . quietly strong, selflessly giving, undemanding, unambitious . . . of even temperament and almost always in control of her emotions"—and called for a reinvented image of motherhood that would leave room for a woman's real, calamitous, and not always maternal feelings.

In the 1970s and 1980s, many mainstream baby boomer women prided themselves on breaking with the sacrificial roles that they saw their mothers having played within their families. As one boomer writer put it, "We just felt a little sorry for them. Mother was someone who was loving and thoughtful, but who had never really lived up to her potential; who had let herself be trapped in a house . . . who had never read anything spicier than *Joy of Cooking.* Her sacrifices often seemed unnecessary; her naïveté was sometimes embarrassing."

"I didn't want it to happen to me" was the clarion call of the generation, *McCall's* said in 1979, adding, "The 'it' is domesticity."

What many baby boomer women most rebelled against was their memory of their mothers' unhappiness and lack of fulfillment. Their own goal was self-fulfillment, with self first and foremost. As Erica Jong wrote, "What I remember most about the mother of my childhood was that she was always stressed, and often angry. I wanted to break that cycle so, for the longest time, motherhood was secondary." Pamela Redmond Satran, looking back for *Ladies' Home Journal,* reflected, "Was I reluctant to leave my infant daughter? I'm afraid to tell the truth and say no. I was more afraid of staying home and turning into my mother, a bored, frustrated, often angry woman whose energy seemed to have no productive outlet. I wanted to be a calmer, more satisfied mom."

"Without our mothers how would we have known what we did *not* want to be?" was how one magazine writer of the time summed it up.

What baby boomer women wanted to be, in the 1970s, was fulfilled, happy, and by extension—by virtue of being fulfilled and happy—better mothers than their mothers had been. This meant repudiating fully the ideal of sacrificial motherhood. The experts cheered them on, agreeing that not only was maternal self-sacrifice bad for mothers, it was bad for children. Indeed, over the course of the decade, a consensus emerged that made self-fulfillment a *precondition* of good motherhood. "It is time we started to redefine our concept of what makes a good mother," a team of social scientists wrote in *McCall's.* "When a woman bends her own needs and desires out of shape to accommodate the needs of others, the strain of that sacrifice shows up in the quality of her mothering."

The experts agreed that unhappy mothers produced unhappy children. "The mother's emotional state is a key," wrote Columbia University psychiatrist C. Christian Beels in 1976. "Mothers who are not working and would like to, and working mothers whose lives are beset by strain and harassment are the ones whose children appear to suffer in tests of self-esteem and adjustment."

The whole notion of female socialization was shifting. Whereas a decade earlier, the prescription for healthy female adulthood was an (often masochistic) adjustment to the "realities" of her limited life, now the goal was to enhance self-esteem. For a mother to fulfill herself was essential, the experts said, not only for her own personal growth, but also for her children's happiness. For girls in particular, it was necessary to provide positive role models. Self-sacrifice was seen as a poison. "Girls growing up not only see that their mothers have abdicated power and lead restricted lives, but also sense that their mothers have a low opinion of themselves," the social scientists said in *McCall's:*

> Their mothers were not *bad* mothers. On the contrary, they were doing what society encouraged—putting their children first, denying their own wants and needs, investing their energies and talents in their families. As a result, their daughters found it impossible to want to identify with them. . . . From studies of the identification process in children, many theorists conclude that the model a child would most likely choose to identify with is the one viewed as competent, powerful and in control of the sources of gratification. . . . If it is important for a girl's development that she have a positive identification with her mother, then we had better start thinking about the "ideal" mom as something other than a sacrificial creature.

Although some experts took care to write in an evenhanded tone, stressing the importance of a woman's finding her own individual way rather than weighing in on one right and true life path for all women, the majority opinion in the 1970s was that the key to maternal self-fulfillment was work outside the home. Some experts even opined that working mothers were *better mothers* than stay-at-home moms. Bruno Bettelheim, for one, said that the enforced selflessness of stay-at-home motherhood was ill-suited for educated women—and their children. "When work around the house is unfulfilling," he wrote in 1970, "a young mother's children become the natural target for her energies.

> Motherhood has been depicted to her as a tremendous experience, but unless she is fascinated by the minute stages in her baby's development, she seldom finds that any new enrichment has entered her life to replace the old. To fill the emptiness, she turns to watching over her children's psychological problems and educational life.
>
> Sadly enough, the children would often be better off with less watching over and with more real support where they need it. But a nonworking mother is often in a poor position to give her child that support when, for example, he is doing badly in school or in the world. Having over-invested emotionally in her child's achievement, she sees all this investment put in jeopardy when he fails at something. So, as likely as not, she bawls him out when understanding and compassion are needed. She may fail as a mother because her inner needs make her work at it too hard.

A University of Michigan study in 1971 put this theory to the test. Surveying a group of college-educated middle-class women who had graduated with honors, then gone on either to work as professionals or to become stay-at-home moms, it found that the professional women had greater self-esteem and were more satisfied with their lives than the women at home. The stay-at-home moms felt less competent generally than the professional women, even in their abilities to take care of their children. They were lonelier and felt more unattractive and less sure of their identities. When they talked about their children, they stressed the sacrifices they'd made for them, while the professional women talked about the fulfillment their children brought them. Lois Wladis Hoffman, a psychologist commenting on this study said, "The pattern of the able, educated full-time homemakers suggests that they would have shortcomings as mothers—particularly as their children approach adolescence. At that time, when the child needs a parent who can encourage independence and instill self-confidence, the anxieties and concerns of these women and their own frustrations would seem to operate as a handicap."

As for the more limited time that working mothers would have for their kids? Not a problem, the experts said. As a corollary to the argument that for a mother to be effective, she had to be fulfilled, they proposed the notion of Quality Time. This held that for a mother's time with her children to be meaningful, it had to have some edifying purpose. A few well-focused hours with a baby—time spent bonding, perhaps, or doing some cognitive-development–enhancing games—were worth more than whole days spent sending glances his or her way while ironing, cooking, or having a nervous breakdown in a corner. "Even the most interested and able of adults can invest only a maximum of six hours a day in meaningful interaction with a child," *Harper's Bazaar* said. "Thus, the working mother who spends her before-bedtime hours and weekends with her child may have as many successful interaction hours as does the mother who stays home. What may be different is that the career woman's hours with her son and daughter may be more positive, enjoyable ones because she wants to be there."

What is striking, almost painful, to read now in the 1970s writing about motherhood is how optimistic it all was. Common sense and a kind of can-do approach to solving the conflicts of motherhood set the tone. There was faith: The new generation of fathers *would* help. Good babysitting *could* be found. Work and motherhood *could* be balanced. It was all a question of intelligent juggling. And of not falling prey to the trap of self-sacrifice and perfectionism that had tripped up the generation that came before.

That trap, in the 1970s, was called trying to Do It All. "As a mother, do you find yourself compulsively seeking a perfection that just doesn't exist? If so, you may have a malady called 'supermomism,'" warned *Ladies' Home Journal*. *McCalls'* took on "The Myth of the Perfect Parent," who was able, through her perfectionism, to "raise a perpetually happy child." *Harper's Bazaar's* "Working Mother's Anti-Guilt Guide" advised, "Simplify your life, jettison time-wasting trivia and involve your husband and children in running the support systems that keep you all happy and well."

It all sounded so simple. And natural. And possible to achieve.

THE 1980S BEGAN with a great air of congratulation for self-actualizing, self-fulfilled motherhood. "The new sanity—Mothers' Lib," shouted *Vogue* in May 1981. Women, *Vogue* said, were becoming mothers "because they want to be, maybe the most radical shift of all." The magazine quoted the feminist psychotherapist Phyllis Chesler, who said the new ideal mother of the eighties was a woman who didn't let her child become her all. And so, *Vogue* said, the old-style "mom"—possessive, overbearing, and dangerously self-sacrificing—was bound to disappear: "If mothering is not one's primary occupation, it becomes less important to be the perfect mother, perfectly, unconditionally loving and always in control."

In 1983, Betty Friedan, in the twentieth-anniversary edition of *The Feminine Mystique,* celebrated the new mothers' lib: "Choice has elevated an exultant motherhood, beyond mystique." In January 1984, *McCall's* reported that women were now "guilty of feeling guilt free": "Working women don't feel guilty about not being as good a wife and mother as their mothers may have been," the magazine's independent market research found. "They are satisfied with child-care arrangements; they don't feel guilty about serving convenience foods; and few feel household chores are their responsibility." In fact, the magazine quipped, "Untraditional guilts may be on their way in. In fact, are you a mother who is guilty of not feeling guilty?"

By 1986, a majority of all women with children under age three were in the workforce. Baby boomer working moms were remaking motherhood in their own image, and though there were some indications that the personal stamp they gave to it—a kind of nonstop obsession with competition and control—could be a bit excessive, their way of mothering was generally passed off, at the time, as a triumph of choice and self-empowerment. "These mothers know exactly why they're having the baby, when it's best to have it and how it will fit into their lives," said a nurse in the labor and delivery ward of Boston's Beth Israel Hospital in 1983. *McCall's,* in a 1984 article entitled "Are You a Better Mother Than Your Mother?," painted a portrait of the baby boomer mother as a paragon of nonstop high performance, having a life of her own *and* parenting to perfection. "For today's young mother," the article said, "a baby is not the major focus of life. Active and energetic, she is often involved in work activities outside her home. During the time she is with her child, motherhood appears to have become more intense, with more feeding, touching, playing and talking, and the heightened activity level of the '80s babies reflects this."

By comparing 1984 parenting practices with a 1961 survey by anthropologist William Caudill, *McCall's* showed 1980s mothers holding themselves to higher standards than their own mothers had done. Caudill's research had shown that 80 percent of early 1960s mothers were bottle-feeding; in the 1980s breastfeeding was the norm. Mothers in the 1960s believed they would "spoil" their babies by touching them too much; 1980s mothers believed they couldn't touch them too much. *McCall's* found that the 1980s mothers spent nearly three times as much time as their 1960s counterparts on hugging, kissing, lulling, and holding their babies, as well as on talking to and playing with them. The 1960s mothers believed babies needed time alone and shouldn't have their mothers hovering over them all the time. The 1980s mothers believed "unstimulated time is a waste of baby time," and, the magazine noted, this belief "became immediately apparent in the behavior of the children. In similar five-hour stretches of time, the 80s baby kicked, stretched, wiggled and waved arms approximately one and a half hours compared to the 60s baby, who moved only about a half hour." Author Lois Leiderman Davitz suggested that the 1980s babies were trying to mirror their mothers' "on-the-go lifestyles."

By the mid-1980s, mainstream women's magazines were citing studies showing that working moms were happier, healthier, and *less stressed* than nonworking mothers. *Parents* magazine heralded the "Supermom," telling women "busier is better." It reported that new research had found that "the more roles the women had, the greater their sense of self-esteem. They felt more competent and proud of what they had achieved, and they believed their lives were more interesting and satisfying."

As late as 1990, despite the fact that on TV, in the movies, and on the political scene, the storm clouds of anti–working mother sentiment were growing angrily dark, many women's magazines were keeping the happy story of liberated motherhood alive. Readers stressed that motherhood was *"not"* their "sole reason for being." *Ladies' Home Journal* attacked such "myths" of motherhood as the assertion that, given the choice, most women would prefer to stay home with their kids. "In fact," the magazine said, "when asked if they'd continue to work even if they didn't need the paycheck 53 percent of employed moms said they'd stay on the job."

And then, somehow, everything changed.

4.

Selfish Mothers,
Forsaken Children

A child forsaken, waking suddenly,
Whose gaze afeared on all things round doth rove,
And seeth only that it cannot see
The meeting eyes of love
    GEORGE ELIOT, *MIDDLEMARCH*
    CITED IN JOHN BOWLBY, *ATTACHMENT AND LOSS,*
    VOLUME 1

SUDDENLY, as the 1980s turned
into the 1990s, the word "guilt" was everywhere in the magazine stories on motherhood, and it wasn't guilt about "not feeling guilty" anymore. It was guilt about working, guilt about *not being there* enough
for the children. Working mothers were no longer heroines, symbols
of the new and healthy freedoms won by Mothers' Lib. They were vil-
lains, selfish and "unnatural." Symbols once again—only now what
they were said to symbolize was everything that had gone wrong in
the days of Women's Lib.

A seismic shift had occurred in American thinking about mothers
and their children. The central focus was no longer on women's self-

esteem and self-actualization, as it had been in the 1970s. It was on children's self-esteem and self-actualization, with children represented now as the *victims* of their mothers' self-fulfillment.

A great deal of this had to do with one man and one idea: John Bowlby and his notion of "maternal deprivation."

Bowlby was a British psychoanalyst who studied birds, then war orphans in the wake of the Second World War, to eventually develop what are probably the most important ideas to date on the nature of mother-child bonding. His biggest idea had to do with "attachment"— how an infant forms a bond with his or her mother. Bowlby believed that the kinds of bonds infants forge with their mothers determine the kinds of relationships they will have with other people for the rest of their lives. This came to be known as attachment theory.

Attachment theory is so mainstream now that we pretty much take it for granted. We call it bonding. We do it until we're blue in the face. After all, the most widely read parenting experts in the period when we became mothers—Penelope Leach and T. Berry Brazelton— were steeped in attachment theory. (Brazelton, the Boston pediatrician whose books have become so popular that he even warranted an angry mention by Tony Soprano, has said his "whole thinking" was based upon attachment theory.) Bowlby's theories are now part and parcel of what we consider good parenting. Normal parenting. But back in the early 1950s, when they were new, they took the study of child development off in a radically new direction.

The received wisdom among the psychoanalysts and behaviorists of Bowlby's day was that an infant's attachment to his mother was, for the most part, just a matter of physical need. Bowlby argued that, on the contrary, it was based on psychological need—a psychological need so deep, powerful, and determinative that if a child's bond to his or her mother was damaged, that child would be damaged for the rest of his or her life. "Children raised in orphanages without the consistent attention of mothering persons suffered major and irreversible psychological setbacks in later life," he wrote in a 1951 report to the World Health Organization. "Mother love in infancy and childhood is as important for mental health as are vitamins and proteins for physical health."

After Bowlby began publishing his great three-volume work, *Attachment and Loss,* attachment theory caught on like wildfire. It changed the whole notion of child psychology so profoundly that soon Bowlby's language of "attachment" and "loss" and "maternal deprivation" became *the* basic vocabulary for understanding early childhood. This meant some very good things—like the fact that, with Bowlby's influence, the study of child psychology came to center on real children, rather than on the childhood memories of adults. But with time, it led to some troublesome things as well.

For one thing, the potential to do damage, to cause one's child unbearable and lifelong pain, became part of the very definition of motherhood. And the ability—indeed, the propensity—of an infant to experience unspeakable loss became melded to the definition of early childhood. The images, the words, associated with infancy were no longer just those of a baby seeking to suckle or trying to control and master his world. They were now the empty eyes of war orphans. René Spitz's horrible pictures of infants dying of grief in foundling homes. Harry Harlow's pitiful baby monkeys "bonding" to a terrycloth mother substitute. And such gut-wrenching prose as D. W. Winnicott's terrifying warning: "It is necessary not to think of the baby as a person who gets hungry, and whose instinctual drives may be met or frustrated, but to think of the baby as an immature being who is all the time *on the brink of unthinkable anxiety.*"

It didn't much matter that the children Spitz and Bowlby had observed, and whose examples had formed the basis for their theories, had undergone real and awful trauma. (Bowlby's initial work on attachment had come from observations of homeless children; Spitz had studied babies in foundling homes who'd first lived with their mothers and then, when they were six to eight months old, been separated from them for as long as five months.) The fear of causing children to experience feelings of abandonment, "unthinkable anxiety," or any form of emotional deprivation became the ghostly epidemic haunting motherhood in the post-Bowlby years. And the linking of nightmare experiences of children lost and abandoned to mundane everyday situations of short-term separation became attachment theory's problematic legacy.

This fear and this legacy were the emotional backdrop to motherhood for the women of my generation (and for baby boomers who had children in the 1980s as well). In our college years, we encountered them in textbooks if we studied psychology. We conceived of ourselves and our life stories through them if we entered therapy in the 1980s or simply read popular self-help books. They filled the media, informed our political debates on "family values," and provided the theoretical grounding for much of the pop psychology that oozed through our world.

For example: Nancy Friday's 1977 book, *My Mother/Myself.* You couldn't enter a right-thinking household in the early 1980s without finding a copy of it on the bookshelf. Friday's mega-best-seller about the difficulties of the mother-daughter bond brought attachment theory to the supermarket checkout line. It sold 250,000 copies in hardcover and more than 2 million copies in paperback and was accompanied by a PBS documentary and a mini-library of popular big sellers dealing with the dysfunctions and difficulties of mother-daughter "separation."

Soon women's magazines were filled with articles with titles like "How Not to Do to Your Daughter What Your Mother Did to You." Many women began, retrospectively, to label their Spockian mothers' pragmatic parenting style as rejecting. Retrospectively, their problems in adulthood were linked back to "abandonment issues." Bad mothering (once again) became the catchall cause of adult suffering—the "narrative point of origin," to borrow a phrase from the psychologist Daniel Stern—for each person's life story. All of which led *Mademoiselle* magazine to wonder, "Why Is Mom the New American Punching Bag?"

The notion that you could trace back not just your problems but your very identity to your relationship to your mother became common knowledge. And looking backward to your childhood to find yourself in the present became such a pervasive and banal habit of mind ("your voyage into the past," in women's magazine terms) that it was unremarkable, like blinking and breathing. For many young women, it was a rite of passage. And like many youthful rites of passage, it could veer toward dangerous extremes.

One of my friends, I recall, in the late 1980s briefly got into channeling, and looked back into herself so far that she reached the Middle Ages, where she recalled having been held down flat, with nails driven into her hands and hot wax poured on her body. Another friend, in the early 1990s, dropped out of life after realizing she needed to heal within herself the anxiety of having been made to sleep in a small, dark alcove as an infant.

These were not crazy women, but talented and smart, up-and-coming professionals. And their therapeutic "work" was different only by degrees from much of what was happening in mainstream psychotherapy and, in particular, in the highly popular recovery movement.

For this was the period of "recovered memory" and "survivors'" groups. It was a time when, on any given day, you could turn on the TV and find a victim of childhood abuse producing personality after personality at the prompting of her puppet master–like psychotherapist. It was a time when magazines like *Ms.* ran wild exposés of unthinkable forms of child torture at the hands of well-organized and secret satanists. In some quarters of the feminist movement, plumbing the depths of a legacy of abuse was not just the means to an end of achieving psychological health, it was constitutive of empowered womanhood. And so demonic-abuse stories, gory witness testimonies, and complex conspiracy theories circulated on the feminist left—equaled only in atrocity to those circulating among the pro-family warriors of the Religious Right.

The "recovery movement" had begun in the early 1980s, with the children of alcoholics and substance abusers and victims of incest or other forms of physical abuse. As the movement diversified, however, it managed to define victimization down to the point where parental *insensitivity* was classed as child abuse. Which meant, essentially, that anyone with a humanly fallible parent (even one who did no harm other than to pass on his or her own "legacy of pain") could claim the status of victim. After all, as Susan Forward, author of the megabooks *Men Who Hate Women & The Women Who Love Them* and *Betrayal of Innocence: Incest and Its Devastation,* wrote in her 1989 book, *Toxic Parents,* "All toxic parents, regardless of the nature of their abuse, basically leave the same scars."

The "cult of the abused Inner Child," as critic Robert Hughes once put it, became a nationwide pop-cultural religion. It spurred support groups like the National Association of Adults of Dysfunctional Families. How-to guides like Ellen Bass and Laura Davis's *The Courage to Heal.* There were workshops and tapes—all proliferating so wildly and profitably that in 1990 *American Health* magazine was moved to comment, "Blaming parents for what they did or didn't do has become a national obsession—and big business."

The "wounded child mythology," as one family therapist called it in 1990, got to the point where mental health professionals were complaining that their adult patients were so wedded to their inner children that they were refusing to grow up. Even the shock of having children—real children, as opposed to "inner" ones—didn't necessarily lead patients to separate from their little selves. Because parenthood, for "adult children," was a continuation of the "journey" of recovery. And rather than being a selfish enterprise, getting "in touch" with your inner child was considered a *prerequisite* for being a good parent. Otherwise, you might pass on, unaware, "original pain" and start a whole other cycle of suffering. You might pass on the evil seeds of your own insecurities, fears, and self-hatred, and you might not even know you'd done it until it was way too late, because your children might, like you, "repress" the pain you caused them.

For many baby boomers, parenting in the age of recovery, fixing the past and perfecting the present became something of an obsession. "We were the generation that was going to make everything perfect in the world—and that clearly included our children," one woman in her fifties, a clinical psychologist, told me about how she and her friends had approached motherhood in the 1980s. Much of this goal of correction turned around the idea of *being there* more completely and profoundly for their children than their own mothers had been. Not being there physically, necessarily, as in being home full-time, but being there emotionally, as in being *on* and *tuned in* twenty-four hours a day. "We felt that our parents somehow hadn't *seen* us," another mother in her late forties told me as she ran after her late-in-life child on the playground. "We would do a better job."

Inherent in all this was a powerful new message about motherhood: to do it well, you had not only to take care of your children but to be mindful of your children's *inner children.* This wasn't just self-indulgent, "neurotic" mommy stuff. It was accepted wisdom. As Robert Karen put it, in the *Atlantic Monthly* in 1990, "The terrible certainty some of us have that we will re-enact the worst aspects of our upbringing with our own children is not only widespread but seems distressingly well-founded. The abused child does indeed often become the child-abuser, and evidence suggests that many other behavioral and emotional tendencies are passed down through the generations. . . . Which of us are at risk of being parents who will raise insecure children, and what can be done to minimize the risk?"

By the time most of us in the post–baby boom generation started having children, the mass hysteria over things like satanic abuse had passed. There'd been a significant backlash against the recovered-memory movement and, in the wake of such horrors as *Ms.*'s loony "Cult Ritual Abuse Exists!" story, a new generation of young feminists were speaking out to denounce the victim mythology of their elders. And yet the legacy of the 1980s lived on inside us. It was unavoidable. We knew too much. We were overinformed of all the ways children could be wounded; we were terrified of inflicting any form of emotional harm. We had a surfeit of knowledge about the pitfalls of parenting and a huge vocabulary with which to articulate memories and sensations that another generation might have "repressed."

And so, thinking over our own psychic aches and pains, and hunting down all possible causes in our parents' less-evolved psyches, we swore, deep in our souls, that when we had children we wouldn't do any of it to them. *Any of it*—whatever "it" was. Until, by the turn of the millennium—at a time when not providing transportation to and from high school extracurricular activities could be construed as a form of abuse (and invoked as a significant factor at the trial of a daughter who arranged to have her father killed)—the *it* of abuse or neglect could be, on some weird, personal, psychological level, not getting your child into private school; not scheduling your child for enough play dates; or not managing to hunt down each and every piece of the requested Hello Kitty party set.

The total lack of proportion between the severity of our "crimes" (real and imagined) and the amount of guilt they inspired should have set off warning bells. But it didn't—in large part, I think, because it meshed so perfectly with our sentimental education in the years of the recovery movement. And, of course, because it followed so naturally from the hyperventilating version of attachment theory that had trickled its way down into our popular culture.

This hyper-concern with separation was in the work of Penelope Leach, who in her 1994 book, *Children First,* warned about the potentially devastating effects of any and all maternal separation: "The grieving of a baby who loses her one and only special person—her lone mother who dies, for example, or the lifelong foster mother from whom she is removed—is agonizing to see because we know we are looking at genuine tragedy. But the pain of separations we arrange and connive at every time we change caregivers or leave a baby in the daycare center that has new staff—again—or with an agency babysitter she has never seen, may not be as different as we assume."

And it was in the words of T. Berry Brazelton and his coauthor Stanley Greenspan, when they likened the deprivations of American day care to those suffered by the horribly neglected children found in the post-Ceaucescu Romanian orphanages. The orphanages—in which children were starved, severely neglected, and tied to their beds—Brazelton and Greenspan wrote, were "the most dramatic recent example of the results of neglecting a small child's needs . . . warning us about the impact of institutional care." They warned American parents against feeling complacent that such neglect was not common in the United States. "This type of care is part of every community," they wrote. "Approximately 50% of young children are now reared for significant parts of the day by persons other than their biological parents."

A grotesque manipulation of attachment theory ran rampant in the punditry of conservatives like George Will, who in one 1990 *Newsweek* column invoked the language of "maternal deprivation" to take aim at poor unwed mothers and upper-middle-class working mothers—all in one shot. Serving up video images of a young unmarried mother and her six-month-old baby, he showed how the quality of attachment was so poor that the baby, seeking warmth and attention, vomited each time her mother fed her, and how the mother, avoidantly, held her away. From this, he catalogued the incidence of "failure to thrive" among the children of unwed mothers. There were, he said,

> many babies with bald spots in the back of their head, evidence that the babies are left for long stretches on their backs. A child care—actually non-care—product popular in some ghettos is a pillow made to hold a bottle next to an infant so the infant can take nourishment without an adult in attendance. . . . Depressed, unstimulating or unavailable mothers produce in babies "maternal deprivation syndrome" which suppresses their infants' development. . . . The merry-go-round goes around only once and the infant does or does not get the brass ring of the full enjoyment of the potential that was his or her birthright.

"Nonorganic failure to thrive" is a medically accepted condition diagnosed sometimes in low-income children born in good health whose weight drops afterward and who face an increased risk of medical and mental problems. It is not the kind of thing one normally sees in families who are not in economic need. But lest middle-class mothers have concluded that they were out of the woods, Will put his own gloss on the maternal-deprivation research: "As regards incompetent parenting, there are also . . . gilded ghettos. Their residents include 'privileged' children of parents too affluent for their children's good, parents able and eager to give children anything but attention, measuring out what these parents are pleased to call 'quality time' in dribs and drabs. There are more ghettos—and more damages to children—than meets the eye."

Signs of abandonment and loss were everywhere in the world we read about in our early adulthood. They were in Romania—in the miserable crib of twenty-eight-month-old Simona Young, who, the *New York Times* reported, had spent the entirety of her life lying on her back, unattended and alone: "Unable to sit up by herself, she would push her torso up on thin arms and rock back and forth for hours, trying to soothe the aching void that had replaced her mother." They were in the heartland of America, where, the *Atlantic Monthly* reported in 1990, fully one-third of middle-class homes were producing "insecurely attached babies." And they were in New York City, where one prominent child-development expert said that same year that *half* of all four-year-olds were "insecurely attached."

By the late 1990s, haunting phrases like "failure to thrive," once reserved for children wasting away in extreme situations, were batting around in our heads, haunting our thoughts like the residue of a bad dream. If our children didn't gain weight, had colic or reflux, didn't smile, didn't want to be hugged as badly as we wanted to hug them, learned Spanish from the babysitter, or weren't reading before kindergarten—it was Failure to Thrive. We couldn't leave home—could barely leave the room—without worrying about the long-term effects on our babies. The stakes were so high. The cost of our self-actualization (or preservation) was, potentially, a child *forsaken.*

Given all this, is it really any surprise that we constantly feared for the worst? Or that anything we did for ourselves—"selfish" acts like stepping out for a quiet cup of coffee—could bring on a whole mess of guilt? (*"The feeling of guilt can be healthy,"* said attachment parenting guru William Sears. *"Guilt is an inner warning system, a sort of alarm that goes off when we behave in ways we are not supposed to. . . ."*)

WHETHER OR NOT parenting our children's "inner children" makes us better mothers is an open question. But what's not open to question is that our efforts to do so have created some crazy contortions in the American culture of motherhood.

A few examples:

A mother feels that her creative spirit was stifled as a child, so she refuses to have her son bound by of rules and regulations. As a toddler, he eats when, where, and what he wants to and goes to bed and to school when it suits him. "I don't want him to feel he has to fit other people's ways of doing things to be okay," she explains.

Another mother practices attachment parenting as a way to cancel out the coldness she remembers in her European parents. She exhausts herself to the point of physical collapse. Her daughter looms large in the family bed and her marriage splits apart.

All around me, in recent years, I've seen women living motherhood as an exercise in correction, trying to heal the wounds of their childhoods and, prophylactically, to seal their children against future pain. They tell their children they love them, over and over; they give them nothing but positive regard; they reward each block placed over the other with a cry of delight, every action short of bad behavior with a shout: "Good job!"

They wield their psychological literacy as a shield. With it, they can do no harm. Cause no pain. Avoid fatal errors.

"My sister was sexually abused by my father. My mother didn't know. My mother now says, 'We have *Oprah* now. If I knew then what I know now, I'd have done something about it,'" a stay-at-home mom and former lawyer in Texas told me. She continued, summing up the attitudes of the mothers around her, "We're smart. We've read the 0–3 stuff. We took the basic psychology courses. We learned the value of early attachment. We have a vocabulary for this stuff that earlier generations didn't have."

True enough. But there is also a funny aspect to much of this. It is, in the end, all about *us. Our* unmet needs. *Our* fears. *Our* desires to make everything perfect. As *Glamour* once put it, "What do I want to soothe in me?" is always the question that accompanies "What is it that I don't want my kids to grow up feeling?"

All of which raises the question, Whom is all the "therapeutic parenting" we've come to practice really meant to help? Where do *our* needs—as opposed to our children's—really begin and end?

TIME AND AGAIN, when mothers I spoke with talked about their fears regarding abandonment and separation anxiety, it was *their* feelings, not their children's, that they shared.

"If I get too busy with work, I actually get desperately jealous of women pushing strollers. . . . I feel exiled, as if I'm wandering in the wrong world and I can't get back to the other. It's insane but I can't stop it, so I've got to give myself more time with my baby and be careful not to overschedule myself until I've worked it through or had the experience with him that I need to have," one New York City mother told me of her decision to cut back her work schedule and spend more time with her son. "I couldn't stand leaving him," she said. "I felt bereft, as if I were the one being left. I was feeling my own feelings from childhood, and it made me profoundly depressed. . . . I was also obsessed with feeling that [my son] didn't know me as a mother, that I would be to him as I felt I was to my mother— uninteresting, not good enough, unimportant, expendable. . . ."

For mothers suffering from separation anxiety, forming a "total-reality dyad" with their babies makes them feel better—until it sucks the life out of them. At least, this is what one forty-seven-year-old Maryland working-at-home graphic artist and mother of two described to me when she detailed the lengths to which she'd gone to create the bond she felt she'd never had with her own mother:

We did the nursing thing, the family bed à la La Leche League. I nursed my three-year-old daughter until I miscarried in pregnancy number two. I got pregnant again shortly after and then nursed my boy until he was three. . . .

Four years into mommyhood, my energy had waned, as had my self-esteem. The queen-sized bed had three other individuals in it, and my day was booked in service to my kids, each day, every day, relentless—no grandparents, no babysitters. . . . It was hard to see my friends with local grandparents and with regular nannies leaving the kids for romantic vacations. Eventually I had to protect myself from those conversations among friends about their vacations by excusing myself.

To counter my feeling of despair, I tried distraction. While in the family bed nursing my one-year-old boy, I read every fiction book on King Arthur I could find in the local library system. I fixed a space in the unfinished basement to work in. After nursing my son to sleep, I would to go to the basement and paint until two or three in the morning for about a period of two years. . . . The bad side effect was no short-term memory as well as fatigue. At forty-two years old, I went to the doctor and thought I had Alzheimer's. I thought the trade for memory and sleep was well worth the bargain. I was always tired during the day . . . but I had my identity coming back into focus.

What became obvious to me after listening to these women was that much of what we do these days in the name of perfect motherhood is really about "reparenting" ourselves. It's about compensating for the various forms of lack or want or need or loneliness that we remember from childhood.

Our pop culture and education have taught us to attribute these feelings to "separation" or "abandonment." So we separate as little as possible. We insist on being physically present or, if this isn't possible, mentally engaged with our children twenty-four hours a day. But what we overlook entirely in doing this is the fact that, for the vast majority of us, *separation* from our mothers wasn't the cause of whatever problems we had in childhood (or have now). It certainly wasn't the kind of separation we dread our children will undergo in day care. After all, in the late 1960s, when many of us were preschoolers, only 2 percent of American children were in group care such as day-care centers, after-school care, or even *nursery school.*

No—having had a working (hence, absent) mother is not the thing most mothers today cite as the cause of their mom-related psychological woes. It's having had an *unhappy* mother. A divorced mother, perhaps, who was crippled with worry over money. Or a mother who was stoically sticking it out in a bad marriage. Or as was very often the case for the women I spoke to, a mother who'd been sucked into *her* era's version of total-reality motherhood, and who'd been bored and frustrated and overinvested and angry as a result. Who was too much in her children's faces, as a result. Who'd *mothered* too much.

Much as we mother today.

WHY DID attachment theory take root so deeply—and how did things get so out of control?

Jerome Kagan, the Harvard University child psychologist, has some interesting theories. He argues, in part, that attachment theory became so big—so very life-defining—in our time because it reinforced what we naturally feel to be true about babies (they need their mothers). Partly, he says, it was accepted by the psychological establishment and has endured so well because, in a "soft" field of science always eager to produce demonstrable results, the major testing method of attachment theory—Mary Ainsworth's Strange-Situation test, which could evaluate babies in a laboratory setting to see whether they were "securely" or "anxiously" attached to their mothers—was easy to carry out and replicate.

And partly, perhaps most important, attachment theory stuck because it fit into the big picture of contemporary American society.

After all, the years of publication of Bowlby's *Attachment and Loss* trilogy (which came out between 1969 and 1980) corresponded more or less exactly to the span of years during which American mothers reached critical mass in the workforce. Attachment theory—with its focus on the problems of childhood separation and of maternal absence and inadequacy—fit the bill all too perfectly at a time when many people, in the social sciences and without, were worrying themselves sick over the change in women's lives. René Spitz, for one, the American psychoanalyst whose work in the 1960s in many ways echoed Bowlby's, bashed the growing movement of mothers into the workplace as "mothers' absenteeism," demonized babysitters as potential producers of "emotional cripples," and bewailed the fate of the children raised with their help: "infants without love, they will end as adults full of hate."

SOCIAL SCIENCE doesn't exist in a vacuum. It doesn't spring from an absolute universe of "pure" inquiry and observation. Instead, it tends to hew closely to social anxieties—what Kagan calls "historical nodes of worry." And these nodes of worry determine not only what social scientists study but, often enough, what results they find (because of the way their research is focused), and also, afterward, which of their findings are picked up by the media, and which ideas take hold and become popular with the public at large.

As we look back now, it's easy to see how the social science on motherhood dovetailed with politics and social anxieties over the decades. In the 1960s, most experts, like Spitz, continued to believe that work and loving motherhood were essentially incompatible. Then, in the early 1970s, all the talk was of breaking with the past and liberating mothers through out-of-home work. The movement of large numbers of mothers into the workforce was new enough to inspire optimism and confidence that good and worthy new child-care solutions would become widespread in the future. And so child development experts set out to refute the accepted wisdom of the postwar period. The extreme importance of the at-home mother was denounced as a myth.

In part, this was due to the coming-of-age of a new generation of researchers in the social sciences, more of them women, more of them feminists, eager, as the sociologist Alice Rossi once put it, to be "free . . . from many of the doubts and conflicts we in our generation have experienced and are surmounting only with considerable pain."

Another goal was to challenge the dogma that any and all maternal separation left children forsaken. And so, in the early 1970s, books like Michael Rutter's *Maternal Deprivation Assessed* began to reexamine the issue of bonding and to argue that while children did indeed need to form secure attachments, they did not need them to be exclusively with their mothers. The anthropologist Margaret Mead was forever being quoted for her views that having many caretakers early on was better for a child than always and only being taken care of by his mother. Columbia University psychiatrist C. Christian Beels, writing in the *New York Times Magazine,* called the notion of the all-important, all-exclusive mother-child bond a matter of "folklore" and "myth." Concepts from animal studies like "imprinting" were discredited. A child's relationship with his or her mother (or other important caretakers), the experts now said, didn't just take on meaning in infancy—it developed over a period of time. A number of studies were published arguing that infants' development was not linked in any clear and linear cause-and-effect way to specific actions on the part of their mothers. The authors of these studies, eager to challenge the blame-the-mother thinking that had held sway so strongly in the years after World War Two, began to argue that in order to understand child development, you had to look beyond the mother and her allegedly all-determinative influence, and examine the child's own temperament and personality. And a growing number of researchers came to agree, as authors Stella Chess and Alexander Thomas put it, that "just as the child's nutritional requirements can be met successfully with a wide range of individual variation, so can his psychological requirements."

But then, in the early 1980s, there was a reversal. Optimism fell sway to a sense of dislocation and anxiety, after social change came on too fast and furious, child-care solutions weren't found, and the right-wing "backlash" began. (And, it could be argued, after our self-identification as a beleaguered "nation of victims" began too.) The motivations—the *emotions*—behind the research into motherhood (and the reception that research received) shifted. And so, as the decade advanced, with the problems of working motherhood mounting and no real answers in sight, a new slew of social science studies emerged to reinforce the importance of children's early and exclusive relationships to their mothers. Attachment theory came back in full force, and with further refinements—like the notion that there were "critical" or "sensitive periods" for bonding and learning.

And working mothers got it coming and going.

From the mid-1980s onward, they were pilloried—by right-wing politicians and pundits and even by the nominally "liberal media," which ran endless scare stories about day care, replete with nightmare anecdotes of abuse and sobering statistics from leading social scientists suggesting that group care itself—even the very best kind of group care—could be harmful for children. This was all done, it was said, on the basis of the newest and best scientific evidence—like the 1986 study by Penn State University developmental psychologist Jay Belsky that suggested that one-year-old babies who spent more than twenty hours a week away from their mothers were at risk for adjustment problems in later life.

Belsky had made a name for himself in the late 1970s by arguing against the idea that day care disrupted a child's bond to his or her mother. So, ten years later, when he appeared to reverse himself, the media had a field day. No one minded the fact that Belsky said publicly that his new research was being misconstrued—that he'd intended it to serve not as an indictment of day care per se, but to illustrate our country's need for *better* day care. "My purpose was not to castigate the institution—just the institution as it exists today in this country," he protested. Neither did anyone, in the years following, notice that Brazelton and Leach, too, if you read them carefully enough, were basing their arguments in favor of stay-at-home motherhood partly on the fact that child care in America was so woefully inadequate.

There was just no place for that kind of nuance in the pitched battles over working motherhood that punctuated the culture wars of the early 1990s. There was hardly any room for rationality at all in those years, what with Dr. Laura's diatribes against working mothers; conservative denunciations of the Family and Medical Leave Act as "another example of yuppie empowerment," as Republican representative John A. Boehner of Ohio put it; films like *Mrs. Doubtfire,* which showed working mothers as self-obsessed and cold; Marilyn Quayle's speech at the 1992 Republican National Convention, which stated that mothers did not want to be liberated from their "essential natures as women"; and, of course, the rabid vilification of ur–working mother Hillary Rodham Clinton.

The evil babysitter, the demonic day-care worker, became figures that loomed large in the public imagination, showing up, most famously, in Rebecca De Mornay's deranged mother-substitute in the 1992 film *The Hand That Rocks the Cradle* and in the spate of witch hunts that sent child-care providers like Kelly Michaels to jail on grotesque (and later discredited) charges of child sexual abuse.

When South Carolina mother Susan Smith drowned her two sons in 1994 by strapping them into their car seats and allowing her car to roll into a lake, she was denounced as an example of modern maternal "selfishness." (And her case was cited by Newt Gingrich as a reason why Americans should vote Republican.) When the nineteen-year-old British au pair Louise Woodward was convicted in 1997 of second-degree murder (later changed to involuntary manslaughter) in the death of her eight-month-old charge, Matthew Eappen, public sentiment turned most angrily not against the sullen-faced au pair but against Matthew's mother, whose crime, in many commentators' eyes, was that of having hired an au pair in the first place.

After detailing the baby's injuries ("a swelling brain, fractured skull, bleeding in the head and eyes"), columnist Mike McManus called the parents "negligent" in the baby's death: "The mother was not a divorced woman who had no choice but to work, but the wife of a physician who clearly earned enough for her to remain at home with her infant son. True she did only work part-time and did come home to nurse the child. But why was the au pair needed at all?" Talk-radio callers labeled Deborah Eappen "self-absorbed" and "materialistic" because she worked part-time. One issued a particularly harsh judgment: "Apparently, the parents don't want a kid and now they don't have a kid."

Partly, the attacks on privileged working mothers like Eappen were a kind of veiled class war—stoked, perhaps, by the recession of the early 1990s and then continued, in the middle and late 1990s, when the boom years bore their inconsistent fruit. After all, in the early 1990s in particular, the most famous working mothers singled out for pillorying weren't typical working mothers at all. They were overachievers—Hillary Clinton, Zoë Baird, Kimba Wood, women with choices out of reach for most women. The hand-wringing on the part of (other affluent) female commentators about how difficult it was for these women to resolve their "work/family" issues grated terribly on the nerves of women who could only dream of law partnerships, high-profile political contacts, and full-time nannies, illegal or not.

The message coming from the feminist movement didn't help.

In 1989, Felice Schwartz, founder of the nonprofit working women's group Catalyst, published a soon-to-be-infamous article in the *Harvard Business Review* that argued that businesses should recognize that some female employees would be happier working less, and advancing less, in exchange for more flexibility and family time. "The high-performing woman who does want to participate in the rearing of her children and is willing to trade off some career growth and remuneration for the freedom to do so will be happy at middle management for a significant part of her life," she said.

Many, many women agreed. Indeed, surveys in the early 1990s consistently showed (as they do today) that the vast majority of mothers wanted to work part-time. But feminist leaders railed that the Mommy Track would ghettoize women and reverse decades of workplace progress. They continued to focus on breaking through the "glass ceiling," even though most women would never rise close enough to the glass ceiling to touch it and wanted—desperately needed—to find a way, quite simply, to balance *some* work and more family time. It was a classic case of the perfect becoming an enemy of the good. And it allowed the perception to endure that feminism was concerned primarily with the elite, that child care was a luxury, and that working mothers were selfish and spoiled.

The moralizing forces arguing against working motherhood in the 1990s received more scientific reinforcement, in the middle of the decade, from the burgeoning national obsession with early-childhood education. In 1994, the Carnegie Corporation published a report describing a "quiet crisis" among American children, whose minds, it said, were being neglected by their overworking parents, incompetent caretakers, and inadequate schools. This was followed in 1997 by an onslaught of media coverage of "new" scientific data showing the importance of brain development between birth and age three. *Time* and *Newsweek* turned over their covers to special reports on the infant brain. Hillary Rodham Clinton organized a White House conference on early-childhood development, in conjunction with a national communications campaign, which included a prime-time TV special, *I Am Your Child,* narrated by Tom Hanks.

The news came out of the White House conference that an adult's potential vocabulary was determined largely by the words processed by his or her brain before the age of three. Soon, studies showed, almost 80 percent of parents with a high school education or more were buying flash cards, brain-teasing puzzles, and other educational aids to spur their babies' intellectual development. A mini-industry arose of Baby Mozart tapes, sold as a way to enhance spatial reasoning and musical and artistic talent, and Baby Einstein bilingual products to train the brain—all of which came with warnings about the limited "window of opportunity" during which a parent could enhance a young child's intellectual development.

With all this information came a crushing sense of responsibility— and also of challenge. For if, as *Psychology Today* claimed, child prodigies were "made, not born," and "parental encouragement and exposure" were more important than "genes or a natural 'gift,'" then any properly ambitious parent could turn his or her offspring into a young Mozart (provided he or she acted fast, for the "critical period" for producing a prodigy ended at age seven). The flip side of this was, if you *neglected* to nurture and—let's admit it—*create* your child's talents, then you could hold yourself responsible for a lifetime of future academic and professional (not to mention social and psychological) failure.

Accompanying all this, of course, was a creeping message that it was impossible to properly monitor and stimulate your child's intellectual development if you worked. *Time* magazine said, "In an age where mothers and fathers are increasingly pressed for time . . . the results coming out of the labs are likely to increase concerns about leaving very young children in the hands of others. For the data underscore the importance of hands-on parenting, of finding time to cuddle a baby, talk with a toddler, and provide infants with stimulating experiences." The message to educated, middle-class parents was clear: turning their high-caliber offspring over to women of lesser educational skills could be a real liability.

As time passed, a chorus of expert opinion would rise to discredit many aspects of the baby-education movement. The idea that as-yet-undeveloped brain faculties can be stimulated was roundly debunked. Experts began speaking more of "emotional intelligence"—knowing how to share and get along with others, for example (which sounded benign enough, until preschool teachers started making noises about getting children "evaluated" because they hugged their classmates too much). The magical powers ascribed to classical music (Build Spatial Skills! See Baby Ace the SATs!) were brought down a notch when it was revealed that studies had found it helped college students on paper-and-pencil tests for only fifteen minutes after a listening session. It was also later disclosed that many of the studies used to buttress early-education claims had been conducted with rats or with children raised in very deprived environments who had developed learning problems.

People close to Hillary Rodham Clinton watched with bemusement as early-learning warnings aimed, at heart, at improving the care of the nation's needier and more vulnerable children were adopted, with ambitious excess, by the upper middle class. Even the news magazines, if you read carefully enough, started to sound semiapologetic for the collective fit of apoplexy they had stoked. "Cutting-edge science is confirming what wise parents have always known instinctively: young children need lots of time and attention from the significant adults in their lives," Barbara Kantrowitz wrote, in an introduction to *Newsweek*'s special early-childhood issue. But, she added, "This does *not* mean parents have to go out and spend a small fortune on specially designed developmental aids that prey on parental insecurities."

What reason there was coming from the media or from a well-meaning White House, however, did not necessarily fall upon reasonable ears. My first daughter was born on the date of publication of that *Newsweek* special issue, on April 28, 1997. It was almost eerie to have the magazine waiting for me in my overnight bag as I came down from the delivery room with my baby. I came out of my five days in the hospital not having read a single newspaper, unable to recall a word of what the doctors said to me, my mind completely taken up with the image of my daughter's face, reacting to warm water for the first time in her bath. But in my postepidural fog, *Newsweek's* words—"Every lullaby, every giggle and peek-a-boo, triggers a crackling along his neural pathways, laying the groundwork for what could someday be a love of art or a talent for soccer or a gift for making and keeping friends"—had seeped into my consciousness, so much so that when I revisited them, while researching this book, I found that I had them half-memorized.

As the months went by, I took Hillary Clinton's advice—that "the activities that are the easiest, cheapest and most fun to do with your child are also the best for his or her development: singing, playing games, reading, storytelling, just talking and listening"—to heart. The *New York Times, What to Expect,* and my mother, an educator, all issued ringing endorsements: read! talk! sing! And so I did. I talked and sang and made up stories and did funny voices and narrated car rides and read at mealtimes until, when my daughter turned four and a half, I realized that I had turned into a human television set, so filled with twenty-four-hour children's programming that I felt as though I had no thoughts left of my own. And, as I listened to the maddening chatter of the playground moms around me in America, I realized that I hadn't been alone in my excess.

And the irony, of course, was that in 1997, as I began my quest for über-motherhood, welfare reform had pushed poor women—those most in need of enlightening messages about early brain development—out of the home, leaving their children, very often, with *no one* to talk to at all.

5.

Millennial Motherhood

IF THE CLIMATE for motherhood in the early and mid-1990s was angry, anxious, and tinged with irrationality, the turn of the millennium was sheer madness.

Nineteen ninety-six had brought us the "soccer mom," defined, in the pollsters' imagination, as a woman living and breathing domestic political concerns like education, health care, and family safety. She was a woman who, unlike the "supermom" of the 1980s, had pretty much renounced all interests or ambition outside of the family, as Republican pollster Kellyanne Fitzpatrick put it to the *New York Times:* "If you are a soccer mom, the world according to you is seen through the needs of your children."

But by 2000, the soccer mom had been outperformed. In the paroxysm of productivity that swept the United States into the dot-com age, to sit alongside a soccer field drinking a latte was little better than to be a slacker. In the Bush versus Gore election year, the icon of contemporary motherhood was defined, by the pollster wordsmiths, as the "minivan mom." As her wheels implied, she was a mom on the move, driving to school, piano, fencing, violin practice, Brownies, Cub Scouts, Sunday school, PTA meetings, volunteer work, *and* some kind of part-time, vaguely edifying, remunerative activity.

The new definition of good motherhood was, in the popular imagination, the state of being "almost always on-duty." Yet the duties of parenthood had now reached epic proportions. It wasn't enough, if you were "at home" or working part-time, to be there to pick your kids up at school if you wanted to clock in virtuous mommy hours. You had to do homework with your children, bake for their bake sales, and volunteer in their schools. You had to give quality *and* quantity time—and if you wanted, at the same time, to set your child on the path to a productive future, you had to model productive behavior, and keep yourself in a state of constant busyness. Your love for your child was judged not just by the amount of time you spent with him or her but by the amount of time you spent *doing for* him or her.

No act was too asinine, if it was done in service to the demands of "being there." Thus a New York mother could quit her job to better intellectually stimulate her preschool son after testing showed that his "pencil grip" wasn't right, and flaunt it, unembarrassedly, at birthday-party time, when she asked friends to bring "gifts" like bow-tying boards and other fine motor manipulables. And a Washington, D.C., stay-at-home mom (forced back to work by her husband) could fret aloud unself-consciously, about her daughter's alleged angst: "She doesn't like the fact that I'm not at home when she's in school."

There really was no way to achieve a laudatory level of child-centered devotion if you were a full-time working mother. But then, if you read the newsweeklies and women's magazines in those years, this was almost a moot point. Working full-time was *out*. Staying home was *in.* Words like "sequencing" and ideas like "having it all (just not all at the same time)" were breathing new life. Coaches and lifestyle consultants were weighing in on the "issues" confronting women transitioning back home.

A 2002 Census report showing that between the years 1998 and 2000 the percentage of women in the workplace with infants had declined from 59 percent to 55 percent—the first such drop in a quarter century—gave all this statistical weight. *Redbook* announced a new demographic: the "New Nesters." "Top Corporate Women Are Quitting to 'Have It All,'" said the *Wall Street Journal.* Stories abounded about high-profile women who were choosing to hang it up professionally and head home—from Brenda Barns, CEO of Pepsi-Cola North America in 1997, to Rosie O'Donnell, Jane M. Swift, Cokie Roberts, and Karen Hughes in 2002. Even *Working Mother* devoted a whole issue in 2002 to women choosing career paths that let them essentially be home with their kids.

The very same women's magazines that had once spoken out on the virtues of working motherhood now began to advertise the goal of stay-at-home motherhood as something as desirable and attainable as the quest to lose those troublesome last five pounds of baby weight. The "Can You Afford to Stop Working?" headlines of 1996 were answered, by 2000, in the affirmative: "You Can Afford to Stay Home." The argument that it didn't pay for a mother to work out of the home when her children were small was now accepted wisdom. Whereas, half a generation earlier, a woman's work was believed to be of intrinsic value, now it was balanced against a laundry list of day-to-day expenses: haircuts, new clothes, dry cleaning—none of which, the magazines said, could measure up to the invaluable experience of stay-at-home motherhood.

Whose life was "worth" more—the mother's or the child's—was the ugly equation that underlay this math. The argument was clear: if a woman "chose" to work, she was doing so at the "expense" of her child. Staying home, *Business Week* said, in a 2002 profile of top achievers, was the way "it's supposed to be."

There were a number of problems with this ur-story of new domesticity, which struck guilt and self-doubt into the hearts not just of full-time working mothers but also of part-timers and at-home moms who found, in fact, that they *couldn't* afford to keep doing it. For one thing, the women profiled in places like the *Wall Street Journal* seemed to have sprung from a test tube. They were either psychotic overachievers—like the former top executive profiled by the *Journal* who was regularly working online from midnight to 2 A.M., attending events at her children's preschool in the mornings, *and* planning to double her income in the course of the following two years—or shameless self-promoters whose claims of at-home consulting, creating, cottage-industry operating, and high income earning stank of bad faith.

Another problem: the magazines' use of the new "facts" regarding mothers' movements back home was itself grounded in bad faith. As anyone who looked at the new data carefully enough knew, it wasn't "women" who were leaving the workforce and heading back home at the turn of the millennium; it was wealthy women, pretty much exclusively. Most working moms' salaries weren't going for extras like haircuts and dry cleaning. They were going to pay the rent and buy shoes for their children. Their jobs brought their families health insurance. They paid for the second cars—much maligned as yuppie extravagances by the you-*can*-afford-to-stay-at-home enthusiasts—which were becoming more and more essential as skyrocketing real-estate costs pushed more and more families to buy houses farther from the areas where they worked.

Working mothers, furthermore, when asked why they worked, said they did so not only because they had to for money, but simply because they *liked to*. Even the women polled for *Redbook*'s "New Nesters" story felt this way; when asked by the magazine whether, if they had their "dream jobs" and their husbands could afford to support them, they would quit work, 63 percent said no. *Redbook* also noted that a 1999 Yankelovich poll had shown that 55 percent of women aged twenty-five to thirty-four agreed with the statement "Having a career is not as rewarding as I thought it would be." The issue, then, for most women, wasn't the idea of work (or the idea of stay-at-home motherhood) but the *reality* of life in the workplace.

Despite these inconvenient nuances of fact, the story that women were "choosing" to go home in order to be better mothers to their kids stuck, and soon became de facto reality. And the new equation—that the time a woman spent on herself was necessarily at her children's expense—dominated the thinking of the turn of the millennium.

It informed the reception given to Arlie Hochschild's book, *The Time Bind,* a three-year study of a corporation dubbed Amerco and the people who worked for it, in which Hochschild described how the awful pressures of total-immersion family life were actually pushing women to *flee* their homes for the relative calm and sanity of their offices.

Instead of becoming a broad critique of the increasingly insane demands of family life, the coverage of Hochschild's book turned into a widespread bashing of the selfishness of working moms. *Newsweek* started scolding about "The Myth of Quality Time" and quoting experts on the "apathy" and "depression" they saw in kids whose parents gave them nothing more than that. And *U.S. News & World Report* soon was blaming working "parents" (a nonsexist touch, though the article focused only on mothers weeping with guilt as they dropped their children off at day care) for the "lies" they told themselves about their commitment to parenthood.

There was, generally, a kind of punitive purism in the air as the new millennium dawned. You could hear it when preschool stay-at-home moms whispered about the behavior of working moms ("the ones, you know, who don't *really care* about their kids"). It was in the words of a Washington-area child psychiatrist who told a mother with advanced cancer that she had to give her son more "quality time." It jumped out from the pages of Marie Winn's 1977 anti-TV diatribe, *The Plug-In Drug,* which was reissued in 2002 in updated form for the VCR-and-computer age. Winn's argument was not just that excessive TV-watching was bad for kids (something that's beyond dispute), but that even in the smallest doses it was a mark of bad parenting. "It is, in fact, the parents for whom television is an irresistible narcotic, not through their own viewing . . . but at a remove, through their children, fanned out in front of the receiver, strangely quiet," she wrote. "Surely there can be no more insidious a drug than the one you must administer to others in order to achieve an effect for yourself." In contrast to the lackadaisical, VCR-in-the-minivan parenting practices of today, Winn joyfully recalled the days of long family car drives without filmed entertainment: they were "tough on parents," she writes, but "memorable for the kids. . . . Nobody is likely to forget the time . . . Mom burst into tears in the front seat, sobbing, 'I can't take this for one more second. I'm losing my mind!'"

Virtually no one lived up to the new standards of parenting perfection. (In 2000, for example, 87 percent of parents reported ignoring the widely disseminated new standards from the American Academy of Pediatrics stating that children under two shouldn't watch any TV at all, just as, for that matter, 90 percent of parents, bucking the experts, admitted to spanking their children.) But they hung over our heads like a sword of disapproval.

And the glorification of being driven to distraction as a form of good mothering bore its own perverse fruit. I frequently saw mothers who were loath to set limits to their children's behavior suddenly snap into a rage that was way out of proportion to the incident that provoked it. I came to wonder, too, if those of us set on parenting "properly" (i.e., totally) didn't in the end wind up relying *more* on the TV, because our parenting styles created the need for passive entertainment. After all, our children, overstimulated by us, couldn't play on their own, and we, stressed and exhausted to the breaking point, desperately needed a break.

THE WOMEN in my interview groups in 2002 often said they wanted to be "everything" to their children. They wanted to do everything they were supposed to do and be everything they were supposed to be and feel everything they were supposed to feel and, topping it off, to "model motherhood," as one very unhappy stay-at-home mom I spoke with put it. Being a "good-enough mother" didn't begin to cut the mustard. The word that cropped up, time and time again, was "perfect."

It all amounted to a great leap backward—at least in terms of the standards by which women's liberation had been understood in our lifetimes. It became common, in the early years of the new millennium, for example, to hear women talk about raising their children as their "life's work." To see them make a fetish of hand-sewn Halloween costumes and homemade baby food. To see them subordinate their life's goals to the furtherance of their husbands' careers. Some of the most basic tenets of 1970s feminism—things that we in the "postfeminist" generation grew up taking for granted—were being undone. Things like the idea that, on the most basic, human level, men and women were largely the same. Or that equality in marriage meant "equal freedom from household tedium," as the 1970s feminists had put it.

Housework now was back. That is to say, the *idea* of housework was back—in a kind of cool and slick and somehow postmodern form—promulgated by the popularity of "shelter" magazines like *Martha Stewart Living* and *Real Simple* and of books like *Home Comforts*. How many women actually did this homemaking is unclear. But even if they didn't want to do it, many revered the idea of it and berated themselves for not doing it as they should.

Something akin to the old-fashioned wife was back, too, largely by default, as the demands of the millennial marketplace pushed everyone to work such long hours that wives who could afford to dropped out and their husbands faded into the background, working so long and so much that they could not (or would not) participate in any meaningful way in planning or running their domestic lives. With the husbands too preoccupied by work to set up play dates or teacher conferences or remember to move the car seats, the mental work of motherhood fell entirely upon the moms. "When one parent works ninety-two hours a week, the other one, by necessity, has to start picking up the slack. Otherwise, some fairly important things—like keeping the refrigerator stocked, or filing income taxes, or finding a reliable baby-sitter, not to mention giving a child some semblance of security and consistency around this place, for God's sake—won't get done," wrote Hope Edelman, a contributor to the 2002 book *The Bitch in the House,* in a piece entitled "The Myth of Co-Parenting" that could have been called "Memoirs of a Dot.com Wife."

"I feel like we forced ourselves into that situation because of the groundwork we laid when [our first daughter] was born," a Washington, D.C., mother of two who works part-time from home told me. "I decided at that point that I was going to work part-time and then I stopped working and then I started working freelance. I pulled myself out of the competitive marketplace so my earning potential plateaued right there, whereas [my husband's] was still taking off and he still has focused more on work because now we can't afford to do it any other way because we need him working to the extent that he is in order for us to live."

The old adage "a woman's job is her husband's career" was breathing new life, too. Women who once went to power lunches now prepared client dinners for their husbands in their homes. One told me how she burned inside, playing hostess to one of her husband's most important female clients, who refused to include her in their conversation. A working mom who had scaled her own ambitions down for a lesser job on the Mommy Track said, "My husband has an assistant at work and an assistant at home, and I am the assistant at home."

Even "adjustment" was back. Only instead of being called "adjustment" it was now called "surrender." As in *Surrendering to Motherhood,* Iris Krasnow's 1997 book that advocated "downsizing Self" to embrace motherhood. Or in *The Surrendered Wife,* Laura Doyle's 2001 guide, which recommended abdicating control as a means to happier marriages, and inspired a wave of self-help "surrender circles" around the country. Or even in the patronizing way some of our leading female (and erstwhile feminist) social commentators started to mock other women who still were tacky and not-with-it enough to believe that the world needed changing.

"American women—can-do daughters of their country's optimism—still secretly nourish a poignant hope that there is An Answer to the dilemma of work and family," scoffed the *Washington Post's* Marjorie Williams:

> On a person level, and as a matter of social policy, we often seem to be waiting for the No-Fault Fairy to come and explain at last how our deepest conflict can be managed away. (Perhaps if we called it "blending" rather than "juggling"? What if we told ourselves that day care improves the infant immune system?) This endless quest entails an earnestness too deep for satire.

And so, as the century turned, while some women seethed over the new domestic arrangements ("Coparenting seemed to mean that I would be entirely responsible for [my daughter] and would be free to apply myself to my work only to the extent that we could call in a third party to relieve me," writer Lindley Shutz said, of the new family order that took root when she became a mother and discovered that her physician-husband's commitment to work "was not up for evaluation"), many more took refuge in the notion that it was all the work (sigh!) of Mother Nature. "So-and-so needs these materials for an art project and so-and-so needs these health forms," mused a working suburban mother of two with a doctorate in art history. "I take on 90 percent of that sacrificial burden [because] it just seems to go through our minds so naturally."

True, many of the women I spoke with said, this wasn't quite what they'd signed on for when they'd married. But they weren't angry about it. ("I've just sort of talked myself out of that frame of mind," said one. "It's nonproductive for me to feel that way.") And *no,* this wasn't tantamount to "sucking it up," they insisted. (They hated it when I posed the question that way.) They weren't giving in. They were just "accepting the strengths or weaknesses of your spouse or the good and bad in your relationship," as one woman who prided herself on her coparenting arrangements put it. It was just a matter, said others, of accepting that men and women were *different.*

Popular social critics packaged the situation as a return to a previously existing, more natural state of being in which men and women, liberated *to* their true natures, were two profoundly different animals. What was good for the gander wasn't good for the goose, said writers like Danielle Crittenden, who built her argument against working motherhood on the notion that it twisted and perverted mothers' natural needs to be with their children all the time.

The ideal of the sacrificial mother, once an object of derision, became the stuff of Hallmark card sentiment, invoked reflexively and thoughtlessly, as the *Washington Post* did, in 2001, when it chose to headline a story about a miserable but persevering mother of ten whose husband drank and beat her "Tribute to a Winning Mother." When the women I spoke with remembered their mothers, their first words (before they gave the matter much thought) were very often ones that would have made the baby boomers shudder: "She was just Mom," "the ultimate mom," "Always there for us, always accessible," "very steady and very present . . . utterly dependable . . . incredibly, quietly devoted to her job," "unwavering," "attended every school performance and piano recital, put on fantastic and clever birthday parties with themes and handmade decorations, invented Halloween costumes . . . told us stories, recited poetry from memory . . . hosted great parties that boosted her reputation as the Hors d'Oeuvres Queen . . ."

Even *Donna Reed* was back—her name and image invoked ruefully (but not disdainfully) by as unlikely a fan as the hardworking *Washington Post* reporter Lonnae O'Neal Parker, a self-described perfectionist ("obsessive, compulsive, a little freaky when it comes to control") who wrote, in "The Donna Reed Syndrome," of having left her job to experience what she dreamed of as the world of traditional stay-at-home motherhood: "a model of routine and order and organization and competence . . . a life where women kept house, raised kids and kept their eyebrows looking really good." Back too was June Cleaver—invoked as a role model most memorably for me by a forty-one-year-old mother who'd made her career in the Air Force maintaining bombers, tankers, and F-15s, then had quit because, when both her husband and she were called away on active duty, there was no one to take care of the kids. "There never was anyone like that of course," she sighed about June Cleaver, as a conference room of like-minded stay-at-home moms sighed along with her. "But for some reason we think there was. And those of us who wanted to make a home took her as a role model."

We had come full circle. Back to "adjustment." Back to separate spheres for men and women. Even back to a hipper, more high-tech version of the "happy housewife heroine."

It was perhaps not surprising, then, that as the millennium turned, the kinds of common female ailments that in the early 1960s were understood to be the result of a too-intensive, too exclusively "selfless" lifestyle came back in full force. Things like depression and anxiety and incredible, grinding fatigue and a whole bevy of stress-related ailments like insomnia, headaches, and rashes. ("I used to be the healthiest person, I really was," said the woman who'd told me she'd talked herself out of "nonproductive" anger, of the irritable bowel syndrome, asthma, and insomnia she'd developed as a mother.)

Depression alone was said in 2003 to affect up to 30 percent of mothers of young children. Experts said this was caused, in part, by sheer exhaustion. Our refusal to let our children "cry it out" at night and our penchant for cosleeping were producing a generation of dangerously sleep-deprived mothers, plodding through life in what one study called a generalized "state of despair."

"I have been tired for years and years and years," one stay-at-home mom I spoke with said. "It makes me feel vulnerable and weak." Many other mothers told me they were suffering from anxiety or depression or a combination of the two. "Anxiety is just accepted," said a thirty-one-year-old working mother of two in Texas. "It's not something that is openly acknowledged, it's just subtly brought up in conversations as we talk about busy schedules and coordinating events." A single working mother in Los Angeles knew she wasn't well but waited years before seeking help—and medication. "I think that mothers often believe, as I did," she said, "that it simply goes with the territory."

Perhaps because of feeling so vulnerable and weak with fatigue, some of the mothers I spoke with had developed new phobias since becoming mothers. One African-American woman, married to a white man, said that she sometimes feared her children, who were light-skinned, would be taken from her and she wouldn't be able to get them back. "I would be hard-pressed to prove I was their mother because of my dark skin." Another, a former mountain climber, said she was now afraid to get into an airplane.

A fair number of the mothers I spoke with were taking or had taken medication for depression and anxiety. ("First there was the incarnation. Then there was the resurrection. Then there was Prozac," a

Protestant minister in the Northwest told me.) And many more were or had been in therapy, often pulling their husbands in with them to try to figure a way out of the mess of their lives.

Their sex lives, in particular, were often a mess. For there was a special, depressing twist to the denial of self that underlay millennial motherhood: a pervasive, dreary loss of sexuality. It wasn't just that women didn't feel like sleeping with their husbands anymore. They didn't feel like sleeping with *anyone* anymore. They didn't feel like sexual beings. In part, the problem was that the passion they bestowed on their children emptied them of their sexual energies. "I loved and cuddled and breastfed, and by the end of any given day I was sort of 'all touched out'," one forty-year-old mother of two in Washington State remembered of her first marriage, which ended in divorce. "Being touched related to being needed, and I was giving all I had to give to the baby. Ergo, nothing left for Daddy."

In part, the problem was just sheer exhaustion. And partly, it was a failure of sexual fantasy: how still to feel sexy when you were no longer free, no longer in control, no longer able to take advantage of the watered-down version of the sexual revolution that many of us had imbibed, and which consisted, as one formerly sexy-feeling mother put it, in the belief that "we can all choose to have as many sexual partners as we want." But most important, the problem had to do with the loss of self demanded by millennial motherhood—in this case, the electric inner self that could come alive with sexual thoughts and fantasies. "When I have no spare thought for myself, then it's really hard for me to get in the mood," said a thirty-nine-year-old full-time working mother of an infant in Virginia. "I wish I had more cells in my brain to devote to sex; they are all consumed and my line of credit is running low."

For the purist adherents of total-reality motherhood, this was considered all well and good: "It is a physical reality that there is only so much physical affection a woman can channel through her body in a twenty-four-hour period," said a stay-at-home mom who prided herself on her ability to make her self "subordinate" to her kids. "Children require a large amount of physical care and affection themselves, leaving little tolerance for intimacy with a spouse."

But most women said that feeling the life go out of their flesh was pretty depressing. They often tried to make a joke of it. ("What's sex?") But that was only if they thought of it. Which most of them tried not to do.

An old friend, who'd been joking about her lack of a sex life for years, grew serious as she told me that not only did she not have any desire for sex, she couldn't even remember what it *felt* like to want it. "That part of my life is completely dead," she said. "I don't even miss it. It feels like it belongs to another life. Like I was another person."

One woman had a picture of that other person displayed prominently in her home. It was her wedding photo. In it, she still had the skinny, ready-for-office-wear body she'd had before leaving her job, adopting a child, becoming a stay-at-home mom, and gaining a transformative amount of weight in a matter of months. Sometimes, her husband would pick up the picture and say, *"That's* the girl I married."

"I try not to think about it too much," she told me.

AS THE PSYCHOLOGISTS who treated them in the 1960s knew, depression often is the province of women who make their kids their life's work. There's something sad and scary about losing yourself, particularly when it stands your life's ambitions on their head.

One woman I spoke with, a painter whose dreams of a life as an artist had taken a backseat to her husband's career, tried to articulate this. She was a person who'd pretty much had everything: a wonderful education, a wonderful husband, a nice big house, two children, and full-time help. Still, she wondered, over dinner, why her life felt so joyless, why her husband and she had to work so hard at having fun together, where her ambition had gone, where her life had gone, when was the last time she'd had a truly interesting conversation.

Of course, she said, bringing up her children was now her great creative act. It was the greatest creative act anyone could ever hope for really, and she wouldn't give it up for the world, she said, but "What happens when you look back at these years and say, 'Where is the body of work?'" she asked, her voice cracking.

There was a long silence then. The molding and making and sculpting and creating of the children's lives did, of course, amount to a body of work, she said, gesturing elegantly. But then her hands fell flat to her sides.

IT SHOULDN'T PERHAPS have been surprising to anyone that, at the turn of the millennium, a certain vice was resurrected, along with the values, virtues, and habits of mind of the prefeminist era: recourse to "mother's little helpers" as a way of getting through the day. Only, in an appropriate twist for a generation of overachievers, the little helper offering shelter from the craze of motherhood was no longer Valium, but speed.

There was speed for moms, in the form of methamphetamine, or crystal meth, which in 2002 was crowned the drug of choice for supermoms. Around the country, said newspapers as diverse as the *New York Times* and the *Salt Lake Tribune,* desperate mothers were using meth as a way to keep themselves momming twenty-four hours a day. Said one former addict, of the thrill of life on speed, "I felt I could paint the side of the house with a toothbrush." Said another, a mother of three whose urge to keep up her children's "standard of living," postdivorce, landed her with a thirty-five-year prison term for drug dealing, "The house, the kids, the cars, the groceries, the flower beds—

I thought I had to be perfect at all of it. . . . For my self-esteem I didn't want to let anything go. . . . I didn't want to let go of the fantasy that I could do it all perfectly."

There was speed for children, too—in the form of Ritalin and related stimulants widely prescribed to treat attention deficit disorders. One of these drugs, Adderall, was explicitly marketed to mothers as a little helper to counter the impulsive and squirmy, mommy-irking behaviors associated with ADHD. In ads that ran in a number of parenting magazines, a mother, with a smile of contained hysteria, played with her manic-looking son. The text read, "Thanks to ADDERALL XR, David's Mom is learning a whole new language. . . . *I'm proud of you. . . . Thanks for taking out the garbage. . . . Do you want to have your friends over on Saturday? Good job with your homework!*" The message was clear: prior to Adderall, she would, no doubt, have been screaming, *"I want a Valium!"*

IN 2001, after Andrea Yates murdered her five children by drowning them, one after one, in a bathtub, it wasn't lost on a number of female commentators that her plight, before she went completely over the edge, was different not so much in kind as in degree from that of a great number of American women.

Andrea Yates baked, made costumes, home-schooled her children. She was overextended, undersupported, and filled with an overwhelming sense of failure. And, topping it all off, she ascribed to a very literal form of the Motherhood Religion. She read Scripture constantly and literally, believed women were the cursed daughters of Eve and that sinful children were the spawn of sinful mothers. "My children were not righteous. I let them stumble," she told psychiatrists. She cut herself off from friends, stopped outside activities that she enjoyed, turned down the idea of hiring a nanny, and allegedly refused her husband's offer to cut back on his working hours so that she could have an outside life. "I'm a mother now," she explained. She worked herself to a state of nervous exhaustion; she pushed herself harder than any person could sanely be allowed to, and *still* she felt she *couldn't take good enough care of her children.* She went insane—and so the circumstances of her life combined with illness to produce tragic results. But what is also insane is that the circumstances of her life—doing so much unsupported, and with the whole weight of the Motherhood Religion bearing down upon her—were not, in and of themselves, seen as a sign of sickness. And this is because they could pass (without psychosis) for a form of normal life in our time.

Yates's insanity was undoubtedly organic. It was perhaps inevitable that her mind would snap. Yet mental illness takes different forms at different times and in different cultures. Cultural pressures don't *make* people go crazy but they do lend their craziness its specific symptomology. Yates would perhaps have become psychotic in any time, in any place. But at another time, in another culture, without this era's particular set of pressures, would Andrea Yates have become a supermom gone unhinged? *Would she have killed her children?*

6.

The Motherhood Religion

*I wonder how these kids will grow up feeling about their parents.
How much resentment and how many theories will come out about
the negative aspects of this overzealous involvement? It just does not
look healthy or normal to me, especially with the mothers typically
on the edge and stressed all the time. How much of this stress will
be reflected on the kids? My mom was upset and stressed all the time
and I know how profoundly this has impacted my whole attitude
toward life.*

A THIRTY-NINE-YEAR-OLD WORKING MOTHER IN VIRGINIA

THERE'S A STORY we mothers tell ourselves these days, in books and in magazines and in movies and on TV, and even in conversations with our friends.

And that story—which is usually told over the head of a toddler, or accompanied by the visual image of a mom making dinner for six while she does homework for four—is that we now live our lives in the totalizing, ultra–child-centered way we do because we have realized that liberated motherhood wasn't all it was cracked up to be.

It wasn't good for children and it wasn't good for mothers. And so now we are using all our freedom and choice to set the situation right. We are giving our children what they "really" need. We are giving ourselves what we "really" need—a degree of intense child-bonding that both feminism *and* Spock denied to previous generations.

All of which is good. And right. And, on a very basic level, the way things were always meant to be. The only problem is that this story—the Gospel According to Which We Mother—has no actual basis in fact.

There's no proof that children suffered in the past because their mothers put them in playpens. There's no proof that children suffer today because their mothers work. None of the studies conducted on the children of working mothers—in the 1950s, 1960s, 1970s, 1980s, and 1990s—have ever shown that a mother's work outside of home *per se* has any impact upon her child's well-being. (The quality of care a child receives while the mother's away, on the other hand, has a *major* impact on that child's well-being, but that's a whole other story.)

Studies have never shown that total immersion in motherhood makes mothers happy or does their children any good. On the contrary, studies *have* shown that mothers who are able to make a life for themselves tend to be happy and to make their children happy. The self-fulfillment they get from a well-rounded life actually makes them more emotionally available for their children—in part because they're less needy.

All of this research has been around for decades. But somehow, we've managed to miss it. Just as we manage, each day, not to notice the fact that the pained-faced Mommy getting down on her knees at kindergarten drop-off time and draping herself over her son's tiny shoulders isn't a very happy person. We manage *not* to acknowledge, despite endless clues from our children's doctors and teachers, that our preferred parenting style is *not* terribly conducive to promoting future happiness. We persist in doing things that are contrary to our best interests—and our children's best interests. And we continue, against all logic, to subscribe to a way of thinking about motherhood that leaves us guilt-ridden, anxious, and exhausted.

Why do we do this? I think it's because, as far as motherhood is concerned, our beliefs don't come from experience or observation. Real life, science, or even common sense has little to do with these beliefs. They're articles of faith. Matters of religion—the American Motherhood Religion. And as such they have a life and an inner logic all their own.

WHEN I TALK about the Motherhood Religion, what I mean is all the ways that motherhood in America has been unmoored from reality and turned into theology. Or how, time and again, motherhood has been made into an overdetermined thing, invested with quasi-ecclesiastical notions of Good and Evil. And while the definitions of Good and Evil have sometimes changed, one thing has always remained the same: in times of trouble, making a religion of motherhood has provided people with a kind of refuge. It has offered a psychological fix, a collective salve for people weary of a soul-bruising world. The Motherhood Religion soothes anxiety. Over and over again.

It did so in the late eighteenth century, when the ideal of mother as sacred teacher and moral guide came to American shores. It came from England and it had sprung there from some new and very potent sources of anxiety: middle-class life was changing. The nature of work was changing, pulling fathers out of their homes and into a separate world of moneymaking labor. This meant that family life was undergoing a major revolution. Whereas in the past, child care had been woven into a whole tapestry of work done in and around the home by mothers and fathers and servants together, now children were more and more alone with their mothers. Fewer middle-class households could afford to have servants. And what servants they did have now were much lower class than in the past. These servants were deemed untrustworthy, coarse, and uncultured. Potentially, even, corrupting for children. And so, to a much greater degree than ever before, it fell to mothers to make sure their children came out all right. Particularly as regarded moral and spiritual guidance.

Out of this situation, from the sermons and the parenting books that made their way from England to American shores, the Motherhood Religion was born. Ministers and authors taught English and American mothers that their hands-on duties were not just essential but sacred. If they did everything right, their children would be saved. If not . . . well, it was better not to contemplate the consequences of bad motherhood. For they were nothing less than Evil.

In the nineteenth century, the Industrial Revolution pushed even more fathers out of the home. It relieved mothers of many of their non–child-centered duties, as they could now buy many of the household goods they'd once made themselves. The new era also raised a lot of new fears: What would happen to a world taken over by the ever-encroaching demands of business? Where would spiritual life reside? What would be left of the human? And what would become of comfort and care in a world of rapacious competition?

The Victorian cult of motherhood answered all these anxieties. The exclusive domesticity of the "Angel in the House" provided a refuge from the world of commerce. The idea of mothers' sweet tenderness offered an antidote to the callousness of the world of industry. And the notion of motherhood as woman's *one and true calling* compensated nicely for the fact that, in truth, middle-class married women simply didn't have much else to do anymore.

In the early twentieth century in America, the birth rate was falling. The first wave of feminist activists were demanding the vote, education for women, self-determination, and independence. Many Americans reacted with horror. And their fears helped sustain the new maternal ideal that rose at the turn of the century: Mother as a doting angel with vital responsibility for every aspect of her child's spiritual and physical existence.

Another period of acute anxiety came in the years immediately following World War Two. During the war, many mothers had gone to work, filling essential jobs left empty by the men who had gone to war. This was considered a good and patriotic and socially necessary thing. And the stamp of approval bestowed upon mothers' work even extended to day care, which the government subsidized for some women working in the war industries. Women working for the industrialist Henry J. Kaiser, for example, had access to day-care centers staffed by certified teachers, doctors, psychologists, and nutritionists. There were infirmaries and, for additional fees beyond the one-dollar-a-day cost of child care, there were extra services on offer, like dinners to go, mending, grocery shopping, and child immunizations. Topping it all off, by availing themselves of these services, women were told they were doing the Right Thing. As a Kaiser brochure put it, if a mother's load was lightened, "the better able she would be to give love and affection to a young child."

After the war, the GIs came home needing jobs and wondering what had happened to their families while they'd been away. Had their wives been faithful? Did their children remember them? What roles would they play now that women had been running the show? And, more generally, how would a sense of comfort and normality be returned to life after the horrors of the battlefield?

Most women went home from their jobs, comforted and encouraged, beatified by the Feminine Mystique. This dogma of domestic sanctity guaranteed that there was still such a thing as a man's world in America. And a woman's world, for that matter. And something that could be called home. All of which was anchored in place by Mother's loving care. As one contemporary domestic guide put it, "She it is who will create the world after the war."

But real life didn't live up to the Mystique. It kept changing. Increased wealth, in the decades after the war, created a hunger for

former luxuries—things like cars, vacations, and college educations—
that now felt like middle-class necessities. A wife's salary was often
what a family needed to make these things affordable. Then, in the
mid-1960s, came inflation. Now women's salaries were needed not
just for luxuries but for *real* necessities. And so more and more
women—mothers included—left home to earn the money needed to
buy them.

It's commonly believed that the women's movement came along
and then, in its wake, women dropped their aprons and headed off to
work, seeking self-fulfillment and personal liberation. But that's
really not the way things happened. Women left home first. They
started going to work in big numbers in the 1950s. Because of an un-
usual confluence of demographics (the small size of the Eisenhower
generation, and the huge size of the postwar baby boom), there was a
great demand for labor—and for female labor in particular. By the
mid-1950s there was a national shortage of teachers, nurses, and clerical workers. Manpower Inc. was so desperate for woman workers
that it was offering them incentive gifts for sending in their neighbors and friends. To persuade women to take on more jobs and work
more days, the temp agency offered prizes for productivity and point-
ers on household efficiency.

The kinds of jobs women took were not necessarily fulfilling.
They were *jobs,* after all, not careers, and *women's* jobs at that. But they
paid the bills. And as the 1950s advanced, women's workforce participation skyrocketed. By 1956, at perhaps the height of the period we
think of as the at-home-mom Feminine Mystique years, one third of
the workforce was female. About two-thirds of those working women
were married, and more than half of those married women had children
of preschool or school age.

Over the course of the 1950s, the number of working mothers
alone grew by 400 percent. By the late 1960s, almost 40 percent of

mothers with children between the ages of six and seventeen were employed. And after that, as the cost of living kept rising, the numbers just kept going up. In 1971, almost half of all American women with school-age children had jobs, as did almost one-third of women who had children under age six. By 1972, for the first time, more mothers of school-age children were employed than not. By the mid-1970s fully half of all mothers were working, including 39 percent of mothers of preschool children, and after that the rate increased—particularly for mothers with young children—with each passing year.

This was a massive change, and it happened very fast. Faster than people could get their minds around it. Faster than our institutions could change to accommodate it. And, of course, it left a massive amount of anxiety in its wake. How could a family without a mom at home work? What were women going to do? What were children going to do? You could hear this anxiety in the outraged tone with which the psychological establishment reacted in the 1950s to the first set of statistics showing the steady stream of mothers into the workplace. It showed up in the early writings on attachment theory and, notably, in the horrified protests of psychologists like René Spitz. And then came the trickle-down effects: the catastrophizing over the lives of "latchkey" kids and "insecurely attached" day-care babies. The warnings from politicos and pundits that mothers' work might very well condemn whole generations to grow up as sociopaths.

This catastrophizing was no doubt a symptom of extreme cultural anxiety—like that, writ large, of a person with an anxiety disorder whose autonomic nervous system can't distinguish between a crowded subway car and an attack by a grizzly bear. And that cultural anxiety lasted so long and fused itself so totally to the issue of working motherhood that, as the decades passed, it became all but impossible to separate it out from the reality of working motherhood. The result was that by the 1990s, when 73 percent of mothers with children over age one were working (as were 59 percent of those with infants), certain beliefs—that mothers' work was bad, that separation was agony, and that children needed full-time mother care—no longer sounded like mere worries or opinions. They were articles of faith.

LOOKING BACK now at the 1990s, the anxiety is clear—as is the way that motherhood was called upon to quell it. The early part of the decade was marked by a recession. College-educated white men (the infamous "angry white males") were particularly hard-hit, both by unemployment and, if they were employed, by the increasing pressures of a hypercompetitive marketplace. What was their future? they worried. What was their purpose? Would they ever again be able to coast self-confidently through life? Would there ever again be enough jobs to go around?

There was plenty of anxiety on hand for women, too. For they also were hard hit by the recession. In the job-poor years of 1990 and 1991, for the first time since the end of World War Two, their influx into the world of work actually *stopped*. (It picked up again when the economy revived.) Many women lost jobs. Many others (of the baby-boom generation) who kept their jobs discovered that just as they were getting to the point when they might have risen to the top, their work lives were becoming unmanageable. There was no guaranteed family leave—only 40 percent of women in the workforce then had the right to take maternity leave and to have a job waiting for them when they returned. Only 10 percent of employers were providing their employees with child-care assistance—and most of the time this took the form of little more than counseling or referral services. Only 5 percent of business and government employees offered day care or helped their employees pay for it. It was an impossible situation. After two decades of advancement, women were maxing out in their careers. They couldn't even think of breaking through the glass ceiling if they wanted to spend any time with their kids; in fact, in many professions, if they wanted to devote time to their families, they could barely hold down a job at all. The optimism of the 1970s had run aground with experience and left them in a rut.

Women worried: What was their future? What were they to do about the unforeseen and now seemingly unresolvable conflicts in their lives? How could they make sense of the fact that they couldn't live up to the full scope of their ambitions if they wanted to have kids? How could they get their minds around the fact that—despite all the boosterism of the you-can-do-it-all 1980s—they *couldn't* do it all?

All this anxiety set the stage for the reemergence of the sacred stay-at-home mother. With her holistically healing message about returning to the hearth. The new stay-at-home dogma offered salve for bruised professional egos. It helped men remember that they *were* still men, and helped women see that if they didn't succeed as they'd planned they weren't failures, they simply had redefined their "priorities" and had joined in the trend toward "new traditionalism." (What was true for mothers, however, wasn't true for fathers. When men went home and took care of their kids—as increasing numbers did in the early 1990s—there was no talk about the dads' having found new "priorities." They were just unemployed. So that, in 1993, when the job market improved, and the proportion of dads staying home fell back down to 16 percent, from a high of 20 percent in 1991, it came without fanfare, in contrast to the enormous hype generated in 2001 when the percentage of mothers with infants in the workforce dropped—also 4 points—from 59 to 55 percent.)

Then came the New Economy. With a new set of realities, which made mothers' work—indeed, *all* work—all the more difficult to reconcile with the needs of families. There was, first and foremost, the fact that good, affordable child care was getting harder and harder to find. The full-employment economy meant that the caliber of people entering the child-care profession as nannies or day-care workers was getting lower and lower. The quality of day care available to *most* families was abysmal. Day-care work was considered the province of the extremely unskilled—like women transitioning from welfare. Nannies had to earn a living wage, and in cities where the cost of living had sky-rocketed, the cost of at-home care for children was pushed out of the reach of all but the best-off families.

After two decades of political leadership intent on shrinking our government, there was virtually no political will to make things better. When the Clinton administration proposed a series of measures to improve the quality and availability of child care, they were met by a chorus of commentators who said people didn't want them. (*Do you want the government raising your children?*) Addressing the most glaring problem in American child care—the lack of national standards—was simply considered a hopeless cause.

Some (in fact, relatively few) women could now choose to stay home. Many more women were effectively put in the situation of *having* to stay home—either because their now sixty-hour workweek was incompatible with family life or because their husbands' seventy-hour workweek meant that if they didn't stop working there would literally be *no one* at home with the kids.

All this led to a *lot* of anxiety. And to a new cult of domesticity, which, like the cult of domesticity that coincided with the Industrial Revolution, helped soothe the stresses of living life in an increasingly rapacious age. There was the stress of raising superchildren to compete in a fiercely competitive world. There was the stress of raising a family with virtually no social safety net. The stress of keeping up with the newly rich neighbors. There was the need, once again, for an oasis from the world of money and work, because with cell phones and e-mail and a 24/7 economy, oases of tranquillity were hard to find.

The new cult of motherhood offered peace. A sense of greater safety. The promise of *getting out*.

With the old promise of the 1970s and early 1980s—that women could proudly and happily lead multifunctioning lives—giving way to a grinding sense of impossibility, and with the notion of the "balanced life" teetering into oblivion, the idea that it was, after all, better for a women to be home with her children emerged as the "truth" of the day. The fact that families were being buffeted by economic forces beyond their control was replaced by a story of how women were taking control and "choosing" to go home and dedicate themselves to full-time motherhood, or "choosing" lower-paid dead-end jobs without benefits because they offered "flexibility." A response to economic conditions was reencoded as a new social ethic.

And this remained true when, in the next turn of the screw, a *lack of jobs,* post 9-11, was once again redefined by the terms of the Motherhood Religion. To capture this, I think of Belen Aranda-Alvarado, a member of Harvard Business School's class of 2002, who told the *Los Angeles Times* how the mind game of turning necessity into morality worked. Explaining how her male peers (and erstwhile competitors) cheered her decision to stay home and work as an "entrepreneur," she said, "They kind of see me as having the perfect solution [to the recession] that is socially acceptable."

The new cult of domesticity of the boom years—and the sad years that followed—created its own set of anxieties for mothers. How could they fit the self-sacrificing demands of total-reality motherhood into their prior self-conception as self-determining women? How could they make their worship of success jibe with their new devotion to the idea of family life?

The Mommy Mystique helped make it all come out okay. The revived ideal of raising kids as a woman's "life's work" comforted those uncomfortable with their decision (by choice or by default) to stay home with their children or to downgrade their workplace ambitions once they'd seen that ambitious work was incompatible with ambitious motherhood.

The Mommy Mystique soothed the anxieties caused by lifestyle changes—caused by economic changes—that had not been (indeed, have yet to be) entirely acknowledged and digested. This is different from the recent past, when the Motherhood Religion helped people deal with their anxiety over women's changing roles. People have largely accepted the idea of those changes now. What they haven't accepted (or even really conceptualized) is what we have to do to make those changes *work*.

Think about it: women might have responded to their anxieties differently at the end of the twentieth century. Instead of losing themselves in planning perfect birthday parties, they might have demanded more of their employers or of their government. They might have asked more of their husbands. But doing that—even *thinking* about that—would have exposed them to an even greater degree of anxiety. Because it would have meant tackling the sources of their problems. Because it would have meant trying to *do something* about their lives. Which would have meant destabilizing their marriages (and being confronted with the fact that, most probably, their husbands wouldn't change), or knocking their heads against the wall in seeking new government policies for social change. Women have known, I think, deep in their guts, that neither route would reap rewards. So they shut that sort of thinking down.

And having shut down their willingness to confront real-life motherhood, with its real-life problems and anxieties, they took refuge instead in the morality play version of modern motherhood that we see performed—and debated and discussed and dissected and critiqued—all around us every day.

That was an unfortunate decision. Because the moralizing, the pontificating, the hypocrisy, and the pressure that keep the Motherhood Religion alive in our time aren't doing mothers any good. In fact, they are doing many mothers a lot of harm.

ANDREA YATES, of course, is a very extreme example of how things can go haywire when motherhood is made into a religion and its every act is invested with the moral weight of Good and Evil. But lesser examples proliferate: in the endless self-flagellation, the guilt, and the utter idiocy of so much of The Mess:

> "For my daughter's fourth birthday I didn't make a cake from scratch and write 'Happy Birthday, Emma' on it. I had to work. I made the cake from a mix and put on whipped cream and Emma said, 'Where's Emma?' and I felt just terrible."
>
> "If I have a day where I have someone who comes to the house to take care of my daughter, I feel very guilty if I'm doing something other than doing the groceries or going to the dry cleaner."
>
> "My guilt comes from a school environment where you can never do enough, and there are always people who are doing more than you."
>
> "I feel guilty that I don't know how to enjoy my children!"

The maddening chant of our Motherhood Religion haunts working mothers and stay-at-home moms alike. Working moms have to run from a chorus detailing their evils. If their children seem fine, they must constantly question their just-fineness. If their financial situation isn't dire, they must constantly justify themselves to others, to make their working acceptable. Because they are told that it is unnatural for them to be working, because they are told it is selfish for them to work unless there is a dire financial necessity for it, many are plagued not only by guilt but also by a pervasive feeling that there is something *wrong* with them if they don't feel guilty about working.

Stay-at-home mothers are made, by our religion of productivity, to feel they have no worth if they are not earning money. The religion of feminism makes them feel that they are letting down the Girls' Team. The cult of total-reality motherhood tells them that they are saints—which would be flattering except that they don't generally *feel* like saints (they often feel bored and impatient and frustrated and tired)—which leaves them wondering what is wrong with *them* for feeling that way.

All this moralizing we routinely do is a ridiculous waste of time and energy. And it also rests upon assumptions that have no basis in reality. Chief among them: that mothers do what they do most of the time out of choice.

"CHOICE" is the fetish word of our generation, perhaps the most sacred of all our articles of faith. It runs through all discussions of motherhood, and inspires most of the quasi-moral fables we read so frequently in the press. It was the buzzword that recurred endlessly in the coverage of Sylvia Ann Hewlett's 2002 book, *Creating a Life: Professional Women and the Quest for Children,* which depicted the stark "choices" made by childless top female professionals and advised younger women to be "intentional" about marrying young and having children as soon as possible. It comes up again and again in the stories of how college women are taking the long view in planning their lives—choosing easily Mommy Trackable careers, for example, which will allow them to stop, have children, then start up work all over again. And it's the founding principle of the so-called Mommy Wars—which wouldn't exist without the notion that there are two warring camps of moms who've made diametrically opposed life choices, one camp having chosen the "selfish," modern track of ambition and the other having taken the "selfless," natural track of stay-at-home motherhood.

People repeat these ideas about our "choices" all the time. Even working mothers buy into them. And yet, they *just aren't true.*

I have by now talked to hundreds of women. And what I see is that working and stay-at-home moms do what they do not so much by choice—by choosing from a series of options arrayed before them like cereals on a supermarket shelf—but out of a very immediate and pressing sense of personal necessity. There are many aspects to that sense of necessity—money, status, ambition, the needs of the children and of the family as a whole—all of which play themselves out, in various ways, in individual women's lives. And all of those aspects of personal necessity are part and parcel of the condition of motherhood—not external to it, not accessory to it, not a "selfish" deviation from it. They grow naturally out of what women have done—and who they have been—throughout their lives. So their paths as mothers are not so much "chosen" as *devolved* from who they are, who they've been, and what the material conditions of their families require.

Penelope Green once put this succinctly, with remarkable honesty, in an essay called "Family Value" that ran in *Vogue* in 2001. In response to a friend, who had remarked on Green's having had to "shelve her career" for her baby, she wrote that her nonjob of writing thirty hours a week had "never been a question of 'choice' or 'sacrifice.'"

"I work the way I work," she said, "because it gives my parenting life the only shape that feels right to me. . . . Maybe you could even say it is not so much the fact of my child as it is a lack in me—of talent or love or maybe a little of both—that keeps me out of circulation. Hell, maybe I just went as far as I was able, career-wise. Maybe I got bored; certainly I got lazy. Probably my daughter is a convenient excuse."

We all know the reasons why working mothers work (since they must constantly justify themselves): money, above all, but secondarily, satisfaction, adult companionship, intellectual stimulation, a sense of security and independence and status—the ability, in short, to provide for their families and remain true to themselves. But from talking to women, I've found that the reasons that stay-at-home moms stay home are not all that different, in that, at base, they spring both from a psychological need for self-fulfillment and an effort to meet the material needs of their families. (And *not,* as many commentators would have us think, from a moralistic idea of what was the "right thing to do.")

Very often, the material condition that makes them stay home is a husband's nonstop work schedule. But there are other concrete reasons as well: Child-care costs that amount to more than a mother's take-home pay. Or working hours or a lack of job flexibility that simply makes being a working mother impossible. ("When my daughter had chicken pox it was not an excusable absence," one stay-at-home mom who formerly worked at a large telecommunications company told me. "When I was pregnant, with partial paralysis, it was not an excusable absence—even though I couldn't drive.") Some stay-at-home moms I met had had a bad experience with child care: "I went through nine nannies in two years," said a Washington professional on an open-ended leave. "I think the sequence of changes had a really high cost. I can't quantify how it was for my children, but for me it was really hard." Some quite simply had had joyless, low-paying jobs that weren't worth keeping—particularly when balanced against the cost and low quality of day care.

"I didn't have any kind of life before that I enjoyed," admitted one stay-at-home military wife with two children. "If I were not going to stay at home, it would have to be for something really meaningful."

The psychological reasons for staying home were varied and complex. Women whose mothers had worked out of dire financial necessity and hadn't been able to afford to have nannies simply associated working motherhood with stress and deprivation and anxiety. "My mom had five kids and often worked two jobs," recalled a twenty-eight-year-old former clerical worker for a government agency turned stay-at-home mom. "Often she'd go through jobs because they'd want to fire her for taking a couple of hours off to come with us to the doctor's office. I watched, and I didn't want it to happen to me. I didn't want my only contact with my kids to be in the morning rushing out.

My mom was always rushed, worried about getting it all done. There's no joy in that." Some women, who'd had working mothers in communities where most mothers stayed home, remembered feeling uncomfortably different. Those whose mothers had not been able to afford babysitters—at a time when there were no after-school programs—remembered feeling very much alone. "At the other kids' houses it was warm and there was food cooking. Their moms were there after school and could go on field trips. I would lose my key on purpose in elementary school so I could go home with one of my friends," recalled a thirty-five-year-old Washington, D.C., stay-at-home mom who went home with her brothers and sisters after school to an empty house after her parents' divorce sent her mother back to work. "I wanted to be Doris Day when I grew up."

Others just couldn't deal with being physically separate from their children. "Before I started staying home, I was the breadwinner," says a Washington, D.C., mother who recently, after years at home, began part-time work again. "I was making three or four times what my husband was making, easily. And then, after my twins were born, I said, 'I'm not going back.'

"We could not afford it. We had just bought a new house. We had a lien on our bank account from the IRS. We could not pay our taxes. We went into counseling. It was awful. But it was a nonnegotiable for me. Because I couldn't live with that kind of feeling."

There were status reasons, too—often unstated but clear—like wanting to be a homemaker because of early shame at being the *one* child in the neighborhood with a working mom. There were women for whom stay-at-home motherhood was a mark of success, of having *arrived* solidly in the middle class. "I grew up around people who had to work. I didn't know anybody who stayed at home unless they were on welfare," said a stay-at-home Washington mom with three kids. For these women, whether they came from middle-class, lower-middle-class, or poor backgrounds, stay-at-home motherhood was the culmination of a lifelong ambition, one that had been nurtured, and worked at, consciously or not, the whole of their adult lives, necessitating the choice of the right kind of husband with the right kind of earning potential to make a stay-at-home future possible.

I found that when women were able to act in line with their natural inclinations and ambitions—whether to work or stay at home—they were generally happy, and generally felt that their children were happy, too. Whereas those whose natural inclinations and ambitions had been thwarted—*whether they were working or stay-at-home moms*—were sure that they and their kids would be better off if they changed course, and either went to work or went home. The morality of the situation—whether they felt it was good or bad for their children—derived, not from some external sense of the morality of their "choices," but from the amount of happiness generated by any given arrangement. And that general sense of happiness or well-being began when a mother's sense of personal necessity was satisfied.

THERE'S A REALLY interesting way to illustrate what I mean about personal necessity and motherhood and the idea that you can't separate personal necessity *from* motherhood. It means taking a look, not just at mothers today or at our foremothers in past decades or centuries, but also at our relatives, the primates, as I learned from reading Sarah Blaffer Hrdy's fascinating 1999 book, *Mother Nature*.

Hrdy, an anthropologist trained in sociobiology, became personally interested in the mess of motherhood when, early on in her career, she stumbled between the twin pulls of her work and her young daughter and wondered why it was so hard to make everything fit together. She had read Bowlby and believed in his ideas about bonding and didn't want to do anything that would disrupt her connection to her daughter. But at the same time, the desire to work was so strong within her and felt so natural . . . Could it really be so out of line, she wondered, with motherhood?

Thinking about contemporary human society didn't offer Hrdy much by way of answers. But thinking about our primate relatives did.

While studying other primates, Hrdy was struck by the fact that, unlike human mothers today, other primate mothers have always managed to pull together what we consider to be opposite and mutually exclusive goals: providing for children and nurturing them with loving, hands-on care. Moving into the human realm, she noted that in the Pleistocene era women carried their babies as they foraged or gathered firewood. What was it, she wondered, that made their multi-tasking lives come together so naturally? There had to be, she thought, an "ancient female motivation" that explained how they Did It All.

That ancient motivation, she came to see, sprang from certain material realities of primate life: High-status female primates ate. Low-status female primates were eaten. Or were chased away from food. Or saw their babies eaten by other females. And so primate mothers, in order to keep their children alive, had to be ambitious. They had to secure "status" for themselves and their offspring so that they'd have access to fought-over resources like food and shelter. Hrdy writes:

> Establishing an advantageous niche for herself was how Flo, the chimpanzee female that Jane Goodall studied for so many years, stayed fed, guaranteed access to food for her offspring, and kept them safe from interference by other mothers. Eventually, Flo's high status made it possible for her daughter Fifi to be among the few females who would remain in her natal place to breed—in Fifi's case, inheriting her mother's territory. Even more impressive data documenting the connection between female status and all sorts of reproductive parameters . . . have been compiled for Old World cercopithecine mon-

keys like macaques and baboons. These data strongly suggest that generalized striving for local clout was genetically programmed into the psyches of female primates during a distant past when status and motherhood were totally convertent.

Primate mothers' "striving for status," Hrdy saw, was every bit as natural and necessary a part of their mothering as was the care and feeding of their young. Their ambition helped their children to survive and, as a result, was *the* ultimate form of mother care.

We've dropped this "striving for status" function from our contemporary definition of motherhood. But Hrdy is convinced that we are more tightly linked to our ancestors than we think. For one thing, we are still struggling for limited resources. And for another, the sense of the necessity of providing for our children—securing them the status and resources that will allow them to "survive or prosper," as Hrdy puts it—is still hard-wired into our brains. Which means that "natural" motherhood today should know no conflict between providing for our children (i.e., "working") and nurturing them (i.e. "being a mom"). *Both* are part of our evolutionary heritage; both are equally "child-centered" imperatives.

What's "unnatural" about motherhood today, if you follow Hrdy's line of thinking, is not that mothers work but rather that their "striving for status" and their "maternal emotions" have been compartmentalized. By putting the two in conflict—by insisting on the incompatibility of work and motherhood—our culture does violence to mothers, splitting them, unnaturally, within themselves. And the nature of work today makes this split worse. The demands of the contemporary workplace, which often require long working hours and long commutes, force mothers to separate from their children for excessive periods of time. Lack of flexibility completes a picture in which women really *are* forced to choose between providing for and nurturing their children. This means that mothers' instinctual drives to "seek status" are put in conflict with their children's instinctual needs for succor. "The conflict . . . is not between maternity and ambition," Hrdy writes, "but between the needs of infants and the way a woman's ambition plays out in modern workplaces."

No wonder motherhood in America today feels so messed up. No wonder so many mothers feel incomplete, like something's always lacking from their otherwise chockablock-full lives. No wonder so many suffer from anxiety—a kind of existential anxiety, a feeling of powerlessness, as though disaster lurked around every corner.

For me, Hrdy's findings, whether or not they're applied literally to understanding the lives of modern mothers, provide a very apt metaphor for understanding the mess that plagues us today. For they show that the so-called "choices" most of us face in America—between more-than-full-time work or 24/7 on-duty motherhood—are, quite simply, *unnatural.* They amount to a kind of psychological castration: excessive work severs a mother from her need to be physically present in caring for her child, and excessive "full-time" motherhood of the total-reality variety severs a mother not only from her ability to financially provide for her family but also from her adult *sense of agency,* as it sucks her so deeply down into the infantile realm of her children.

In saying this, I am not necessarily making an automatic argument for working motherhood, for in some marriages, I believe, the nature of the husband's work is such that the wife has to stay home in order to provide for and protect her children. And staying home clearly is the fulfillment of some women's strivings for status. I am just making the argument that if a woman loses her sense of agency—of her potential ability to provide for her child—she will, very slowly, crack apart. As did so many postwar moms, urged back home in the days of the Feminine Mystique. As do so many stay-at-home moms today. And if a mother is deprived of her ability to nurture and care for her child—as are women today who must work excessive hours or consign their children to inadequate care—she too will suffer deep within her core.

. . .

BOTH WORKING MOTHERS and stay-at-home moms are ambitious. Both are status-seekers. These facts are obvious to anyone with the eyes to see them. (Life on the soccer field is rapacious. The world of play dates can be inhuman. Running volunteers for the school auction can be an exercise in cruelty.) So why can't we acknowledge that what we do is value-neutral? Why do we continue to invest goodness in stay-at-home motherhood and evil in work? *Why must we take refuge in theology instead of dealing with real life?*

Imagine how productive it would be if we stopped obsessing on the morality of staying at home versus working and focused instead on the material conditions that stress all mothers to the point where they founder and drown in The Mess. First of all, we would find that working mothers and stay-at-home moms' interests, ambitions, goals, and needs were strongly aligned. And then, by focusing on the facts of their lives, we would be able to start to define some national priorities for policy that would actually help ease families' lives.

For the moment, all this is little more than a pipe dream. Because it's impossible, in a culture that's constantly making a religion of every-thing, to stop and look at the facts. It's almost impossible to *get* at the facts, because they're constantly being couched in the terms of our favorite theologies. This is true of the way we talk to one another, of the way journalists write about motherhood—even, says Shari Thurer, a psychologist who reviewed decades of thinking and writing about motherhood for her 1994 book, *The Myths of Motherhood,* of social science:

> The psychological research to date continually looks for bad outcomes from maternal employment and other-than-mother care *instead* of looking for bad outcomes from the lack of societal supports to mothers. In other words, the way psychologists

have been framing their research questions reflects the culture's idealized myth of motherhood. So while research has failed to demonstrate the deleterious effects of day care, it has also failed to demonstrate the deleterious effects of *no* day care—because it did not set out to find them. The unfortunate result is that our psychological research has inadvertently contributed to the maintenance of the status quo, instead of stimulating questions about social change and help for mothers.

This is precisely what happened with Jay Belsky's day-care research in the late 1980s. It happened at the time of the publication of Stanley Greenspan and T. Berry Brazelton's 2000 book, *The Irreducible Needs of Children,* in which the authors made an argument for better day care, and challenged society to come up with more ways to help families. (*USA Today* headlined its coverage "Stay Home with the Kids If You Can.")

It is what happened in 2002, when newspapers across the country ran with the news that mothers' work made their children unable to learn—despite the fact that the study that occasioned this news, conducted by researchers at Columbia University, had found that mothers' work, per se, didn't do *anything.* It was poor-quality care that was keeping kids back. (Three-year-olds with working mothers who were emotionally available to them and could afford to pay for "the best child care possible" scored just the same, researchers found, as the kids of stay-at-home moms.) It happened again in the summer of 2003, when the largest long-term study of child care in the United States was summed up by journalists to say that day care was making kids aggressive. This even though the study had concluded that what was really going wrong for aggressive kids in day care was, once again, the poor quality of the care.

Both the 2002 and the 2003 studies concluded that what really mattered for children wasn't whether or not their mothers worked but whether or not their families could afford to provide them with top-quality care. But, as has happened over and over again, these results pointing to the effects of class and of inadequate child care in America were recast to denounce working motherhood. ("Here's Another Thing to Feel Guilty About," was the subject line of the group e-mail sent my way.) The net result was that talk radio was swamped with the usual crusading callers; politicians were spared the need to come up with solutions, and mothers were left with no greater option than to throw up their hands and take their nightly Ambien. Because there was nothing else they could do in the face of such an impossible situation.

Except, of course, to refuse to accept that the situation was impossible.

"Instead of saying, 'I feel terrible. I feel guilty,' maybe [women] can take these results and advocate for [national] family-leave policies that create more options for mothers of babies," said researcher Jeanne Brooks-Gunn, the lead author of the 2002 day-care study, as she expressed her frustration with all the hand-wringing and guilt expressed in the study's wake by working mothers. "Every other industrialized nation has done it. Why can't we?"

MOTHER IMAGE PROBLEMS

The way we mother today isn't entirely new.

Back in the 1920s, the converts to "scientific motherhood" were already practicing a (more emotionally ascetic) form of total-reality motherhood. It meant constant vigilance, a perfect monitoring of food intake and activities, chauffeuring children to and from music and dancing lessons, and total immersion in the advice books of the new child-care experts. As one upper-middle-class mother in Middletown, Connecticut, proudly put it, in 1929, "I accommodate my whole life to my little girl."

Teach-your-kids-to-read books have been around since the early 1960s. R. Fitzhugh Dodson's 1970 best seller *How to Parent* boasted a reading list of guides to help parents intellectually stimulate their children and encouraged mothers to apply their teachings to lay the groundwork for later intellectual growth and professional success. But new levels of wealth and our own postboomer generational peculiarities have brought the demands of being a "special kind of mother" to a new fever pitch. Our Spockian mothers may have been told to make us their life's work, but they appear, mostly, to have taken expert advice with a grain of salt. Many now express horror with our way of taking what the experts say literally. They see us singing and rolling on the floor in our sweatpants, getting glitter glue and soy milk everywhere, and they think we're crazy. Our children have no "boundaries," they say. They're spoiled rotten. They think it wouldn't be a bad thing if we were to go out for an evening with our husbands. Do something with our hair, at least. *Get a life.*

So much for progress.

It would be easy to categorize the shift toward self-sacrificial motherhood that began in the late 1980s as part of the widespread cultural reaction against women's advancement detailed in 1992 by Susan Faludi's *Backlash.* It's true that the broadening of messages advocating self-sacrifice and a devotional form of stay-at-home motherhood corresponded to the coming into its own of the Christian Right as a force in mainstream American politics. But I don't think that's a sufficient explanation. Cultural messages don't just come from outside and above. If they don't take root in fertile minds, they can't stick.

And these new messages about motherhood stuck with us despite the fact that many of our own mothers turned up their noses at our excessive mothering techniques, despite the fact that many pediatricians were highly vocal in warning us not to fall into the most popular forms of hysteria du jour, despite the fact that there were always some experts appearing in the media, writing books and issuing appeals for rationality and calm. Despite the fact that, in our heart of hearts, we knew that self-sacrificial motherhood wasn't really a very good thing.

After all, plenty of us, in the 1960s and 1970s, had had overinvolved mothers—the kind that experts warned about back then. Mothers who too closely monitored our homework, got overbusy at our schools, or generally bordered on living our lives for us. Those of us who did came out of it with no illusions about the virtue of practicing such a "selfless" form of motherhood. "My dad didn't stand a chance against us." . . . "The bulk of our life was and is spent with [my mother] mad at us for one reason or another, since to her we never appreciated her and did not love her," women told me as they remembered the double bind of being on the receiving end of another person's total ambition.

Many women I spoke with recalled their mothers' immersion in the minutiae of their lives as a way of exerting some control within families where they really had no power. And they said that they did not want to repeat that pattern in their own families now. "One golden rule for me, based on observing my mom, is: to always be a little bit selfish and take care of myself, otherwise I will resent my child and she will bear the brunt of my dissatisfaction and stress," said one working mother in Virginia. "I want to take care of myself better in order to be able to give her more love and affection, and not torment her by making her feel guilty for all that I have given up for her willingly or as a result of having her."

But these sentiments, so common and so commonsensical, don't generally get much airtime today.

For some reason, our cultural receptors are tuned differently. In our abuse-wary, separation-averse time, we hear the cries of abandonment and loss and pain that we believe issue forth from our children and not the words of warning against overinvolvement that experience, expert opinion, and common sense provide. Trying to be perfect, we mother in ways that we know *full well* aren't healthy.

It is as though, as one woman I interviewed put it, we all suffer from "mother-image problems." And these "mother-image problems," like the body-image problems rampant in our society, where average models are 5'11" and weigh 117 pounds and average women are 5'4" and weigh 140 pounds, have a kind of funhouse-mirror effect on our self-images as mothers. They push us to strive for impossible goals that diminish and undermine us—*and aren't even good for our children.*

Something about the ideal of motherhood we carry in our heads is so compelling that even though we can't fulfill it and know that we probably shouldn't even try, we berate ourselves for falling short of succeeding. It is in service to that "something" that we continue to pursue the goals of total-reality motherhood. It is not, I believe, because we really, truly believe in our heart of hearts that a good mother is deeply self-sacrificing. No—I would argue instead that, like a woman obsessively trying to weigh 117 pounds, what we are trying to do, in religiously following the rites and rituals of ideal mother-hood, is assuage some kind of deeper longing inside us.

For some women, I think, it is a longing for the world of their childhoods, when someone was there to take care of things. For other women, who did not feel sufficiently cared for by their mothers, it's a desire to give their children the kind of comforting childhood they didn't have—and to "reparent" themselves in the process. Overall, I think, it's a longing to *get things under control.*

For it is the sense of control that underlies the appeal of Donna Reed, with her world of "routine and order and organization and competence," as Lonnae O'Neal Parker put it. It is the sense that *somebody* has things under control and is able to achieve with graceful ease all the things that we find so painfully challenging.

And this, I think, is the real reason why we mother the way we do. It gives us a feeling of control that is very comforting (and very fa-miliar). It suits us psychologically. It allows us to assuage our anxiety. And it fits where we are as a society.

PART 3

Ourselves, as Mothers

7.

A Generation of

Control Freaks

H AVE YOU noticed how hard it
is these days to get together on the weekend with another family?

First, you have to find a time slot free of kids' activities. No soccer, lacrosse, or baseball, no ballet or SAT tutoring or religious school.
No tae kwon do or fencing or occupational therapy or speech therapy
or violin practicing or homework. Then you have to find a group activity that will please (or at least palliate) every member of the group.
Indoors or out? Museum or not? Well, the problem is . . . this one's
husband doesn't like to leave home on Saturdays (he works so hard all
week), and that one doesn't tolerate the playground. There can't be
any ice cream because this one's son gets all funny with ice cream (actually, he's never had any, but his mom gets funny with ice cream,
and if he sees the other kids having some, he'll want some, and she
doesn't think she can deal with that), and this one's daughter has said
she won't play indoors anymore. Not until she's ten. And then—the

activity needs to have some *intellectual* quality. It needs to have some *athletic* component. (Otherwise the kids will be too crazy.) But it can't be *overstimulating* (the kids work so hard all week). It has to be convenient, it has to be easy, it has to be over early, please, so everyone can be gotten home in time, fed in time, lulled into a cooperation-conducive mood in time so that the bedtime rituals can happen without Mom's going *totally crazy.*

This is a very unpleasant situation. But it's not entirely unfamiliar.

In the 1980s, you couldn't invite a friend over for dinner without her opening the oven door and doing a quick calorie count before she mentally committed herself to eating.

In the 1990s, she brought her *own* dinner—because she was, inevitably, allergic to whatever you served.

We have long been a generation of control freaks.

For decades now, we have had a tendency to act as though contagion—the contagion of out-of-controlness—lay behind every corner. Behind every pot lid, every menu, every play date.

Once, we controlled against that contagion by erecting a cordon sanitaire around ourselves. Now we do it by micromanaging our family lives. Because it feels, very often, that if we don't do the exactly right thing, master all the details, control every moment, then our children will be . . . not just shut out from, say, the best ballet class, but . . . cast adrift . . . left behind . . . limited . . . passed over. They will get fat, they will be immature, they will lack muscle tone, and focus, and a competitive edge. . . . They'll end up as losers.

To many of us today, it feels as though the pie of life—the ultimate rewards spelling success and happiness in adulthood—is becoming ever smaller, and if we don't prepare our children well now to seize their piece, they may end up going hungry altogether. And on the other hand, if we give them just the right combination of winner-producing things—the right swimming lessons and ballet lessons and learning-to-read books and building toys—we can inoculate them against failure.

This is, of course, ridiculous. And raises a set of questions: If we don't want to be feeling anxious and out of control, why don't we do something productive? Why, if we're worried about our kids' not getting their fair share of the pie, don't we devote ourselves to making sure the pie's made large enough to feed them?

I believe that it's for the same reason that, as young women, so many of us renounced pie altogether, and instead enacted our anxieties in food obsessions and body control.

From the beginning of the time that, as adolescents, we began to contend with the complexities of life as adult women, we have had a tendency, in the face of anxiety or challenge, to shut down. To block out the big picture of our worries and responsibilities. To *microman-age* as a way of getting things under control. With the sad result that, as young women, many of us constricted our horizons at precisely the point when life was opening up before us. And that, as mothers, we have tended, overwhelmingly, to turn our eyes inward at precisely a time when we should be looking outward. We have developed a tendency, as a generation, to *privatize* our problems. To ferociously work at fixing and perfecting ourselves—instead of focusing on ways we might get society to fix itself.

This speaks of a kind of hopelessness—a kind of giving-up on the outside world. It's as though we believe that, in the end, *we* are all we can count on. And that our power to control ourselves and our families is all the power that we have.

This is a lesson we learned long ago. Ironically, its roots date back to the days when we were taught that *everything* was within our power.

GIRL POWER

We were the girls who could Do Anything. This was not something we had to shout about, or something we had to prove, it just *was*. It was our legacy as the inheritors of feminism, our "entitlement," as Barbara Findlen put it in the 1995 collection of essays *Listen Up: Voices from the Next Feminist Generation.*

Our mothers were our greatest fans. They made it very clear to us that they didn't want our lives stunted by the kinds of limitations they'd encountered in adulthood. They wanted us to be independent and competent, to make our own money and control our own destinies. They didn't teach us to do housework, to sew on buttons or to bake bread. They were endlessly supportive as we explored our options and took risks, even if our options took us far from what was familiar to them, or from the beliefs that had shaped their lives.

Our culture was supportive, too. On the surface, at least. It gave us coed gym and woodworking shop, and told us never to let the boys drown out our voices in class. Often enough, we did better than they did in school. *Even* in science and math. We called our teachers "Ms." We went to college in classes that were more than 50 percent female. And our passage into adulthood was marked by a steady stream of increasing numbers of women in the professions. We believed that we could climb as high as we wanted to go, and would live adult lives that would allow us to be the people that we wanted to be. Other outcomes—like the chance that children wouldn't quite fit into this picture—never even entered our minds.

But a very strange thing happened to us on the way to adulthood. Even as our horizons continued to widen, we began to shrink. We began to shut ourselves down.

In the 1980s, while our baby boomer elders continued their quest to achieve firsts in the worlds of business and politics and elsewhere, we earned the dubious distinction of being the first generation ever to register an "epidemic" of eating disorders. Anorexia nervosa and bulimia—which afflicted only 2 percent of American women overall—were suddenly showing up in 10 percent of women in our age group and in *20* percent of young women on some college campuses.

At Yale, Naomi Wolf, who had her own battle with anorexia in her early teen years, put the incidence of bulimia at more like 60 percent. "The norm, then, for young, middle-class American women," she wrote, in *The Beauty Myth*, "is to be a sufferer from some form of the eating disease."

In 1989, social historian Joan Jacobs Brumberg, reflecting on the generational character of the students she was teaching at Cornell University, called anorexia nervosa "the characteristic psychopathology of the female adolescent of our day." She linked this pathology directly back to our collective psychology as a generation of do-anything-and-be-anything overachievers.

"Even though feminine dependency is no longer in fashion," she wrote, ". . . young women combine traditional expectations with a quest for equity and power. To be brainy and beautiful; to have an exciting $75,000-a-year job; to nurture two wonderful children in consort with a supportive but equally high-powered husband—these are the personal ambitions of many in the present college generation."

Our problems, she said, were inseparable from our sense of personal promise:

> In order to achieve this level of personal and social perfection, young women must be extremely demanding of themselves: there can be no distracting personal or avocational detours— they must be unrelenting in the pursuit of goals. The kind of personal control required to become the new Superwoman . . . parallels the single-mindedness that characterizes the anorexic. In sum, the golden ideal of this generation of privileged young women and their most distinctive pathology appear to be flip sides of the same record.

In other words, there was a fault line running through the girls-can-do-anything messages of our youth. *No one* can do just *anything* if it also involves doing *everything* and doing it all at an incredibly high level of performance. Men have always known this; they don't even try. Prior generations of women knew it, too. But not us. We had a sense of omnipotence. Which we confused with real empowerment.

SOON the experts were saying that, as far as generational meltdown went, anorexia nervosa and bulimia were just the tip of the iceberg. A much bigger problem, the *real* epidemic, was that so many young women—*normal* women—were obsessing and hypercontrolling and *just plain weird* about food. The psychiatrist Judith Rodin started calling women's preoccupation with their weight a "normative discontent." Chronic dieting, compulsive exercising, and intermittent binge eating were so common, and so worrisome to mental health professionals, that by the late 1980s they had given them a new official label: "subclinical eating disorder."

When I was in college, it seemed that disordered eating—whether of the full-fledged bulimic or anorexic type or of the run-of-the-mill, pain-in-the-ass, dressing-on-the-side and no-butter-on-the-potato variety—was so widespread that it provided a kind of background noise to my coming of age. There were eating-disorder memoirs. Dog-eared copies of Kim Chernin's *The Obsession* everywhere. Posters all over campus for eating-disorder support groups. And an enthusiastic and energized array of mental health professionals to lead them. A new strain of feminist psychology was emerging, devoted to "listening" to the "rebellion" the anorexic expressed through her body. The eating disorders were a cultural *event.*

And no matter how much concerned noise the experts were making, being a control freak, in the 1980s, didn't feel like a bad thing. It was a way to fit in. A way to bond with like-minded friends. It was a good way to *get your way*—in your family, at social events, and particularly with boyfriends (who never seemed to really get what was going on).

Perhaps that's why, soon enough, control-freakishness was not just a way of dealing with food. It was a way of dealing with *life*. And it morphed, in the early 1990s, into a whole new slew of other newly "epidemic" maladies—various syndromes involving aches and pains and vapors and intolerances, which had in common the net effect of allowing those suffering from them to exercise a rather remarkable degree of control over their environment and those around them.

At the extreme end of this, there was multiple chemical sensitivity, called the "twentieth-century disease" or being "allergic to everything," which required its sufferers to live in bubble houses, carry oxygen tanks, or retreat from the world altogether. At the lesser end there were, for example, the food allergies—chiefly to dairy and wheat—naturally occurring in only 1 to 2 percent of the population, magically occurring, as I recall, in the early 1990s in about 75 percent of the young women around me. Lactose intolerance was so very common, so recognizable as a with-it foible, that Meg Ryan, cast as a control freak American Everywoman in the 1995 comedy *French Kiss,* got easy laughs when she contorted and screamed "Lactose intolerance!" after breaking down and eating a cheese plate in France.

In her 1994 book, *Consumed: Why Americans Love, Hate and Fear Food,* Michelle Stacey presented her own version of the Everywoman: Laurel Schiller, a pseudonymous "restrained eater" on a 1,400-calorie-a-day, no-fat diet. A classic example of a woman with a "subclinical" eating disorder, Schiller called her fat-free diet book her bible. She got a "frisson of pleasure" from eating American Glacé frozen dessert an entire carton at a time. Her other pleasures were few and far between. She couldn't be sure of maintaining her diet if she went out to eat, so she stopped going out. "Every time I'd make a plan, I'd think, I don't want to do this because there's nothing for me to eat there," she told

Stacey. "So I wouldn't want to make plans, or I'd make plans not in-volving dinner. Or I'd just make sure we went to a restaurant where I knew there were things I could order. But I used to love to go out to good restaurants, and at a certain point I realized it was kind of weird that I was staying home just so I could eat what I wanted." Her adherence to her magical rituals took over her life.

I REMEMBER HOW, in the early and mid-1990s, it seemed to me that a suspiciously high number of the women around me were wast-ing their lives away. Not growing super-skinny, necessarily. But mak-ing themselves small and stupid with food and body obsessions. Constricting their horizons with rigid rules and regulations and pho-bias. Making themselves, and their lives, grow smaller. A number of them were afraid to drive. One was afraid of water. Many had re-nounced dairy and/or wheat, and were utterly impossible to eat with. Or else they were impossible to *do anything* with, because they always needed to be at home, ingesting just the right amount of wheat-free cereal with just the right amount of soy milk, then spending just the right amount of time in the bathroom.

This New Neurasthenia, as I came to call it, could be debilitating. There were young women with permanently depressed metabolisms. A friend with thinning hair and translucent skin, suffering from mal-nutrition. But it wasn't without its compensations. Husbands could be sent out in the middle of the night to seek needed foods or stom-ach medicines. Family lives could be entirely reconfigured in order to achieve a needed level of irritant-free sterility—all in the name of right-thinking good living.

In 1990, Donna Stewart, a Canadian psychiatrist, brought this point home dramatically when she studied fifty (mostly female) patients suffering from the usual array of headaches, stomachaches, irritability, and malaise that were then generally attributed to such "fashionable diagnoses" as environmental hypersensitivity disorder, food allergies, chronic fatigue, and yeast hypersensitivity. She discovered that, in a bizarre way, her long-suffering patients *enjoyed* being ill. None of them were actively employed. Less than 40 percent expected ever to return to work—*or* ever to recover their health. They had become permanent invalids. And they were in control. Their syndromes and symptoms, wrote Stewart, "become a legitimate reason for giving up other responsibilities in favor of health concerns or for allowing themselves to be looked after by others. The secondary gains are often obvious and significant."

MANY FEMINIST COMMENTATORS and psychologists, writing about the "epidemic" of anorexia nervosa and bulimia—and weight obsession, generally—in the late 1980s and early 1990s, viewed it as a desperate play for control. Control of the body, of *something,* by young women coming out of their you-can-do-anything girlhoods into you-*can't*-do-it-all womanhood, in which so many things suddenly seemed out of control.

Much of what seemed out of control in their lives had to do with sexuality—both the fact of being a sexual person and that of being, very simply, a woman. For one thing, the sexual revolution hadn't been all it was cracked up to be. Sure, by the 1980s, young women could— were expected to—sleep with whomever they wanted to. But that didn't necessarily save them from being called sluts afterward. It also didn't keep them from falling into the whole round of waiting-by-the-phone dependent behaviors that were supposed to have gone up in smoke at about the same time the "women's libbers" were throwing their bras and girdles into the Freedom Trash Can. Young women in the 1980s often found themselves as man-dependent, insecure, and sometimes self-belittling in their behaviors as were their prefeminist foremothers. The only difference was that now they knew to hate themselves for it. And to think that they ought to be able to get it under control.

The teenagers and young women of the post–baby boom generation certainly had more freedom than their mothers had had to move through life and do things or go places where nice girls en route to marriage in the past didn't go. But it wasn't as though the big wide world necessarily greeted them with wide open arms, or even a basic sense of safety. In the late 1980s and early 1990s, young women who ventured into formerly all-male bastions were routinely subjected to harassment, hazing, even sexual assault. Or, at the very least, some overt drooling. I think particularly of Kelly Flinn, sexually assaulted in her bed at the Air Force Academy; Shannon Faulkner, psychologically broken after just one week at the formerly all-male Virginia Military Institute; the women at the Stroh's Brewery bottling plant in St. Paul who were driven from their jobs after months of insults and physical assaults (one male employee allegedly drove a forklift into a female colleague); and the new classes of young female interns and trainees and junior associates who every Fall proudly took prestigious jobs alongside their male peers in newspapers and corporate offices and law firms and then spent the first few months squirming as their not-entirely-rehabilitated male superiors undressed them with their eyes.

The gender-neutral universe our generation had grown up believing in simply didn't exist. Young women in the late 1980s and early 1990s could embark on their careers with all the self-assurance in the world. That wouldn't keep male bosses from visibly checking out their legs. Or keep female bosses from viewing them as competition. Or keep the rumors from circulating that if they did well, they had necessarily slept with someone to earn their stripes. Age-old sexist *stuff* played itself out time and time again. The face of the professional world might have been changing. But its hidden face wasn't—not much. The general mood of the country, in fact, was shifting *backward*.

The glory days of the women's movement—the time when Representative Bella Abzug said there was "no opposition" to equal-rights legislation for women in Congress—were gone, leaving a lot of anger and resentment in their wake. Part of the way that anger and resentment expressed itself was in a generalized atmosphere of sexual threat.

In the mid- to late 1970s, it sometimes seemed that you couldn't turn on the TV without seeing some woman raped, pawed, or otherwise sexually humiliated. The roles given to the new girl-woman actresses our age—Jodie Foster and Brooke Shields—were those of child prostitutes. They were sinister. Indeed, beauty, glamour, sex, generally, by the late 1970s had often taken on a sinister tinge—like Helmut Newton's photographs that were so popular then in *Vogue*. The images may have been stylized and high-concept, but they were creepy nonetheless. Downright scary, if you were just stepping out of childhood and seeing them, as many of us were.

Some feminist writers have suggested that all these dark, violent atmospherics around sex were a kind of pop cultural punishment for women—a message that they'd gone too far in freeing themselves and would now have to pay. I don't know whether or not that's true. But I do agree that—indeed, I recall how—in the mid- to late 1970s, there started to be a pervasive, creeping anger toward women in the air. Sometimes it took the relatively banal form of fathers and other older, male commentators who ranted against the frustrated, unfeminine, lonely, and unfulfilled "women's libbers." (After tennis player Billie Jean King's 1973 defeat of Bobby Riggs, my father took it upon himself to tell me, whenever relevant, "Men are the world's champs.") That kind of thing was relatively harmless, if maddening. But other kinds of hostility were out-and-out menacing. Like the way, in the

1970s, it became all but impossible for a young woman to walk down a New York City street without undergoing the most stomach-turning kinds of verbal or physical harassment.

Writer Betsy Israel provides a vivid memory of this in *Bachelor Girl,* her 2002 history of single women in America: "It seemed very dangerous all of a sudden. I remember the week I was flashed by three guys, once right in the subway . . . once when I came home and found a guy on the steps with his dick hanging out . . . and once as I waited to be buzzed in at a friend's. . . . That's when I got a purple belt in karate," a woman she interviewed told her. In the 1970s, writes Israel, if young women weren't fearing the threat of sexual violence on the streets, they were reading about it, *constantly,* in the press. Whether or not the reported wave of violence against women was really new, was really on the rise, or had really to do with a new surge of anger in men, it became part of the zeitgeist. Israel quotes journalist Lucinda Franks on the effect all this had on young women in New York in those days: "Anxiety had slipped around their lives like a back brace."

The "fear of sexual assault and rape," the psychologist Maria Root would later write, was an "insidious trauma" that shaped us all in those years. I believe it was what lay behind the "victim feminism," with its emphasis on rape, pornography, and other forms of sexual violence, that became popular among women our age (that is to say, among that minority that still called themselves feminists) in the late 1980s and early 1990s. I also think it was more generally true that, no matter where they lived or whether or not they called themselves feminists, many women growing up in the 1970s and 1980s learned to associate danger with their sexuality. Perhaps that was why, in the early 1990s, a magazine as mainstream as *Redbook* would find that violence against women ranked as a greater concern for its readers than abortion rights or even workplace equality.

Young women coming of age in the 1980s and early 1990s faced an identity problem: How did you grow up from an empowered girl into an empowered woman in a culture that wasn't growing up with you? The baby boomers had been battling this dilemma forever. But the post–baby boomers didn't want to be like them. And yet what other role models did they have for who they wanted to be? Not their mothers, certainly, with their frustrations, their disappointments, and their second-class status in marriage. Not to mention their lack of control, which was particularly striking, all too often, in mothers who had gotten divorced, and who had lost, along with their husbands, most of their household money, their identities, and their lives generally.

I RECENTLY ASKED one older woman, who divorced in 1977, how many of her friends' marriages had similarly ended in divorce. "Almost all of them," she said, without batting an eye. It may have been an exaggeration, but it was how it felt for those of us who lived in communities where divorce was prevalent at that time. If our own parents didn't divorce, our friends' parents did. And prime-time television was full of sitcoms with gritty divorce-survivor moms as stars.

In the late 1970s and early 1980s—when the divorce rate peaked, topping out at 52 percent—left-behind women whose lives had fallen apart through divorce loomed large on the cultural scene. They were called displaced homemakers, and they were so worrisome that Congress funded an umbrella organization, the Displaced Homemakers Network, to oversee the many support centers that had opened around the country to help them. "Most therapists know women [being left by their husbands] who are in their forties and fifties," *Glamour* reported in 1978. "They are not just depressed. They are frantic."

Many girls and teenagers in the 1970s and early 1980s saw their mothers, or their friends' mothers, settle into a nunlike existence, pining away for the life that once was and living their future through their daughters. There was a message these daughters took to heart from the experience of divorce: relationships were untrustworthy.

Life could very easily and unforeseeably veer out of control. The daughters of these mothers swore that nothing like that would ever happen to them. They built their lives around the premise that they would always be in control. But their push to succeed and control their lives was in many ways a haunted quest. Very often, the image of the left woman, the disempowered woman, lived on in the back of their minds.

WE KNEW very well who we didn't want to be. But we had few role models to follow to where we *did* want to be. There were famous women, of course, doing fabulous things, but they usually seemed far from our lives. The older women we encountered, in college or in our early years at work, seemed to view us more as challengers than as heirs. Our mothers may have supported us, but they had not had the lives we wanted—or that they wanted us to lead.

All of this, I believe, led many young women, pummeled by the gathering clouds of adulthood, to narrow the scope of their growth. They wrapped themselves tight to turn off their sexuality. They shut down their potential for being the women of the future and focused narrowly upon *not being* the women of the past.

Journalist Peggy Orenstein recalls, in her generational saga, *Flux,* how as a teenager in the late 1970s she saw "anything that smacked of conventional feminine behavior—from motherhood to female-dominated professions—as retrograde, a threat to my new-found self-hood, unthinkable." Before she made it to college, she was diagnosed with an eating disorder. "I still don't know exactly why it happened. Perhaps I believed that being thinner would attract boys, or maybe it was just the opposite: I was trying to keep the confusion of sexuality at bay. I may have been aping unrealistic media images of women, or honing my physical self to conform to the world of men I strove to enter. Individually, each of those explanations seems both plausible and insufficient; together they speak to a profound ambivalence, an unresolved tension about female identity that went far beyond my own case."

Psychologists who worked with women with eating disorders noted how their fears of turning into their mothers were rife with food imagery. And what that imagery betrayed was not just a fear of overeating and losing control; it was a fear of growing up, becoming a mother, and *being devoured.* In *Solitaire,* Aimee Liu's much-cited 1979 memoir of her battle with anorexia, an anorexic makes it clear that if she gained weight, her breasts would "blow up like zeppelins. I would probably start having periods again as well. I would probably look and function just like my mother. . . . I don't want to be such a victim of fate." In *The Obsession* psychoanalyst Kim Chernin used a stand-alone quote from the psychoanalytical anthropologist Geza Roheim to make the point: "If you are a mother you must let yourself be eaten, you must share yourself out at the feast." The image of the giving-tree mother, so violently renounced by the baby boomers, terrified many of us as well. As writer Anne Glusker put it, in a 2002 *Washington Post* article on how she adapted herself to motherhood, "I saw my identity as something to be shielded from children who, I thought, would inevitably gnaw away at their mother's sense of self until there wasn't much left."

When baby boomer women looked at their mothers and saw all that they did not want to be, the burgeoning culture of feminism provided them with a political vocabulary to guide their new efforts at self-creation. But this was much less true for those of us who came of age in the 1980s. However unfairly, feminism had already been largely discredited. We used the words of self-creation that were available to us in our time. And so, when we tried to differentiate ourselves from our mothers, to cast off the diffuse images of dependence or low status we associated with them, we did not seek "self-actualization" so much as success. We did not seek "liberation" so much as "control."

Why, if we wanted power, if we wanted control, didn't we, the most privileged and accomplished generation of American women yet born, just take it? And if we couldn't just take it, why didn't we, like the baby boomers before us who joined the feminist movement, take to the streets and demand it? Why didn't we, like them, ask for more—ask for change? Why did we scorn them and seek empowerment through cutting out dairy? Why did we turn our social anxieties inward, and work them through in the intimacy of our bodies?

Because, I think, it didn't really dawn on us to do otherwise.

FEMINISM IN THE AGE OF NARCISSISM

Turning away from the public realm, replacing social consciousness with an exclusive focus on self, had been the norm in American society since the late 1970s. The "culture of narcissism," characterized by a "retreat from politics and repudiation of the recent past" that Christopher Lasch detailed in his 1978 book of that name, was the only political culture many of us ever knew. By the time we were aware enough to think about it, the political currents of the late 1960s and early 1970s had become little more in our lives than the psychedelic plastic Peace and Love signs we stuck in the backs of our closets, or the crying-Indian public service announcements we remembered from Saturday morning TV.

The grand social visions of a Great Society had petered out, by the time of our teens, into the tightfisted rugged individualism of Reaganomics. The more socially aware, activist political culture that had hummed in the background of our childhoods was, by the time we were teenagers, getting to seem as out of style—as tacky, even—as platform shoes and bell-bottoms. The look of our generation was Ray-Bans and oxford-cloth button-down shirts. The sound of our generation was arrogance and irony. The book of our generation was *Less Than Zero*. The man of our generation was Ronald Reagan. The emotional reality of our generation was the coming-of-age of the "diminishing expectations" Lasch had identified a decade earlier. Children under Nixon, we did not believe in government (and neither did our elected leaders). Children of divorce, we did not believe in relationships. Our songs were defiantly *not* about love. It was an age of "ironic hopelessness," wrote eighties novelist David Leavitt.

What we *did* believe in was money and our own power to succeed. We voted overwhelmingly to reelect Ronald Reagan in 1984—ringingly endorsing his "small-government" policies that would, or so it was promised, allow us to pursue success unchecked and reap the maximum rewards for our efforts. Our lack of belief in just about anything larger than ourselves or money did not go unnoticed. As David Lipsky and Alexander Abrams wrote in their 1994 book, *Late Bloomers: Coming of Age in Today's America,* "The worry about people of our age was that we were *too* single-minded, *too* careerist. That we had no values at all, except for achieving our own ends."

We weren't big on social activism. We weren't exactly civic-minded. There were exceptions, of course: those among us who campaigned for nuclear disarmament or pushed our universities to divest themselves of investments in South Africa. But they sounded, in the air of the times, somewhat tinny, somewhat off.

The women of our generation rode into their professional futures on the backs of the women who had come before them, thumbing our noses at them all the while. This was not lost on slightly older feminist commentators like the communications professor Susan Douglas, who, in her 1994 cultural memoir of feminism and the media, *Where the Girls Are,* excoriated the new vision of depoliticized, decontextualized personal liberation that took root among young women in the 1980s: "For women in the age of Reagan, elitism and narcissism merged in a perfect appeal to forget the political already, and get back to the personal, which you might be able to do something about," she wrote. ". . . Women's liberation metamorphosed into female narcissism unchained as political concepts and goals like liberation and equality were collapsed into distinctly personal, private desires. Women's liberation became equated with women's ability to do whatever they wanted for themselves, whenever they wanted, no matter what the expense."

The one major feminist issue that resonated loudly with us was abortion rights. We were consistently, definitely, as the slogan came into being, "pro-choice." Like the businessmen who propelled Ronald Reagan to power, we did not want the government placing limits on what we could do with ourselves. This didn't make us feminists (indeed, throughout the decade of the 1980s we would insist that we were *not* feminists). It didn't make us progressive or reactionary, pro-family or anti-family, anti-motherhood, pro–sexual freedom, or anything else, for that matter. It just meant that we were *for* ourselves—for our own individual liberties. For our freedom to do with our bodies what we chose.

In this, we were very much in step with the mood of our country. We were also in line with the thinking of the Supreme Court, which, in decision after decision in the 1980s and early 1990s, proved that abortion rights in America were more a matter of abstract principle—the libertarian principle of noninterference by government—than of a concrete commitment to making women's equality a reality. We were also following the lead of the abortion-rights movement, which in the mid-1970s had begun aping the libertarian rhetoric of free-market conservatism simply to keep abortion rights alive.

The backlash, after all, against *Roe v. Wade,* the Supreme Court's landmark 1973 decision that legalized abortion, had been immediate and fierce. Within three years of the decision, leading Republicans had started calling for the states to take it upon themselves to issue new laws restricting abortion. The Christian Evangelical movement and the New Right achieved national prominence with their fight to turn back the clock, not just on abortion rights but in all areas of non–church-sanctioned sexuality. The leaders of the women's movement found themselves struggling to maintain their foothold in what very often looked like a losing battle. They lost out time and again in the skirmishes: the 1976 Hyde Amendment, which banned the use of federal funds for abortions; the 1984 "gag rule," which made it impossible for women's health centers receiving federal funds to even *mention* abortion; the Supreme Court's 1989 *Webster* decision, which dated the state's "compelling interest" in the fetus all the way back to conception; a series of state laws requiring parental notification for minors seeking abortions, or spousal consent for married women seeking to end a pregnancy. There were laws requiring that abortions take place only in hospitals, laws requiring that women seeking abortions undergo a "waiting period" before the intervention, even regulations requiring women to undergo tests to determine the viability of the fetus.

But the abortion-rights movement succeeded in standing its ground in the major conflict—keeping the country's voting majority in favor of maintaining *Roe v. Wade.* And a big part of the way it did this was by changing its rhetoric. Instead of talking about a woman's right to an abortion, its leaders began to talk about women's right to "choose." Suddenly, no one was *for* abortion rights anymore. They were just "pro-choice."

The "pro-choice" movement could have picked other slogans. It could have stressed other aspects of the abortion issue, as it had in the past—like the fact that the right to control her bodily integrity was central to a woman's core humanity. But the movement didn't go that far. It couldn't. *Roe v. Wade itself* hadn't gone that far. It had simply set limits on the government's right to interfere in a pregnancy. And most people could live with that, polls showed, in the decades following *Roe.* Just so long as you didn't push them too hard on it, or go into too many of the gory details.

Rickie Salinger, who has written compellingly about the devolution in the abortion-rights movement's language from a rhetoric of "rights" to one of "choice" in the wake of *Roe v. Wade,* noted how "choice" suited the post-*Roe* political climate:

In a culture weary, after the 1960s and early 1970s, of strident rights claims, "choice" became *the* way liberal and mainstream feminists could talk about abortion without mentioning the "A-word." The term "choice" was attractive for that reason and because it offered American women "rights lite," a package many perceived as less threatening than unadulterated rights, thus easier to sell. . . . "Choice" didn't create a new class of perogatives for all women, an unattractive prospect to many people already uneasy about the expanding number of new sexual and economic perogatives associated with the women's liberation movement. Nor did "choice" impose rights on women who didn't want them. In addition, "choice" could be perceived as an essentially conservative claim of personal freedom from state intervention, a claim that was consistent, of course, with the "privacy" basis of the *Roe v. Wade* decision. And finally, "choice" connotes the private exercise of personal freedom.

Choice fit right and sounded good and covered a multitude of sins—like the fact that in the decades following *Roe,* women's choices actually shrank, as the many rules limiting their access to birth control and abortion multiplied. This continued even in the years of the pro-choice Clinton presidency, when a shortage of doctors and hospitals willing to perform abortions made access to services impossible for more and more women. So that, with time, a great many women didn't have the ability to "choose" at all. And the principle of "choice, for many," became all but meaningless.

Our generation inherited this notion of "choice" as an empty abstraction. We internalized the notion that the granting of "rights" did not necessitate the granting of *access*—that is, giving people (pregnant women, in this case) the ability to *use* their rights. Many committed abortion rights activists refused to accept this, and fought to keep abortions accessible and affordable for all women who needed them. But the political climate of our era pushed these activists to the margins. Most women, by the 1980s, didn't see the cynicism, or the logistical maneuverings that had gone into emptying words like "choice" and "rights" of real meaning. We accepted these words, in their bastardized forms, as the real thing. And the basic terms of our understanding of our world followed: We had choices. It was our responsibility to make good on them (or not). It was not the government's responsibility to make sure we were *able* to make good on them.

Because we bought into these basic definitions of "choice" and "equal rights," we were left without a leg to stand on when we became mothers and suddenly all the "choices" we were making seemed wrong. We couldn't see that those choices weren't really choices. All we could conclude was that we were choosing poorly. We were hemmed in by the limits of our political imagination.

MINING THE BODY

The abortion-rights debate—and the very real situation of women's constricting reproductive rights in the 1980s and early 1990s—had, I think, another long-term effect on our psyches as well: it not only reinforced our tendency to treat all our problems as private concerns (*Roe v. Wade* had, after all, been decided on the basis of something called "privacy" rights), it focalized all the issues about empowerment and identity that swirled in the background during our coming-of-age years onto the issue of control of the body. Our bodies. This gave political reinforcement to our tendency to shrink big issues down to the size of our bellies. And it gave psychological reinforcement to the idea that our status as women could be measured by the degree of control we had over our flesh.

Roe v. Wade could have set a precedent of making women's bodies essentially off-limits to the government—by, let's say, simply ruling that women had the basic human right to do with their bodies what they chose. But it didn't. Instead, Justice Blackmun's majority decision, which legalized abortion in the first two trimesters of pregnancy, based on then-existing medical standards of fetal viability, let the idea stand that a woman's body was something open to outside interference. Such had been the case in the pre-*Roe* era when some states had started liberalizing their abortion laws by expanding the conditions under which a *doctor* could decide to provide a woman with an abortion. Women's bodies had then been conceived of as a kind of communal property, with the state maintaining a "compelling interest" in the fetus and the medical community compellingly involved in decisions regarding the mother.

This didn't change after *Roe*. Instead of making a broad statement establishing women's absolute control over their reproductive destinies, Justice Blackmun's trimester solution maintained the centrality of the medical profession. Because it did not establish the right to terminate pregnancy as an absolute right of the mother, *Roe* just limited the time frame for the state's compelling interest in the fetus and left the way open for future tinkering with, and limitations on, abortion rights.

Thus the message filtered down that despite all of women's advancements, their bodies were *not* theirs to control. Their bodies were a battlefield—*the* battlefield on which the forces for and against freeing women from their reproductive "destinies" would fight right up until today. That fight wasn't just about abortion—it was about all manifestations of post-1960s sexuality: teenage and premarital sexual activity above all.

It wasn't surprising, then, that polls in the early 1990s showed that "battles for control" over their bodies were the most pressing social concerns of young women. Or that, in the 1980s and early 1990s, the watered-down version of feminism that most of us took in through our pop culture conveyed the incessant, obsessive message that personal power resided in body control.

This was feminism in the age of narcissism. Private. Self-centered. Self-consciously apolitical. Jane Fonda was the great standard-bearer for this new self-empowerment ethic. In 1983, the woman who had formerly posed with the Vietcong to protest the war in Vietnam burst on the scene with a message that now reverberated deep within the female heartland: "Go for the burn!" Fonda's introduction to her mega-best-selling *Jane Fonda's Workout Book* was a parable of self-liberation. In it, she described how as a fashion model and actress she'd spent years maintaining an ultrathin weight through the use of vomiting, speed, and diuretics. When she'd become pregnant, however, she'd begun "to realize that my body needed to be listened to and strengthened, not ignored and weakened." She'd come to advocate exercise, not just as a way for women to get fit, but also as a means to creating a more fit society: "The new female consciousness that has developed over the last decade," she wrote, "extends to our right to physical as well as economic, political and social equality." It was all a matter of "Being Strong." Fonda, of course, inspired a legion of imitators, none more memorable than Susan Powter ("Stop the Insanity!"), who in the early 1990s was *everywhere* with her oft-repeated tale of how, through sheer power of will, she had transformed herself from a 260-pound housewife to a muscle-bound, quasi-messianic sensation.

A number of feminist writers have commented on the fact that women shifted their powers of control to their bodies at precisely the point when their control of their reproductive rights began to slip. Roberta Pollack Seid, for one, contemplating body-control trends in the 1980s for her 1989 book, *Never Too Thin,* said, "We might not be able to control the external human and natural environment, but we certainly could control our inner environments and make ourselves into our personal best—strong and muscled enough to be winners." Susan Faludi captured the atmosphere well in *Backlash,* when she described such eighties-era media moments as the Michelob ad that aimed to sell light beer to women with the image of a skinny woman in a bodysuit and the words "You *can* have it all," or the Hanes ad that called a new line of pantyhose its "latest liberating product."

The whittling-down of the focus of women's "liberation" from big social issues to body control wasn't *just* the work of the abortion-rights battle or the media, however. It also stemmed from certain tendencies in feminism. I think in particular of the kind of feminism taught in universities in the late 1980s and 1990s—a feminism in which the focus was on rape, pornography, sexual abuse, objectification, exercise, eating disorders, fat oppression, heterosexist language, and treatment of "sex workers"—even the politics of haircuts. Much of this was small, private, and in a certain sense narcissistic stuff. And unlike the feminist work in the 1970s that took place in the streets—in marches or staged events or in Congress or the courts—this feminism took place largely in classrooms, in arcane, self-referential language that was never intended to reach a wider audience. This was a feminism on which careers were built—books were written, tenure earned, private ambitions achieved. The social change that had made these careers possible was of a different domain altogether.

In part, this new "feminism"—which could consist of bashing Barbie dolls or pasting stickers reading "Feed Me" over posters of the waif-thin model Kate Moss—was a response to a politically hopeless age in which the forces of reaction were overwhelmingly winning out against those in favor of women's progress. The focus on the body was partly dictated by the feminist movement's relentless focus on abortion rights—a priority less of its own choosing than one imposed by the anti-*Roe* backlash. But that was not the whole story.

There had always been in the heart of feminism a kind of overinvestment in the female body. The body was never, for feminist thinkers, *just the body*—its shape and size a function, primarily, of genetics. It was always politicized. Adrienne Rich called it "the terrain on which patriarchy is erected." As a result, the "repossession" of women's bodies was one of the main obsessions of 1970s feminism.

The writers of *Our Bodies, Ourselves* taught women to fight off the controlling paternalism of the medical profession. Feminist academics taught students to love formerly denigrated aspects of femaleness, as writer Meg Wolitzer once recalled:

> At a class I attended at Smith College one bright fall day in the late 1970s, a women's studies professor brought in a speculum and showed us how to use it. We all stood around, some of us in headbands and plaids, gazing into the vagina of a volunteer, who cheerfully lay across the professor's desk with her legs splayed (extra credit!). We peered respectfully inside that woman like a bunch of guys looking under the hood of some late-model MG. . . . For years we had been metaphorically turning that speculum on ourselves, but we scavenged only for imperfections, inside and out, shining pinpoint lights of criticism onto our reproductive systems, our breasts, legs, arms, torsos and our intently worried faces.

Even the *form* of the female body was politicized. Feminists often repeated that big breasts and hips were popular in politically conservative times, when women's reproductive roles were particularly prized—as, for example, after the population losses of World War II—and that thin silhouettes like those of the flappers or of Twiggy came into vogue in moments of women's progress. And so they taught women to denigrate sexpot images of the female body long treasured by men. To reject the ideal of a Marilyn Monroe–style fertility-goddess body ("all boobs and buttocks, a hallucinating sequence of parabolae and bulges," as Germaine Greer put it in the 1970s), in favor of a sleek and streamlined form connoting "strength," as was the buzzword in the 1980s.

A new generation of women learned, in the Reagan years, that remaking their bodies, shedding flesh, and building up muscle was an "antipatriarchal rebellion." Gloria Steinem saw it this way, as she toured college campuses in the early 1990s and heard former anorexics tell of how, through "strength" (excercise), they had found a way out of their compulsions to diet. She concluded, "Suddenly, a skinny, androgynous, 'boyish' body was no longer the only way to escape the soft, female, 'victim' bodies they associated with their mothers' fates." And she compared the now-exercising anorexics to "Vietnam amputees whose confidence was bolstered when they entered marathons in wheelchairs or on artificial legs."

This was the height of irony, political correctness meeting bodybuilding. Steinem, unwittingly, was substituting one ideal female body for another. And, in addition, she was being snowed. She didn't see that, for the former anorexics, exercise was potentially just another more *highly adaptive* form of the same perfectionistic controlfreakishness that underlay anorexia. She and other feminists who taught that one should—that one *could*—take total control of one's body were so desperate to break with the legacy of reproductive determinism that they replaced one fixed idea—that the body was for mothering—with another: that the body was to make of it what you would.

HOW SURPRISING IS IT, then, that those of us who sought to make good on the promises of feminism would come to have quasimagical beliefs about our abilities (indeed, our responsibilities as rightthinking women) to control our bodies?

This thinking has run rife through politically correct takes on pregnancy and childbirth for the past few decades. In the mid-1980s, Renée Rose Shield, making a vain plea for "commonsense" parenting in her book *Making Babies in the '80s,* wrote, "Episiotomies are not a male conspiracy to control women by performing unnecessary operations on them . . . an episiotomy is only an episiotomy." In the 1990s, otherwise well-informed women nursed a sense of omnipotence, believing that, through good living, they could "control" their fertility. Then they turned forty and discovered that they couldn't. And they were shocked. "If you ever told me I'd be having this kind of difficulty, I would have laughed in your face," a forty-four-year-old television producer struggling through fertility treatments told *Newsweek.* "I exercise, I eat well, I keep better work hours, but I'm really not in control of what's happening with my little eggs. It's devastating. It's a terrible sense of failure."

Today, this attitude lives on in the know-better-than the-doctors approach to childbirth that makes so many women feel like "failures" for having cesarean sections, and in the fanatical devotion to breast-feeding that makes others feel they've "failed" if they don't nurse their babies. You see it in the shockingly "organized" way other women opt for voluntary and unnecessary C-sections because they can schedule them at their convenience. And it is manifest in the increasing number of women who eschew medical help altogether and decide to go it alone, forgoing prenatal care for their babies and subjecting themselves to home births.

LIFE'S LITTLE HELPERS

In the early 1990s, a lot of attention was paid to the problem of eating disorders. Most commentators blamed the ultraskinny ideal promoted by our society. They blamed sexism. They blamed men. "Men still set the agenda," wrote Erica Jong, in the *Times* of London in 1994. "And the agenda equates female sexuality with evil, female flesh with the devil."

But the "fashionable" disorders—the intolerances and allergies—passed largely without comment. "Anorexia and bulimia may still inspire horror, but claiming a food allergy or intolerance is socially acceptable," Regina Schrambling, a reformed allergic-to-everything ascetic, noted acerbically in *Vogue.* Food allergies and intolerances were, you might say, politically correct. Indeed, since they were often undiagnosable, and frequently enough dismissed by medical practitioners as problems "in our heads," they became fuel for the feminist fire, a kind of badge of honor of wounded selfhood rising up and speaking out in the face of Establishment indifference.

It was as though there were good and bad kinds of controlling behavior. The bad kind was the kind that played into the hands of "patriarchy"—promoting thinness, for example, or anything else that conformed to what was generally considered male notions of female beauty. The good kind took on patriarchy—in the form of challenging the medical establishment, the food industry, or anything else that smacked of convention.

But all these behaviors really came down to the same thing. And they took root so deeply among our generation not just because they made us look good, not just because they led us to act in a way that earned society's smile, but because they made us *feel* good. As anyone who has ever had an eating disorder, in a full-blown or mundane, "subclinical" form knows, there is a self-reinforcing aspect to it: the mind-numbing, self-emptying pleasure of bulimia, the life-ordering, self-satisfying asceticism of anorexia, the self-and-other–dominating comforts of cutting out dairy (or wheat, or whatever). Food-and-body control is an opiate. A highly effective and highly adaptive way of drowning out the angst of existence.

It might seem nonsensical that a generation with so much potential power—educated like men, coming of age fully expecting to climb the ladder of success—would resort to such self-disempowering tactics. After all, every millisecond spent obsessing about a piece of chicken gristle was a moment in time lost on living out the promises of our freedom. And yet, I think, *that* was precisely why we did obsess. Because, deep down, we didn't really *feel* all that empowered.

What we did feel was a lot of anxiety.

Just as we do now.

8.

Running Scared

MY PARENTS DIVORCED
when I was little. It was hard financially for my mom," a Washington,
D.C., pediatrician told me one morning as we sat out a rainstorm in
our local coffeehouse, talking while we waited for the skies to clear so
we could hop into our cars and get to work. "She always told me to be
sure to be able to provide for myself and create security for myself."

And so, the doctor said, she took control of her life, planning
every step—from school to college to medical school. When she married and had kids, she bought a house in a suburb known for its good
public schools. She joined a family practice that would let her work
part-time so that she could spend a maximum of hours at home.

She did everything just right, and for a while, at least, the demon of
anxiety—a childhood acquaintance that had tortured her throughout
early adulthood with migraines and self-doubt and a never-ending
inner litany of her shortcomings and incipient failures—was quieted.

But then life started veering out of control. For one thing, medicine turned out to be not so lucrative a profession, especially if you were practicing it on the Mommy Track. For another, her children's school district didn't end up being all it was cracked up to be. One district over was said to be better.

So now she was up at night wondering: Should she move? Now? Lock into a school district where the high school was better . . . but . . . could she count on its staying better over time? And anyway, with standardized testing all the rage, did she even want to send her kids to public school? And if not, could she and her husband afford private school? Could her kids even get in?

Her younger son was having trouble just making his way through preschool.

He was a smart little boy with a sweet round face and big brown eyes who liked story time and sports. But he had a tendency to lie down at circle time. He wasn't good at listening and following directions. And he liked to be hugged a lot. A team of specialists had concluded that he had low muscle tone in his upper body and "sensory integration" issues. Not the sensory integration issues the doctor-mom saw all the time in her practice—kids who didn't like to be touched—but . . . the . . . *other kind* of sensory integration issues. . . . The loving-to-be-touched kind.

And so now her little boy was in weekly occupational therapy and, at more than $100 per session, it was worth every penny, she told me. She laughed about it. She was un-self-forgivingly clear-sighted. "OT" might or might not be doing much of anything for her son. But it was proving highly therapeutic for *her.*

"Look, I'm a very high-anxiety person," she said. "I'd rather believe my son has 'issues'—that he doesn't listen to me because he *can't,* because, as the occupational therapist says, he's too busy 'listening' to what's going on in his body—than have to think it's just because I'm a bad mother."

A bad mother? I asked. What could that *possibly* have to do with it? She looked down and twisted her napkin nervously. "If I did things right," she said softly, "he'd listen."

ANXIETY IS—and undoubtedly always has been—a natural part of motherhood.

"There is an enlarged sense of *vulnerability,* personal and social, created by becoming a mother—and accepting the intimate mission of keeping a dependent being alive," writes psychologist Janna Mala-mud Smith, who studied the nature of maternal fear in depth for her 2003 book, *A Potent Spell.* The writer Francine Prose has described a certain kind of visceral fear that shocked her and changed her life when she became a mother: "All at once, we realize what hostages to fortune we are, how fragile and precious life is—our own lives, and those of our children. Even the bravest of us may find ourselves trans-formed almost beyond recognition into skittish, nervous versions of our former selves."

That is true, and has probably been true from time immemorial. But there is something unique about the nature of maternal anxiety that we live with today.

It isn't just that we are so very fearful—and that the world seems so filled with fearsome things, like the pictures of kidnapped chil-dren that, Prose wrote, she used to study every morning as she poured the milk for her children's breakfast cereals. It isn't even just that our fears—fanned by the media—tend to be so out of proportion to the real threats facing our children. No—what's really unique about ma-ternal anxiety today is our belief that if something goes wrong with or for our children, it's a reflection on us as mothers. Because we be-lieve we should be able to control life so perfectly that we can keep bad things from happening.

We micromanage. We obsess. Over this therapy and that therapy.

Occupational therapy and speech therapy. Gluten-free birthday cakes and organic apple juice. Leapfrog toys and bow-tying boards and black-and-white baby toys. No TV; only a half hour of TV; only educational TV. No sugar. No trans fats. No Disney. No pizza.

We make peace offerings to the demons of our anxious perfectionism. We seek magical charms to ward off the unruliness of existence, the uncontrollability of life. The randomness of fate. The impossibility, not of Having it All, but of finally, existentially, Getting It Right.

And we act as though, through sheer force of will (and good planning), we can sway the gods that master our children's fates. Conferring upon them health, a positive self-image, a winning personality, athletic skill, safety, and, above all, success.

We can send them to Just the Right School, which will set them on Just the Right Path in Life.

We can give them Just the Right Pill, which will take away their shyness, or ultrasensitivity, or maladaptive, misdirected, excess energy.

We can enroll them in Just the Right Activity: whether it's soccer, to build organizational management skills, or tae kwon do, to build a capacity for virile self-assertion, or ballet, to counter a girl's organizational management skills and virile self-assertion with an adaptive dose of pleasing femininity.

It is as though, through the power of our prodigious mental energies, we feel we can erect a protective force field around our children, sheltering them against fat, lack of focus, immaturity, lack of muscle tone . . . failure. And if all this doesn't work, then the fault lies with us. So we must try harder. Do better. *Be there* more—and more perfectly.

"How can I go back to work when I've finally gotten my kids in with the best violin teacher in the city and she demands a lot of parental involvement?"

"We want our kids to be perfect. So if something goes wrong, we have to try to fix it."

All these things we do bespeak a terrible anxiety: that our children simply will not be able to make it through life if we do not perform totemic acts to keep them on the path toward self-perfection and keep their lives pure and unfettered by distracting emotion, personality foibles, or less-than-ideal experiences.

We seem to feel as though the life our children have—that we have built for them—is just a delicate house of cards, held together by the most intricate balancing of all its carefully selected components, and that the slightest shock, the slightest jar to all our perfect orchestration, will bring the whole edifice crashing down.

All of which speaks of an almost hubristic notion of our own powers. And attests too to just how deep our sense of vulnerability must be. For if we are setting out to control the world with our minds, and to keep bad or frightening things away through quasi-magical acts of will, then what that really means is that we feel that, through normal means, we can't control our world at all.

ALL OF THIS plays itself out over and over again every day, in the lives of mothers dragging themselves to toddler music class so that their children will have evenly developed brains, in the mothers petitioning their children's schools to remove chocolate milk from the cafeteria, in the mothers tightly monitoring their young children's play dates: *I don't want my daughter to play with so-and-so because she has an annoying habit of talking baby talk that my daughter finds charming; my friend A doesn't want her son playing with boy X, because he has ADHD and she fears her son may too and may start acting up in class; another friend doesn't want her son playing with boy Y (the son of friend A), because he always comes home "crazy," only comes home crazy, only acts crazy in school when he's been exposed to boy Y's dangerous company.*

Parents look at one another with suspicion. They keep their children close and are afraid to take responsibility for other people's kids.

They look at schools with suspicion. They even view *their children* with suspicion. "When your kid has been diagnosed, you look at them differently. Everything they do can be a symptom of a greater problem," the doctor-mom told me. "I'm always comparing him with everyone else to see if he seems normal."

Out-and-out surveillance—of food, of caretakers, of other adults, of other children, of *our* children—is a normal activity. No one really trusts anyone else to properly care for their kids. Not just because they might do them some physical harm (which they might!), but because they might expose them to *bad habits.*

Our ambient anxiety is fed by the news media, which serves up (in slow news periods) story after story about the dangers facing our children. Day-care centers are filled with pedophiles. Fatal food allergies are "epidemic." Autism is up 273 percent, and—and this is the "story"—*no one is telling us why.* No one, nothing, is to be trusted or taken at face value. Not teachers, not doctors, not childhood immunizations. Even milk is an "insidious ingredient."

The media not only fans our fears, it comforts us in our hubris. Nearly every scare story comes with a Message: You *can* take control. You *can* do something to keep bad things from happening to your children and to keep life from throwing you curveballs.

You can protect your children against predatory criminals by buying the right products: like animal-shaped abduction alarms or the "Give Your Kids a Fighting Chance" videos and DVDs, which, the *New York Times*'s Jane Brody once scandalously wrote, can teach kids how to thwart would-be abductors with "strikes, kicks, bites," and "foot stomps" that "make it possible for even a five-year-old to get away from a full-grown man."

You can cure autism by banning dairy, or by purifying a child's diet of all gluten, as was done with near-miraculous results by the author of "We Cured Our Son's Autism," which ran in the February 2000 issue of *Parents.*

You can prevent your allergic child from dying if only you are vigilant enough, *responsible enough,* to make eating safe. In the words of one expert, "If people point at you when you walk down the street and say, 'Look at the neurotic parent' . . . then and only then are you being careful enough."

Perhaps all this gives parents some comfort. Perhaps it makes life seem "less arbitrary," as Alvin Rosenfeld and Nicole Wise suggest in their excellent book about "hyper-parenting," *The Over-Scheduled Child:* "What oversights led to a toddler's fatal plunge from a skyscraper window, what *didn't* happen to prevent an eight-year-old from drowning while away at summer camp, which factors may have fueled the transformation of a seemingly normal high school student into a mass murderer . . . such stories soothe our angst by providing explanations."

But the effect is, nonetheless, pernicious. How many parents of autistic children, reading articles like the one published in *Parents,* come away blaming themselves and wondering whether, if only they'd banned the ice cream and Stonyfield Farms, they might have saved their children from the clutches of a terrible and little-understood disorder? How many parents of severely allergic children will feel justified in blaming themselves if, despite their best efforts, their child has an allergic reaction? How can anyone, in the face of such an unrelenting deluge, come away without falling into the trap of feeling responsible and blameworthy for *just about everything?*

THE IRONY of all this is that we are now, arguably, living at the safest time for children that the world has ever known. The childhood diseases that were once common and deadly have been all but eradicated. Our food is cleaner and safer than it has ever been before. Children are healthier than they have ever been before. Thanks to seat belts, they don't even die in car accidents in anywhere near the numbers that kids of our generation did. Crime stats are down: school violence has dropped dramatically in recent years—despite and with the exception of the Columbine massacre in 1999. And yet—*people are terrified.*

More than a decade of stories about abuse in day care, evil au pairs, and degenerate babysitters has borne fruit: in 1997, more than half of parents in America worried that their children would be victims of a violent crime, and 41 percent feared their children would become victims of sexual abuse. By 2000, *three-quarters* of parents feared their children would be victims of violent crime or abducted by strangers. This despite the well-publicized drop in national crime rates *and* despite reports—which, admittedly, were not so readily available—that less than one percent of children actually suffer abuse or neglect in a child-care setting. The deluge of stories on fatal food allergies has made its mark on the American parental psyche as well: by the late 1990s, fully one-third of American households believed that at least one of their family members had a food allergy. This despite the fact that the most generous expert estimate of the incidence of food allergies among children under three (the most vulnerable group) is no more than 8 percent. And for the population at large, experts agree that it is as low as less than one percent.

The world that enters our homes through our TV sets and news magazines feels out-of-control and randomly terrifying. It is like the world of a fatally allergic child writ large, where death can lurk in the most secret and surprising places. In such a world, it's little wonder that people take recourse to magical thinking. Little wonder that they become rigid and controlling. After all, in such an world—what can people really count on but *themselves?*

The media, however, is only partially to blame for the anxious and controlling habit of mind so many turn-of-the-millennium mothers now bring to parenting. Because their scare stories couldn't fly—couldn't transmit—if they didn't find receptive eyes and ears. Their messages couldn't propagate if they didn't fall on fertile ground. And we are all eyes and ears. Our psyches are the most fertile terrain imaginable.

We are still practicing the same kind of magical thinking that ten or fifteen years ago led us to believe (consciously or not) that Buns of Steel could give us the necessary armor to sail safely through the troubled waters of adult womanhood. The same kind of basic anxiety that drove us to obsess back then is still there, as alive and kicking as ever. Only it isn't, as in the past, about our sexuality (we wish!) or our place in the world as women. It is about the place that our children will inhabit in a world grown so competitive that it seems nothing other than near-perfection (on their parts and on ours) will secure their futures.

THE AGE OF ANXIETY

Turn-of-the-millennium parenthood is all about performance. Our performance and our kids' performance. And there's a reason for that. We are living in an age of such incredible competition and insecurity—financial insecurity, job insecurity, *life* insecurity, generally—that it often feels as if you have to run twice as fast just to stay *relatively securely* in place.

This has really been true since the early 1990s—a time when many people in our generation were getting married and beginning to think about starting families. The economic climate then was hardly family-friendly. There was a recession. It was a time of unemployment—of white-collar unemployment—and, in particular, a new kind of *permanent* unemployment that became so pervasive that, by 1996, one in three American families feared job loss in the near future. Families were working more and (when their incomes were adjusted for inflation) earning *less* than families in the 1960s had. By the time we started having children, economic anxiety in America was such that more than two-thirds of parents were worrying that their children would not live as well as they had, and more than half believed that the American dream was now out of reach for most families. *USA Today Magazine* summed up the new mood: "Many believe the American dream is in danger. . . . [They] seem to be less certain that hard work and the other rules will be rewarded with a better life and are increasingly skeptical, even cynical, about their prospects and the country in general . . . a sense of limits appears to be coming to define this era." The economist Charles J. Whalen called it "The Age of Anxiety."

This feeling of unease colored our generation's ascent into adulthood. Many of us had come of age in the mid-1980s, when the classic story line of young adulthood was that of the yuppie-chic movie *Wall Street* prior to Charlie Sheen's comeuppance: a wealth of career choices, big salaries, and the acquisition of big things that pushed our quality of life—in the *stuff* we had, at least—well beyond our parents' imaginings. But this fantasy never really trickled down very far to embellish the lives of those *not* working on Wall Street. On the contrary, a trend had started that would continue through the 1990s, accelerating madly at decade's end, as the now-burnished Golden Age shined its brightest: the spoils of life were being divided more and more unevenly, with wealth increasingly concentrated at the top. This meant that moving through adulthood, buying a home, and creating a semblance of contented family life became, for those of us not at the very, very top, a tough struggle against credit card debt, big mortgages, and an awareness that at any moment it could all come crashing to an end.

Our age group was particularly hard hit by the new economic realities of the Age of Anxiety. From 1989 to 1995, earnings for recent college graduates alone fell by nearly 10 percent. And benefits continually shrank along with salaries. We were the first generation of college graduates to earn less than our immediate predecessors. Indeed, by the end of the 1990s, we would prove to be the first generation whose lifetime earnings were adding up to be less than their parents.' The menacing vision of a workplace in which "the old notions of lifetime employment and guaranteed benefits gave way to the new realities of sudden downsizing and contingent, or temporary, employment," in the words of the *Atlantic Monthly*'s generational chronicler Ted Halstead, was our birthright.

THE JOB LOSSES of the early 1990s were different from those of prior recessions in that they came *despite* strong corporate earnings. They weren't just the temporary result of a time-bound economic downturn: they were caused by downsizing and "restructuring," and were generally permanent. And they were accompanied by a new ethic in corporate America: the culture of the big paternalistic company that took care of you and your family and expected loyalty in return had given way to the era of corporate raiders and money managers. Maximizing shareholder profits was now the one and only goal of business. Huge executive pay packages were rewarded to those who made stock prices rise—no matter what the cost to employees or to the corporation's general work culture.

Kevin Phillips, author of *Wealth and Democracy: A Political History of the American Rich,* labeled this change the "financialization" of American corporate culture. It was a new moral order. A new value system, characterized by a kind of survival-of-the-fittest mentality, which permeated every aspect of our society. If you weren't at the top, earning the most and buying the best (even of such basic human services as health care and education), then it had to be because you weren't good enough to be there. And so, if you were saddled with crumbling public schools and could afford no better doctors than the second-rate ones provided through your HMO, you were simply getting what you deserved.

The boom years of the turn of the millennium didn't change any of this. Indeed, they just made things worse. For despite all the self-congratulation and the hype—the "new" economy that would never see a downturn, the Hermès alligator bags on back order and the East Hampton time shares whose rents rivaled the costs of Middle American starter homes—the reality of life for most of us was not so very wonderful.

For one thing, for most people, the boom years didn't feel so very booming. They felt scary. And that's because the results of the vastly growing economy weren't equally shared by all parts of our society. Not by a long shot: in 1998, the 13,000 richest families in America had almost as much income as the 20 million poorest households. The richest families had incomes 300 times that of average families. The top 0.01 percent were earning 60 percent more than they had in the go-go 1980s, with top executives earning 20 percent more than they had a decade earlier. Meanwhile, at the very same time that our nation's most fortunate were reaching unparalleled levels of wealth, everyone else was simply working harder and, effectively, becoming poorer. Families in particular were suffering, their incomes having *fallen* almost 4 percent between 1989 and 1998. In middle-class families where incomes did rise, almost all of the gain was due to wives' working longer hours.

This wasn't an indication of women's workplace progress. It was a sign that people were running scared. A *Newsweek* poll conducted in that period showed that 52 percent of parents were afraid they wouldn't be able to afford the cost of college, 36 percent feared not being able to buy the things they needed for their families, and 35 percent feared not being able to afford good health care.

In other words, while the booming economy of the late 1990s made some people very, very wealthy, it made the vast majority of us very afraid.

The middle class was, increasingly, in big trouble. By 2000, while there were an unprecedented 590,000 American households worth $5 million or more, middle-income families' inflation-adjusted incomes were no higher than they'd been in the 1970s, and they were saving at much lower rates than before. The average American household was carrying debt just about equivalent to its disposable income. For families our age, the problem was particularly acute, as we were carrying more personal debt than had any other generation in their thirties in our country's history. More and more people were fleeing their bills, trying to "head for the hills," as writer Vince Passaro put it (*"There aren't, unfortunately, any hills to head for"*) in his essay "Reflections on the Art of Going Broke," which ran in *Harper's* in 1998.

In part, this situation was due to the national push to keep up with the Joneses—which became atrociously difficult as the boom years continued. Americans have always tended to identify with people wealthier than themselves—a habit of mind reinforced by the unrealistic homes and lifestyles of the supposedly middle-class people we see in movies and on TV—but now those wealthier people were *so much wealthier* than us that to try to keep up was financial suicide. Houses were getting bigger; luxuries were getting more luxurious. So much more money was being spent by those who had it that the notion of desirability got ratcheted up a level, pushing upward the very definition of what was a "nice" thing to have or acquire.

Families' increasing expectations for what was normal for a middle-class existence—indeed what was *necessary* for a middle-class existence—clashed sharply with their inability to sustain it. Between 1989 and 2001, credit card debt in America almost tripled. The number of people filing for bankruptcy increased 125 percent. With the net result that by 1998, when the economy was still *good,* there were a stratospheric 1.3 million filings for personal bankruptcy protection. And in 2003, when the economy wasn't good, a record 1.6 million people filed for personal bankruptcy—92 percent of them middle-class.

But the problem wasn't just that of the wealthy trying to outdo one another and the middle class trying to catch up. The crippling burden of debt carried by adults of our generation was in large part due to student loans, which had increased nearly eightfold since the 1970s. We also had to contend with the fact that for people of our generation, life was just too expensive. If we lived in places like New York or Boston or Washington or San Francisco (where the typical price of a three-bedroom house in 2002 topped $1 million), we were priced out of the real estate market. Salaries in the top-earning professions so eclipsed our own if we were, say, teachers or writers or even *doctors* (not to mention blue-collar workers) that to pursue our professions no longer guaranteed our families a comfortable standard of living. And structural costs of family life—*not* luxuries—were a big part of the problem.

Housing, for example: In the 1950s, payments for a median-priced house ate up about 14 percent of the average thirty-year-old's income. By 1987, a median-priced home consumed 44 percent of the average thirty-year-old's gross income. In 2001, about 80 percent of moderate-income and low-income homeowners were spending more than half their income on housing. And in 2003, a family of four needed to spend about 70 percent a year more on a house in a safe neighborhood with a good public school than they would have in 1973.

Health care costs for families had soared as well, with the employee contributions demanded by corporate benefit plans rising 60 percent for a family of four between 1973 and 2000. With the price of insurance premiums rising so high, and so consistently outpacing salary gains, many middle-class families were forced to go without health insurance altogether. Sarah Horowitz, executive director of *Working Today,* an advocacy group for self-employed workers, called this putative lifestyle choice "the new middle-class poverty." Jeff Madrick, writing in the *New York Times,* agreed: "Typical families often cannot afford the high-quality education, health care and neighborhood re-quired to be middle-class today."

And then, of course, there was child care, the average cost of which rose 20 percent from the mid-1980s to the mid-1990s. By 2000, in many places in America, the annual cost of care for a preschool child was higher than a year of state college education. Families were spend-ing, on average, from 9 to 25 percent of their income on child care, with low-income families spending more than a third. It was no won-der that credit card debt was skyrocketing. As a 2003 report by the public policy group Demos put it, families at the turn of the millen-nium were "borrowing to make ends meet." They weren't just paying for their vacations and expensive birthday gifts with plastic, they were borrowing money to help pay for gas, food, and medicine. The cost of living had simply veered out of control. Credit card debt, said Tamara Draut, a coauthor of the Demos study, had become "the Band-Aid holding the family budget together."

The net result was that while some people at the turn of the mil-lennium were able to enjoy the spoils of Midas-like wealth, quality of life for most people plummeted. In 2000, almost 60 percent of women with children under six were telling pollsters that they found it harder to balance the demands of work and family than they had in 1996. More than half also told the Center for Policy Alternatives that the economic boom had not reached them and their families. Many were living "paycheck to paycheck," their families "just getting by" even as they worked longer hours. Six out of ten men and women said they were worried about the growing economic divide in America, about their children getting off to a good start in school, and about their chil-dren being able to get a college education. A majority also said they felt they had "little control over their current economic situation."

The anxiety that the boom years brought wasn't just about money. It was also about a sense of powerlessness, the creeping feeling that many people came to have that because they weren't superwealthy, they—and their children—were now second-class citizens. There were good reasons to feel this way.

Our government was increasingly responsive to only the very wealthy. All others had to fend for themselves in a universe of shrinking resources. (After all, advantageous tax rates permitting the wealthy to spend enormous sums of money on luxury goods were also enabling the government *not* to spend money on public education or infrastructure.) "It's all too easy," despaired Princeton economist Paul Krugman in 2002, "to see how we may become a country in which the big rewards are reserved for people with the right connections; in which ordinary people see little hope of advancement; in which political involvement seems pointless, because in the end the interests of the elite always get served."

With big money calling the shots, the middle class was increasingly disenfranchised and increasingly powerless in the grand scheme of things. Families were increasingly concerned, then, with holding on to what they had. They were increasingly nervous about *controlling* the little details of life that might, in the future, make a difference for their children. Like making sure that their kids had the best grades, activities, community service experiences, and personalities so that they might get into the best colleges and have a shot at living life at the top of the heap.

After all, it was glaringly obvious now that, to succeed, you had to shoot for the very, very top. Because the fruits of success were increasingly and disproportionately concentrated in the hands of the very, very few. More and more professions were operating on a kind of "star system" whereby a handful of people earned astronomical sums, while their peers looked on and drooled. And since "top" firms would only hire "top" people, who could help them maintain their "star" billing to clients, the need to get into "name" colleges became all the more desperate.

Hence the importance of tutoring, athletics, Ritalin, and occupational therapy in elementary school—*and even before*. America, wrote the economists Robert H. Frank and Philip J. Cook, had become a "Winner-Take-All Society." You *had* to compete in this top-driven marketplace, because to coast, to have more modest goals, to decide that what you had was good enough, wouldn't keep you, economically, on an even keel—it would propel you downward, in the rising tide of top salaries and the cost of living. It was like the problem of car ownership in the age of SUVs: with Hummers on the road, buying a fuel-efficient Honda, if you had a family, was not necessarily a responsible decision.

You had to play the game. You couldn't opt out. Because to do so—to thumb your nose (metaphorically or in reality) at the idea of buying a big gas-guzzler—was to put the future security of your family at risk.

THIS IS the economic backdrop—the material reality—that lies behind our experience of motherhood today. We don't talk about it, of course—any more than we admit that, all too often, our much-fetishized family dinners are being interrupted by calls from our credit card creditors. Anxiety simply *vibrates* everywhere. In the busybody fuss of the preschool mother who finds "sensory deprivation issues" in each child around her because her son didn't like the feel of his socks (and how, then, will he handle the sensory overload of kindergarden?). In the stony-eyed, hurried gait of another mother sprinting from the school door to her minivan every morning so that she won't be hit up for the $45 auction tickets she can't afford. In the behavior of the mother who becomes so obsessed with purifying her child's diet that she eliminates whole ranges of necessary foods (*"Allergic parents have allergic children. . . ."*) and ends up with a seriously malnourished child. (This phenomenon reached absolutely tragic proportions in 2003 when a Brooklyn couple nearly starved their baby daughter to death by withholding all dairy products and infant formula from her and adhering to what they understood to be a strict "vegan" regimen. And it landed another well-off child I heard of in the emergency room with a compound fracture after a minor fall—a result of fragile bones that doctors attributed to his strict lactose- and calcium-free diet.)

Anxiety *buzzes*.

In and around Washington, D.C., parents panic if their kids jump at loud noises, don't connect to soccer, refuse to dress themselves, frustrate their teachers, or are just a little bit strange. If there's money for it, they send them to OT—occupational therapy (not the on-the-job-injury kind, the let's-play-with-a-ball kind)—to "fix" these behaviors. Or to "cosmetic" speech therapy if they trip over their tongues or pronounce a consonant or two a bit funny. Some wealthy parents go so far as to send their troublesome sons to a $30,000-a-year special education school (which, if you can afford a good lawyer, you can get paid for by the district), where they can spend a few years learning to be a little bit more like everyone else. One parent, whose son has a serious neurological disorder and attends the school, told me, "A lot of the boys are very bright but somewhat different children, and the parents have them there in order to preserve their self-esteem."

In New York City, parents with money sign their three-year-old sons up for physical therapy if they can't peel and paste stickers with dexterity. (How, otherwise, will they get into private school?) Older kids performing beneath their parents' expectations visit "Dr. Ritalin" and come away with prescriptions to help enhance their performance at exam times.

Around the country, parents panic that their children's quirks of personality are signs of serious syndromes. Psychiatrists are quick to greet their fears with new diagnoses and the newest medication. Children who would once have been called "worrywarts" are diagnosed with "general anxiety disorder"—and are medicated. Children who don't

want to go to school are said to be suffering from "social phobias"—
and are medicated. Children who don't want to go to birthday parties
or sleepovers are said to show signs of "extreme separation anxiety
disorder" (with a lesser manifestation of this disorder being the children's refusal to sleep in their own beds at night)—and are medicated.
With the net result that, in some communities, it is now the norm to
have a child (usually a boy) on behavior-modifying medication. In
some parts of the country, 50 to 75 percent of children referred to
child neurologists and behavioral pediatricians are being diagnosed
with ADHD—and medicated for it with stimulants like Ritalin.

Such stimulants have a uniquely calming effect upon parents.
Speed, at least, is a known quantity with predictable enough results
in the child who doesn't sit still for his four hours of homework or
isn't willing to go that extra mile to win her gymnastics competition.
The long-term economic and social effects of being a less-than-ideal
student or athlete are not so certain.

We live amid so much anxiety today that, often enough, we don't
even feel it. We are desensitized to it, as to the violence in action movies.
Yet anxiety is the thread of the energy that keeps us going: propelling
us to soccer games, keeping us mentally awake in the evenings to su-
pervise homework, to oversee the perfection of the "high school career."
Susan J. Kraus, writing in *Redbook,* once called this Mommy Panic:
"Many of us are so adapted to a climate of chronic anxiety," she said,
"that we find the adrenaline rush of pulling off the impossible almost
addicting."

All behaviors that can palliate anxiety have the potential to become addicting. And to keep us from ever having to deal with what's
making us anxious in the first place. Which raises an interesting point.
In a 1996 *Allure* article that sought to understand why "women's body
image and self-esteem" were "at an all-time low," writer Barbara Hey
made the argument that there was a little-discussed adaptive aspect
to the popular food-and-body obsessions of the 1980s and 1990s: they

were a way to bond with other women and to keep everyone on the same page, bound up in thinking about things that on a surface level were painful but, deeper down, didn't really challenge anyone too profoundly or destabilize their lives. "Maybe women discuss thighs with alacrity," Hey wrote, "because it goes over better than if they were to speak of being in an abusive relationship, or of the fear of guns in their children's schools, of their sense that the world is out of control." Quoting Becky Thompson, author of the 1994 book *A Hunger So Wide and So Deep*, she suggested that, rather than obsessing over women's problems with their "body image," we, as a concerned culture, ought to question and seek to strengthen women's sense of "embodiment"—whether or not they feel "safe and protected within [themselves] and the world."

I think it's quite possible that a similar thing is going on with maternal anxiety today. The obsessions we hear about—with food, with sports, with the little nodes of perfection that consume us—may well be screens for a much wider, more life-encompassing kind of anxiety.

As I mentioned earlier, I quickly saw in my interviews that there are things you can and cannot talk about regarding motherhood and its vicissitudes. It is, for example, acceptable to discuss your child's "issues"—ADHD, or poor muscle tone, or sensory integration, or whatever. It is not permissible to talk about what anxieties these "issues" raise for you about your child's status and ability to compete in the world and why you are willing to invest so much time and money on problems that even most experts agree may resolve themselves. It is acceptable to hire tutors, even to essentially do your child's homework yourself. It is not acceptable to admit that you think your public school teachers are inadequate, or that you think that, if you don't just give the homework a little extra *something* of your own, your child will end up falling through the cracks and not get into college. It is acceptable to talk about how difficult it is to find child care. It is much less acceptable to talk about how hard it is to pay for it. Indeed, how hard it is to pay for *all* the things—camp and music lessons and swimming and soccer—we consider the necessities of childhood these days. Basically, it is acceptable to air all your dirty laundry about yourself, your husband, or your children. But it is not acceptable to look beyond your family to suggest that there's something wrong with the perfect world you've bought into. It is not permissible to talk about policy, or economics, or culture—these words are, somehow, tacky, strident-sounding, *not the point.* And this is because, I think, policy, economics, and culture are perceived as being things that we have no control over—things as immutable, unchangeable, and *God-given* as, let's say, the weather, or men's hopelessness at arranging play dates.

And so we fixate on those things we feel we *can* control—how our child holds a pencil, whether or not she eats gluten—rather than worry about what we can't control: our economic futures, kids' education, health care costs, whether or not we'll ever be able to afford to retire. The perversity in all this, of course, is that what we're trying to control is precisely what one cannot control; you can't shape and perfect human beings, pre-program and prepare them so that you can predict the course of their lives and protect them along the way. But you can—ostensibly—exert some control over what kind of society you live in. You have the power to elect politicians who can offer to deliver the goods on things like education, public services, and support for families. You ostensibly have the power, en masse, to set the national agenda.

Unless, of course, no one's listening. Unless there is no political space whatsoever in which to articulate your anxieties and look for change. Unless there is no political will whatsoever to make things change.

Unless, at base, it's really your country—and not your child, not your family, not yourself—that is entirely out of control.

. . .

IT WOULD BE EASY (and comforting too) to dismiss the pervasive parental anxiety of our time as so much media-stoked nonsense. Just as it would, of course, be ideal to relax and realize that you cannot control life, another person's life all the less, and to instead parent caringly but calmly, showing what child psychiatrist Robert Coles, author of *The Spiritual Life of Children,* calls the "grace" of acceptance. But to parent in such a state of grace, you have to be able to believe that things will, if you let them fall into place, basically turn out all right. And, frankly, at this point in time, in our winner-take-all society, there is much reason to believe that they will not.

If you do not pay for private school, you can assume, in many districts, that your child will not be adequately educated. If you do not sign your child up for a slate of activities, you can be pretty sure that, thanks to tight spending priorities, he or she will not be exposed to anything much by way of music or art or physical education in school. It's been twenty years since the publication of the much-discussed Department of Education report "A Nation at Risk," which warned that "a rising tide of mediocrity" coming out of our schools threatened "our very future as a nation and a people." School budgets have been dropping ever since. Teacher salaries (adjusted for inflation) have declined precipitously, along with the average SAT scores of those entering the teaching profession.

The current push for "standards" through standardized testing is the final straw sending many middle-class parents out of the public schools or, if no escape is possible, resigning them to constant worry as they see entire curricula rejiggered so that teachers can "teach to the test." It isn't surprising, then, that in the decade leading up to 2002, enrollment in private day schools jumped 24 percent and that home-schooling, once the province of the very religious or the very weird, drew vast numbers of people simply unhappy with public education. People expected—and were getting—less and less from the public sector, and increasingly began to take the cost (in time and money) of educating their children and maintaining their neighborhoods upon themselves.

The situation for families with preschool children is currently even worse. Unless you are able to shell out top dollar for the very best day-care centers (*if* you can find a space in one), you have every reason now to believe that your child will spend his or her days in substandard care. A 2000 study by the National Institute of Child Health and Human Development showed that 61 percent of places that provided child care for young children would be considered poor or fair quality, with care for infants and toddlers the worst. Low wages create enormous turnover. A 2001 study by the University of California at Berkeley found that teaching staff in child-care centers, including preschools, are "alarmingly unstable"—76 percent of teachers employed in 1996 had left by 2000. What staff there is in day-care centers is often unskilled, and take on these jobs with our children when they're too unqualified to find any other.

Not all states require background checks on applicants for jobs in preschools, and those that do often make exceptions for church-based or part-time schools. This means there are very frequently no minimum standards for teachers or staff in these schools. One fifth of the states that *do* mandate background checks don't require potential employers to check into child-abuse or child-neglect registries, which often list people who have been investigated by child-protection agencies. Six states do not even mandate checking candidates' names against state criminal records. And thirty states—including New York, Ohio, and Indiana—do not require running job candidates' names through the FBI's national fingerprint system. So a person with a criminal record in one state would have no problem seeking work in another.

If we were able to feel "safe and protected" within our outer world, we could probably stop obsessing about the little details of our domestic lives. Sure, there are some things in the outside world we will never be able to control—terror attacks or floods or disease, for example. But there is much we *can* do something about: fear of guns, fear of not making ends meet, fear of shortchanging our children because of inadequate child care or schools.

We have come to believe that the fend-for-yourself world we live in today is the natural state of American society. That the enormous economic pressures many of us face trying to maintain middle-class lives are the necessary and natural outcome of living in a country that values free enterprise. And this is the root of the problem.

For none of this is natural, or necessary, or even *normal.* Things used to be different in America. There used to be structures in place that gave families a certain base level of comfort and security. Things like dependable public education. Affordable housing. Job security. Reliable retirement benefits. Things, even, like leisure time—which was a naturally occurring, unscheduled thing just one generation ago, when we were kids, and most fathers came home at night at 6 o'clock and didn't work on weekends.

We tend to think that it is normal for families to soldier on, alone and unsupported and stressed, as they do now. That is because in our conscious lifetime it has never been any other way. Yet before we were born, back in what so many people think of as the "golden age" of the American family (when the baby boomers were born), things were very different. There were actually government programs in place to strengthen and buttress the middle class. This wasn't done by "valorizing" motherhood (that cheap solution so favored by many in the burgeoning "pro-motherhood" movement), but by creating the economic conditions that allowed families to thrive.

In the late 1940s and 1950s, for example, government funds funneled through the GI Bill provided millions of men between the ages of twenty and twenty-four with the opportunity to improve their families' long-term prospects by getting a college or graduate-level education. Government-guaranteed loans, at artificially low interest rates, permitted the generation starting families in the postwar era to buy new houses in the suburbs. The tax code in the postwar years gave an enormous advantage to couples with children: a uniform $600 exemption per dependent, which would be worth more than $6,500 per child today. Tax money was spent to bring public transportation, schools, and utilities to the suburbs. The spending in this period was, historian Stephanie Coontz has said, "the most massive government subsidization of young families in American history" and had the effect of "encouraging family formation, residential stability, upward occupational mobility, and high educational aspirations."

This massive redistribution of public wealth, in the form of tax monies spent on the middle class, gave us the postwar family model of comfort and ease that still lives on in our heads as an ideal. It's often repeated that we can't achieve this ideal anymore because of the fact that mothers work. But that just isn't true. We can't achieve our ideals of family life today because of economic policies and political decisions that have brought a miserable level of stress and financial strain to middle-class families.

After the 1960s, whatever help still existed for middle-class families—like low-interest loans guaranteed by the federal government to help pay for college education—was eroded from the Reagan years onward by tax policies favoring the wealthy and budget cuts that struck disproportionately at the middle class and the poor. In 1974, government spending on infrastructure, education, and research accounted for 24 percent of the federal budget. In 1999, with tax revenues skyrocketing, it was just 14 percent of the federal budget. The cost of higher education soared as federal funding of universities failed to keep up with inflation, and more and more students became burdened with debt as the government turned increasingly to loans, rather than grants, as its preferred form of college aid.

This was not just a question of available tax monies; it was a question of cultural values and priorities. It was a question of shifting public resources away from communities and into the pockets of a relatively few individuals. This was a move that not only widened the material gap between the rich-rich and the not-so-rich but also destroyed much of the similarity of experience that existed between people of varying income levels, eliminating solidarity and sympathy along the way. And making the idea of collective interests and social solutions a thing of the very distant past. The economist Frank Levy articulated this back in 1987: "The welfare state rests on enlightened self-interest in which people can look at beneficiaries and reasonably say: 'There but for the grace of God . . .' As income differences widen, this statement rings less true."

At the turn of the millennium in America, it was all but forgotten. To the detriment of us all. Especially our children.

9.

Winner-Take-All
Parenting

"In the last 20 years, business has become the dominant institution in American society, in many respects usurping the role once played by religion."

THE HARVARD BUSINESS REVIEW, NOVEMBER 2001

CHILDREN PLAY SOCCER at semiprofessional training levels before they start kindergarten. Nine- and ten-year-olds are trained for national basketball championships. Four-year-olds barely able to pronounce the name of their instrument study the violin. Six-year-olds join travel hockey teams.

And parents, despite their best instincts, go along for the ride. "Standing on the sidelines, we guzzle coffee and grumble about vacations missed for tournaments and money spent on coaches and clinics," *Washingtonian* magazine features editor Drew Lindsay complained in a "soccer dad's lament" published by that magazine in September 2002. "But when the whistle blows, we pack everyone up and hustle off to the next practice. If we didn't, we might be shortchanging our kids."

In the winner-take-all society, where the wealthy have the privilege of good education, health care, housing, and, above all, *choice* . . .

and everyone else scrambles to make do with ever-shrinking options and resources, parents know all too well that if they don't groom their children to be winners they will end up, de facto, as losers. They will inhabit the second tier of our two-tiered society and will "sink down into hardship and discomfort," as William Damon, director of Stanford University's Center for the Study of Adolescence, once put it.

This awful reality is, I think, the most basic source of the anxiety that drives our frenetic parenting practices today. And it is fueled by the fact that, in this hypercompetitive and excruciatingly expensive age, more and more parents *themselves* feel like losers.

They want the best for their kids—and push them to do *their* very best—in part because they fear they cannot do the best for them. Often, they cannot give them the best of education, of neighborhood, even of health care, because, for more and more parents, "the best" is out of reach. Yet anything other than the best, all too often, is pretty mediocre.

And so parents riddle themselves with debt buying houses in neighborhoods they cannot afford so that they can be close to the best public schools. Or, in cities with hopeless school systems, they bankrupt themselves sending their children to private schools. They sacrifice their financial futures, immerse their families in stress—just to guarantee them a foothold in the Good Life.

"Things are so difficult now. There are so many layoffs. Everything is so competitive," a forty-year-old mother of four, who grew up in Michigan and now lives in Washington, D.C., told me. "As a mother, you have dreams for your children. . . . I wish they had the standard of living that I grew up with. I hope my children will have the standard of living that *they're* growing up with for their families. It's so scary."

Many parents, for the first time in American history, live with the awareness that they are doing less well, financially, than their parents did. Many now realize that their career choices—in the arts, in teaching, in just about anything other than business or law—

have left them unable to comfortably provide their children with the middle-class lifestyle that they themselves grew up taking for granted.

"My folks expected me to be more comfortably off financially than I am, and I think they are disappointed and sad for me," a thirty-nine-year-old Midwestern mother of two, whose husband works from home as an artist and has always taken care of their kids, wrote to me. "We are sending the kids to private school (on financial aid) and I wish we either didn't have that expense (i.e., could afford to live in a neighborhood where the public schools were better) or had enough money not to worry about the expense of private school. If quality child care had been more affordable and more available, I think my husband would be a little further advanced in his artistic career than he is now. If I were being paid what I was worth I think we'd be more comfortably situated. But I can't control that."

Many parents now live with a precariousness that keeps them constantly on edge. It makes them anxious. It sometimes makes them ashamed. It can make them feel like failures.

It's hard enough living with a personal sense of failure. But worse still is the worry that the career choices you've made have jeopardized your children's future. As in: when the bills and the babysitter are paid, there is *no money left* to save for college—not this month, not next month, not anytime in the foreseeable future.

"My parents were practical and reasonable and measured, and fortunate to have material comforts," a thirty-eight-year-old mother of two who holds an administrative job in a New England university and whose husband is a novelist wrote to me. "The game has changed completely—for some reason, having the same comforts now requires ten times as many hours of work. I could not even aspire to my parents' level of comfort—partly because I am not an executive and partly because it would take two executives to get us there, and that's not who we are, for better or worse."

Most people don't have the time, inclination, or possibility, when they hit parenthood, to suddenly turn around, transform their lives, and magically begin to generate six-figure salaries. And so they try to secure their children's futures through other means. As in early 2000, when, with the New Economy booming and talking heads telling us of a bubble that was never to burst, parents rushed to bookstores to stock up on parenting manuals that promised to assure their babies a lifetime of success: *How to Increase Your Child's Verbal Intelligence; Baby Signs: How to Talk with Your Baby Before Your Baby Can Talk; Baby Minds: Brain-Building Games Your Baby Will Love. Publishers Weekly* commented then, "A robust economy, demographics that have schools across the country bursting at the seams, parental anxiety about setting their offspring on the right track to succeed in a competitive world and concern about societal threats to their kids' well-being—these are some of the forces fueling today's sizzling market for books on childcare and parenting. . . . [T]he amount of money people are now willing to spend to help themselves be better parents has never been greater."

"Better" parents are more performative parents. Parents who model and encourage the kinds of high-achieving behaviors that will allow their kids to rise to the top. No wonder so many "type A" postboomer women end up, when it's financially possible, giving up work and staying home with their kids. Many of them feel they have no choice. For how can they possibly parent to perfection if they have to split their energies between home and work? ("I couldn't give 100 percent to both" is how I have heard it put, time and again.) How can they produce the right results in their children—excellence in shoe tying or violin playing or whatever else they feel they need to achieve—if they aren't "working" with them full-time? And how, after all, can the average babysitter—a low-wage "loser" of limited education—be expected to bring up a winner? She can't possibly. No one but another winner can.

So many well-off overachievers leave their paid jobs to become more perfect mothers. And others, who can't afford to stay home, go through babysitter after babysitter, trying fruitlessly to find one who can live up to their own standards of perfection. A thirty-nine-year-old Maryland mother of two recalled to me how this went:

I had seven different babysitters in the first two years with my elder son. It was constant torture. There were personality issues. They weren't stimulating my son enough. The seventh babysitter . . . she was loving. She was nurturing. She was wonderful. She was not that bright and not that stimulating. I worked three days a week at that time and I was torturing myself: "She's not stimulating him enough." I would come home and they'd be gazing out the window and I'd think, "Oh God, how long have they been gazing out the window?" My husband would say, "He has a younger brother talking to him; you're talking to him and he's napping and he's at the playground." And I kept on torturing myself and even now—my son is a really bright, wonderful kid, a great kid—I sit there playing these stupid mind games with myself, saying, "Would he be reading quicker because for a year and a half he wasn't either with me or with the perfect ideal nanny . . . ?"

The really sad thing about all this is what a terrible message it conveys about how we value ourselves, other people, and even our children: you are a winner—the best, the smartest, most talented, top-notch-achieving kind of person—or you are nothing. That we see ourselves this way is unfortunate. But that we submit our children to that same heartless gaze is tragic. Particularly since, these days, the notion of the ideal, "winning" person has been so greatly narrowed that we tend to force all our children—no matter what their talents or inclinations—to fit the mold of standard-issue, CEO-destined achievement.

"It dismisses our core humanity," a mother of two in a Chicago suburb complained, in an online discussion of motherhood that I participated in during the winter of 2002. "As long as a kid has straight A's, does volunteer work . . . is on a school sports team, is on the student council . . . is extroverted, a student leader, is handsome (without any pimples!) and popular, he or she is a Good Kid. Heaven forbid, your child is generally outer-directed, disorganized, dyes his hair, is artistic but unfortunately not very musical, most certainly not interested in student council and does not have any time to perform community service because there is lots of homework to attend to."

"It's success *über alles,*" another mother agreed. "We want only the best for our kids—but unfortunately, the definition of the 'best for our kid' is interpreted pretty narrowly by society, and with limited emphasis on the individual."

The anxious push to be and create winners poisons our family lives. It makes a mockery of our much-praised ideals of personal growth and creativity, and turns our homes into mini-workplaces enslaved to the values of competition and productivity.

"Conquer, conquer, conquer . . . trying to dominate [the world] at every twist and turn" is how child psychiatrist Robert Coles characterized the turn-of-the-millennium family ethic in 2001. Arlie Hochschild, reflecting on the "commercialized spirit of domestic life" in America in 2003, recalled how that spirit had corrupted the relations between the parents and children she'd interviewed for her 1997 book, *The Time Bind.*

Many parents working for the Fortune 500 company she dubbed Amerco, she wrote, loved their children as "results," and judged the value of their time with them "in terms of future results," as in: "how 'old for their age'" or "how 'ahead'" their children seemed to be. This instrumental notion of parental love and time, she said, was most common among the higher-placed men in the corporate hierarchy— the company's winners. Only relative losers—"women and workers in the middle or lower ranks of the company"—she said, saw their families as "a source of intrinsic pleasure."

In the past, if home was meant to be a haven from the workplace, it was because there was an acknowledgment that the values of the workplace were not ones you wanted in your home. But there is no such awareness now. The making-into-religion of business noted by the *Harvard Business Review* in 2001 has meant that the business ethic has turned into *the* dominant cultural ethos of our time. There is no "outside" to the values of the business world—efficiency, self-interest, and using each situation to maximize profit. There is no other sphere, in which something that might be called domesticity or family values or social consciousness, or simply *caring,* can take root.

It is now commonplace, in public policy debates, to make the case for improved educational opportunities or child care for needy children on the grounds that it *costs less* to educate a child than to keep him in prison once he's an adult. Arguments for parents to spend more time with children are similarly couched in a language of maximized profits. "We need to have parents spending enough time with children so they can produce workers we'd like to hire eventually," the president of the Economic Policy Institute, a Washington think tank, told *Business Week* in 1999. There is, it seems, no notion of the intrinsic value of doing more for children. There are only ways to maximize the returns on our parental or social investments. ("Product development" is what sociologist William Doherty calls our time-and-resource–optimizing form of hyperparenting.)

It is also common now for families to operate—even to conceive of themselves—along the lines of a more or less efficiently run small business. Family time is not spent in relaxing together but in managing everyone's different activities, which become a clash of competing agendas. (Which is why, no doubt, there can be a market for such a book as management guru Stephen R. Covey's *Seven Habits of Highly Effective Families.*)

As always, it appears to be the very wealthiest families who take these practices to the greatest levels of absurdity. This was epitomized,

I thought, in 2002 by a story that ran in the *New York Times* on executives who had taken to availing themselves of the services of Leader-
Works, a management consulting firm, to help them more effectively
manage their family lives. For a $1,000 fee, consultants would use
questionnaire data supplied by family members to create a "growth
summary" report, complete with bar graphs and pie charts, to evaluate the executive's strengths and weaknesses as a family member and
identify "focus areas" needing special work as in: "paying attention to
personal feelings," or "solving problems without getting angry." And
then, wrote the *Times* (this is, I think, worth quoting in full):

> The next step is for the executive to convene a Family 360 Coun-
> cil around the dining-room table, an "upbeat and constructive"
> feedback session where the executive expresses "gratitude for
> everyone's help" and invites the family "to jointly create a De-
> velopment Plan to strengthen family relationships." The com-
> pany also provides an "investment guide" with hundreds of
> specific actions that let you connect with your family as effi-
> ciently as possible: buy a speakerphone for the home so that
> you can join in on family game night when you're on the road;
> go for a walk with your child every day, even if it's only to the
> end of the driveway; create "communication opportunities"
> while doing the dishes with your spouse or waiting in line with
> your child at the store.

At lesser extremes of silliness (and expense), similar practices have
spread. Parents don't just talk to their children, they hold "family meetings." They "conference." One woman I met said she held "office hours"
with her children: "I sat in the family room and one by one I called
them in," she explained. "I said, 'Talk to me. How was your day?'"
Parenting priorities, kids' activities, sometimes even friendships,
have no intrinsic value. Parents know that the best colleges recruit

and give preferential treatment to athletes, so they push their children to take their athletic practice to near-professional levels. They learn that piano lessons enhance math and science learning, so they buy pianos. The point of taking music lessons is not to have a better, richer life but to have a leg up on others. And the point of making friends isn't pleasure but popularity—well-honed "social skills."

Parents make a great show of valuing "creativity" (after all, wasn't it "creative thinking" that created the likes of Bill Gates?) but only, ultimately, if their children's creativity is channeled into wealth-building forms. Otherwise, if their children seriously consider pursuing a lifetime in the arts, they sigh in anxious dismay, as a well-off suburban crowd I interviewed did, when they learned that the son of a beloved local orthodontist had chosen to attend art school over Cornell.

And so children pursue extracurricular activities not so much as an extension of their talents or passions or pleasures but as items to add to the résumé of their "school careers." No one expects to produce more dancers or musicians this way, but rather to raise mini-versions of the well-rounded heroes routinely profiled by publications like the *Wall Street Journal*—that is to say, executives with "hobbies." Like the managing director of an investment bank who also publishes a fanzine. Or the senior partner of a law firm who does trekking or flies a small plane.

There is a decline in interest in substantive learning, replaced, in the public schools, by score-enhancing test prep. There is a changed conception of homework. Instead of being a way to review the day's lessons, it is a way to "add value" to the school day by introducing new material that teachers don't have time to teach. Occupational therapists encourage parents to teach their kids such grade-optimizing school strategies as "previewing, skimming, and scanning" rather than close reading, because then "they don't have to get bogged down by details." (For teenage children, such "visual focus" practice activities as cowatching home shopping with parents were recommended by the *Washington Post* as a quality-time, English-skills–boosting form of study.) Reading, learning, education generally, are now considered means to an end—not valuable activities in and of themselves.

PRODUCING WINNERS—those with the skills and instincts to climb to the top and grab the brass ring in our winner-take-all society, means, above all, teaching children to *operate*. This means learning that appearances are all-important, that busyness is in and of itself a great virtue, that competition is the lifeblood of successful personhood and that the point of playing the game isn't how you play but *being a player*. And, of course, players play to win.

At the extreme end of this infernal vision of life education, there are players like former Salomon Smith Barney analyst Jack Grubman, who allegedly raised the rating of A.T.&T. stock in order to secure an "in" for his twins at Manhattan's most prestigious preschool. There are wealthy families who pay for batteries of educational tests in order to win diagnoses of "learning disabled" for their children so that they can have extended time to take the SAT. ("It's part of our culture that every point matters, so they're looking for any kind of edge" is how an educational psychologist explained this to the *New York Times*.)

And all this game-rigging, this narcissistic achievement-by-proxy, doesn't just occur in the hypercompetitive corridors of big cities like New York. "I think there is definitely a sustained, unspoken attempt to produce a product that [parents] can be proud of and that reflects well on them," a thirty-eight-year-old mother of two reported to me of parenthood in Providence, Rhode Island. "Add to that this desire to compensate—for what I'm not sure—for lives that have spun out of control and that aren't full of meaning or happiness when the motion stops, and there's a real disconnect between what our generation of parents profess (tolerance, peace, acceptance, pleasantness) and the lessons they inadvertently teach their children by not setting limits and disciplining them and teaching them respect."

Playing to win—*no matter what*—is a nationwide dilemma.

OVER THE PAST DECADE, a number of commentators have decried the moral perversion that accompanied our country's transformation into a winner-take-all society. "An especially precious type of equality—equality not of money but in the way we treat each other and live our lives—seems to be disappearing," journalist Mickey Kaus lamented in 1992. "Turbo-charged capitalism is the enemy of family values," wrote commentator Edward Luttwak in 1995. In 2002, *Wealth and Democracy* author Kevin Phillips denounced a "corruption" that had come to extend to every aspect of American life. "The 1980s and 1990s have imitated the Golden Age in intellectual excesses of market worship, laissez-faire and social Darwinism," he wrote. "Notions of common wealth, civic purpose and fairness have been crowded out of the public debate." And referring to the Michael Douglas character, Gordon Gekko, who in the 1987 movie *Wall Street* famously said, "Greed is good," economist Paul Krugman wrote that we as a nation had come to embrace our "inner Gekko."

All of this has had a noxious effect on how we parent. It has inspired a new child-rearing style, winner-take-all parenting, which combines our anxious overconcern with our children's emotional states (May They Feel No Pain) with our fears about their social standing (now and in the future) with an utter disregard for other people (children and adults alike). Particularly if those people stand in the way of our children's maximizing the profit they might reap from the world around them.

We coddle our children when they are little, supplying them not just with love but with a nonstop amniotic bath of praise and stimulation, because, we hope, this will give them the "right start" in life.

We teach them to be "true" to themselves—even if this pursuit of authenticity to self means they trample on the feelings of others. We make sure that our children's needs are honored wherever they go: they must have *their* foods, *their* routines, unchanged. We teach them that their interests must always be served. And served first.

And so we produce a generation of preschoolers who will eat just one brand, one *shade* in orange color, of processed cheese. Who often regard adults as impediments to their will—to be conned, manipulated, or, if necessary, physically shoved from their paths. We make such a fetish of our children's feelings that we step all over the toes of others to indulge them. And, often enough, we train them to be not just indifferent but virtually blind and deaf to the very existence of other people.

A Chicago executive told me how her six-year-old son couldn't have a good school friend over for a play date because the friend's mother said the friend's three-year-old little brother missed him too much when he wasn't home. "She won't even let the little one tag along, because she wants to make sure he is well taken care of and apparently she is the only human being alive capable of this," the Chicago mom told me. "My poor son just doesn't understand why his friend can't come over."

Another mother, in suburban Maryland, explained to me how she permitted her little girl to cancel play dates right up to the very minute that they were scheduled, because she "couldn't force her" to engage in social commitments that now bored her. *"We all like some people better than others,"* she reasoned.

Author Rachel Cusk relates the story of a British couple with a three-year-old child who offered a woman a ride home from a lunch. The woman got into the back of their car next to their child. The child started to complain because she was used to sitting in the back alone. And so the parents stopped driving and asked the woman to get out, leaving her stranded in the middle of nowhere.

"I hesitate to say that we love our children more than our parents loved us," Cusk writes of this episode. "Even if this were true, it is not the kind of love that makes the world go round. That family you see out on a Saturday afternoon, with their cycle helmets and their fear of strangers and their fourteen varieties of apple juice in special beakers, wouldn't stop to help you if you were bleeding to death in the road."

I tend to agree.

While we make a lot of whiny noises about encouraging our toddlers to share when they're pounding each other on the head in the playground, the notion of real cooperation and sharing is all but absent in the libertarian way we now organize our family lives. Our concern for our children's well-being is often a cover for incredible insensitivity. A child feels lazy on the morning of her best friend's birthday party and we find the location inconvenient, so we allow her not to attend. A stay-at-home mom envisions the boring prospect of a school vacation day and schedules a party for her child in the middle of it, knowing full well that the children of working parents won't be able to come.

The demand to be "on duty" all the time for one's children combines with the ethos of the 24/7 marketplace to create incredible acts of virtue-cloaked rudeness. "Good" working parents take time away from the office to volunteer in the classroom—but leave cell phones on so they can be forever on-call to their colleagues. This is not considered disrespectful. It is called creating "balance." As *Variety* once put it, in an article on the "balancing act" carried out by big female players in Hollywood, "Industry women who report the greatest satisfaction balancing career and motherhood say it requires the same organizational skills that made them successful businesswomen. . . . Deals are now struck at soccer games and birthday parties. Their kids' lives are as scheduled as their own."

The self-importance and self-protectiveness of those living their lives on the business model cannot be underestimated. As Arlie Hochschild has noted: "Parents now . . . speak of time as if it is a threatened form of personal capital they have no choice but to manage and invest." As a result, everyone aims now to do what is convenient and hassle-free. The selfishness that results can be astounding:

A well-off couple leaves their four kids for the night with a single mother of two so that they can enjoy a special anniversary dinner and night in a hotel. The next morning, they call to ask if they can pick up their children a couple of hours later than planned. When they're told no, they show up, miffed, to pick up their kids and give their two-year-old a basketball to play with in the living room. The two-year-old throws it at some framed pictures and breaks them. When their friend takes the basketball away and sends the toddler down to play in the playroom, they leave—in a huff.

When emergency preparedness plans were made here in Washington, and we had to fill in contact sheets listing who would be authorized to take our children home from school in the case of a terrorist attack, most parents put down relatives who lived miles away, across potentially impassable bridges, rather than organize with other neighborhood families. Caring for other people's children at a time of *real* emergency, everyone understood, was just too much of an "imposition."

At drop-off time around our local public schools, hurried working parents block traffic with their cars and serve as private-duty crossing guards for their children, who hop out in the crosswalks and then run to school, while the cars pile up behind them. Meanwhile, stay-at-home moms with nothing but time leave their massive SUV-fusion minivans in the drop-off zones while they chat with their friends on the playground. No one complains. No one dares infringe upon another's right to "convenience."

Why should they? Formal courtesy is now considered an excessive waste of time. Invitations need not be acknowledged. Families arrive hours late for social events because they don't want to rearrange their babies' nap schedules. Guests show up at the tail end of religious ceremonies because they conflict with their children's sporting events. Thoughts for others just don't rank high on the priorities of "highly effective families"—just as thoughts of social responsibility can't crowd much into a CEO's consciousness as he works to uphold the bottom line for his investors.

This is winner-take-all parenting, libertarian-style, and it leads to an epidemic of snubs and hurt feelings.

And, potentially, is leading us all to raise a generation of not-very-nice people.

ARE WE DOING ANY GOOD?

When I had my first daughter, my husband was a fourth-year medical student," a stay-at-home mother of three in Oklahoma City told me.

When the baby was six months old, we moved to a small town in North Carolina, where he began a six-year residency, earning little money, working one-hundred-hour weeks.

During all that time, I was raising two kids with very little money, but great friends. I was part of a babysitting co-op. We went to the YMCA. Life was really simple. And when we look back, life was really nice.

Two years ago, my husband finished his residency and is now a neurosurgeon. He has a job making real money; our house is three times as big as before. Our children go to this wonderful private school. It's like never-never land. Now we can do anything with our children. If I want my child to take six different music lessons, I can. It's like being a kid in a candy store—we have so many choices.

This is how we always imagined our life. This is how we dreamed it—this is how we wanted it. But what's funny is that there's no time to be a parent anymore. And we're so busy with our life, we feel like we don't have the time to appreciate all the things we have. My two older kids are in school. They each do one or two activities.

The third-grader does piano and ballet, softball in the spring, bas-
ketball in the winter, and both are in Camp Fire, which is like Girl
Scouts. Last year, my eight-year-old studied ballet and was in a pro-
fessional performance of the Nutcracker. *She spent twenty hours a*
week in rehearsals.

It all made me think: if I've got only twenty-five hours a week
with my children after school and they're spending fifteen hours a week
on activities, when do I get to be the mom? I'm having trouble finding
time to spend with my two-year-old. When my big kids were small,
we just hung out. We stayed home. Now I've actually hired a part-
time nanny so that my two-year-old doesn't grow up thinking he lives
in a car. In some ways, it's so much harder now that we have so much
money and opportunity.

When we had no money, I always found ways for my children to
do things. Now we're having to remind ourselves of what things we
like to do.

The problem with winner-take-all parenting is that it impover-
ishes everyone. There is a kind of spiritual bankruptcy to the ideal
family these days. The rushing around. The selfishness. And, for the
wealthy, the meaninglessness of having so many choices. And the worst
of it is, it doesn't seem to be doing our children any good.

Psychologists report that depression and anxiety are on the rise
among kids. The National Institute of Mental Health reports that
first-time depression is being diagnosed among children at an earlier
and earlier age. There have been steady increases in eating disorders,
alcohol abuse, and other problems related to stress among teenagers,
and the suicide rate among teens aged fifteen to nineteen has jumped
114 percent since 1980. A Harris poll in 2001 found almost 75 percent of teenagers said they felt nervous or stressed at least some of the
time, with half saying they often felt that way. Almost a third of college freshman surveyed by a UCLA team in 2001 reported feeling

"overwhelmed"—double the numbers who said they felt that way in the mid-1980s. Children as young as eleven report being worried about getting into college after hearing adults tell them that their choice of school will "make or break" their future. And among some younger children, the near-professionalization of kids' sports has provided a major new source of stress, with doctors reporting a vast increase in "overuse injuries" among children as young as eight or nine. What this means is that these kids are being pushed far beyond what their young bodies are meant to do. ("No child ever did anything repetitively enough in a sandlot game to cause an overuse injury" is the opinion of Lyle Micheli, sports medicine director at Harvard Medical School and Boston Children's Hospital.)

While hyperparenting can induce anxiety, depression, and stress in older kids, among younger children it now seems chiefly to produce bad behavior. Educators complain that many children have trouble transitioning to preschool because they've been played with so constantly and have gotten so much of what they want all the time at home. They come to kindergarten overprepared intellectually and underprepared in basic social skills. As a result, wrote Judy Azzara, a recently retired school principal who topped off her career with an impassioned cri de coeur in *Education Digest* in 2001, teachers are having to deal with a "spoiled generation" of young children who simply don't know how to behave. "Some five-year-olds actually come to kindergarten reading, writing, talking with extensive vocabularies, and capable of advanced math," she wrote, "but many do not know how to share or play cooperatively and often demand continuous one-on-one attention and entertainment. Ironically, despite these obvious academic gains, educators see more and more children still lacking important developmental gains such as basic social skills or even potty training."

Azzara argued that many problems teachers face now in school stem from parents' inability to simply let go and let their children *be.*

She mentioned mothers sobbing at the classroom door while their children entered kindergarten and said it is now an educational goal among teachers to get parents to "let go." She made a plea for larger doses of parental benign neglect—like, for example, a return to the use of playpens: "I'm convinced through my interviews that playpen-type devices are now viewed by many as little territorial prisons—limiting freedom and expression," she wrote. "But many successful parents in the past viewed playpens as safe havens where children could creatively play, think, and experience limits." And she denounced the trend toward constantly stimulating young children:

> Observation of families and many surveys indicate most young children are entertained and stimulated continually during their waking hours. . . . Most of my colleagues agree that constant playing with parents frequently contributes to a situation where the child is continually in control or the center of attention. . . . We are witnessing more and more family dynamics that contribute to a scenario where children "in control" are literally becoming "out of control."

Azzara's critiques echo in the writings of many other early-childhood educators. Indeed, there appears to be a real backlash now against the hyperventilating parenting style that so many of us practice. Books like *Toilet Trained for Yale, Reclaiming Childhood, Keeping Your Kids Out Front Without Kicking Them from Behind, The Over-Scheduled Child, Worried All the Time, Freeing Our Families of Perfectionism,* and *The Blessing of a Skinned Knee* (lining bookstore shelves just a few inches over from *Baby Minds* and its ilk) warn against the dangers of pushing and coddling kids too much and beg for a return to greater common sense and calm.

Some experts warn that turning kids into "walking résumés" sets them up for feeling for the rest of their lives that nothing they do will ever be good enough. Others question whether our incessant coddling and cheerleading won't eventually lead our children to have *weakened* self-esteem by making them doubt both the veracity of our praise and their abilities to really accomplish worthwhile things. Too much focusing on themselves can lead some children toward the kind of self-obsession that shows up later in depression. And "selfism," some say, can lead children not to care about the outside world at all. "I think this generation will be totally self-centered," a veteran teacher in a Washington, D.C., nursery school told me. "I think they'll feel a real need to produce and have *things*. I don't think they'll have a clue about the human side of our lives."

In 2001, David Brooks painted a rather terrifying portrait of winner kids on the cusp of adulthood as he followed a group of Princeton University students ("Future Workaholics of America," he called them; "power tools," they called themselves) for his *Atlantic Monthly* article "The Organization Kid." He chronicled their eighteen-hour work days, total lack of idealism, and hubristic notions of their own powers of control: "One senior told me that she went to bed around two and woke up each morning at seven; she could afford that much rest because she had learned to supplement her full day of work by studying in her sleep," Brooks wrote. He noted the emptying-out of meaning from the students' lives: "An activity . . . ," he wrote, "is rarely an end in itself. It is a means for self-improvement, résumé-building, and enrichment. College is just one step on the continual stairway of advancement, and they are always aware that they must get to the next step (law school, medical school, whatever) so that they can progress up the steps after that."

Clearly, the upcoming generation of middle-class children will know how to achieve. But will they learn to think for themselves and make choices? Will they be plagued—as children prized above all for their accomplishments have always been—by a pervasive sense of emptiness? A tendency toward depression? An inability to find value in themselves independently of their achievements? A difficulty in finding satisfaction in life? They may well be.

A twenty-something woman I know told me recently of how her friends, newly graduated from college, couldn't settle down and find jobs. They'd grown up being told how wonderful they were by their parents, had come of age in the boom years of the 1990s, and expected, as adults, to find instant glory in the marketplace like the dot-com millionaires just a few years their seniors. Regular jobs weren't good enough for them. Regular life felt somehow empty. "Everyone wants to be a star," she said. "We're never satisfied. We can't make choices or plan our lives because nothing seems great enough to be worth doing."

THE LEADING THEORY right now on fatal food allergies is that parents today may, ironically, have made their kids more prone to life-threatening allergic attacks by keeping them *too* well protected and, in particular, too clean. There is new research showing that children who live on farms develop immunities to allergens that other kids today don't have. This suggests that, in our overly zealous war on germs, we may have weakened our children's immune systems by over-protecting them from the kinds of bacteria that actually strengthened our bodies in the past.

In other words, my Depression-era father was right: You've got to eat your peck of dirt before you die. Otherwise, you may not be strong enough to make it to old age.

Some exposure to dirt may strengthen a child's immune system. Similarly, many experts now say that *some* exposure to adversity—to unpleasantness, sadness, fear, or failure—may give children the tools they need to make it through life with real strength. Our attempts to make our children into winners and shelter them from both pain and failure may actually make them weaker and more likely to fail when they encounter frustration.

Experts have been trying to teach parents this lesson for decades. In 1963, Betty Friedan cited psychologists' warnings that overmothered children were showing "an inability to endure pain or discipline or pursue any self-sustained goal of any sort." In 1978, *Psychology Today* argued that overprotecting children might deprive them of a chance to develop a sense of control over their environment and breed a kind of "learned helplessness"—a habit of giving up in the face of difficulty. By doing too much for their children, overly solicitous parents could make their kids believe they were unable to do for themselves. "Comfortable levels of stress," the magazine warned, "may be better for a child's ego development than things that happen without any effort on the child's part. Self-esteem and a sense of competence may not depend on whether we experience good or bad events, but rather on whether we perceive some control over what happens to us."

In 1987, Bruno Bettelheim warned that the overbearing boomer parenting style was keeping kids from having sufficient mental room— or *spielraum,* as he called it—to develop a rich inner life. This lack of an inner life, he warned, would eventually lead to a situation where children needed constantly to be entertained—either by parents or by TV. In 1996, family psychologist John Rosemond wrote that children were suffering from "hand-and-foot disease, which is usually prompted by being waited on by an overly solicitous parent, usually female." The symptoms of this ailment: "Today's children whine more, are more disrespectful, and throw tantrums long past the age when yesterday's children were over them completely." He also warned that "Frantic Family Syndrome" was causing families to lose their "center of gravity," making them "susceptible to stress."

Is there a center of gravity in the life of the Ideal Mother these days—with her 5:30 A.M. workout and kids' baseball and basketball and diving and weight-lifting practice, and calendars and spread sheets and bake sales and book clubs and miles and miles and *miles* of driving—all at "Mach 3," as a supermom told the *St. Louis Post-Dispatch* not too long ago? (*"If I have too much time on my hands, things kind of get bogged down,"* another mom said.)

Does *anyone* have an inner life?

THE BACKLASH, these days, against our crazy-making form of parenting isn't limited to the writings of educators and child psychologists. Glimmers of nostalgia for another kind of childhood—"when free time was actually free," as Steven A. Cohen, editor of the 2001 anthology *The Games We Played,* has put it—are starting to show up everywhere. Author David Maraniss tapped into it in an essay called "The Sweet Long Days" when he wrote, of his childhood in the late 1950s, "The essential wonder of the games we played is that we played them blessedly free from adults. There were no soccer moms or Little League dads. For better or worse, we defined and lived in our own world."

Everybody Loves Raymond star Patricia Heaton made constant reference to the lost pleasures of her 1960s childhood in her humorous memoir, *Motherhood and Hollywood:* "It was all so much fun back then. It was a different time and the world was a different place. Our parents would let us run the neighborhood wild between meals. In the summer the only rule was to be home when the streetlights came on. The neighborhood was communal. So maybe we were a bit more aggressive, didn't have sensitivity training, got whupped by other people's moms. But it was a blast."

The women I interviewed were unanimous in their recollections of having had much more freedom as children than their children do now. They remembered walking alone to kindergarten; taking the bus with friends to the beach; being sent out of the house in the morning and not returning home until the late afternoon, when their mothers blew horns or rang bells to bring them back in for dinner.

"We ran out and came back six hours later and were involved in all kinds of innocent activities that had me out of the house and with other kids and having my personality forged by those interactions with other kids, rather than how it is now with *my* kids, where I'm hovering around their play dates and their personalities are being forged by having conversations with me," said a forty-one-year-old government lawyer turned stay-at-home mom. "When conflict arises, sometimes they work it out for themselves, but other times I have to work it out for them. When I was a kid, if you were an ass you didn't get played with and after a while you learned to behave. You got socialized."

Children have a need to achieve independence and mastery. They want and need to separate from their parents. That's why they love stories of freedom and adventure. They stare with wide, happy eyes at the little boy wandering, parentless and peacefully, through his city streets in *The Snowy Day*. They devour books in which the parents are dead or otherwise absent: *Pippi Longstocking, Peter Pan, James and the Giant Peach, Harry Potter*. The pleasure children take in reading these stories contrasts sharply, today, with parents' inability to give them enough space to enjoy life beyond our reach. (When my older daughter was a baby, I couldn't even read her the text to *The Runaway Bunny*. I had to rewrite every scene of the bunny's attempted separation from its mother into an exquisite episode of bunny bonding: "'*Do you want to climb a mountain?' said the mother rabbit. 'Let me get on my rock-climbing gear and hat and I'll come with you.'*")

What will the results be for our children of having had a generation of parents who can't separate? What will the long-term effect be of our pervasive anxiety, our rampaging ambition, and our endless desire to control how our children think, feel, and achieve? We have done all we could to shelter them from the cold wind of abandonment. We have done all we could to protect them from pain. We do all we can to set them on the "right path" toward success. But how will our children function when we are no longer there to shout "good job"?

When the mommy light fades, will they shiver in the dark?

And, worst of all, if we make ourselves miserable in the pursuit of mommy perfection, will they leave childhood with the sight of our tense, tight-mouthed faces forever etched in their minds? And will they blame themselves for our unhappiness?

I DO NOT WANT to play into the religion of mommy-as-the-root-of-all-evil by saying that the way we mother today is destined, necessarily, to set our children up for a whole slew of problems down the line. So I have tried to focus on the effects of our parenting style (and it's not only mothers who practice it) that are visible right now. Some of our worst cultural tendencies are currently playing themselves out in our parenting practices, to the detriment of our children. They are stressed and anxious and, at the very least, often badly behaved.

And I would also venture to say that there's another area in our lives which is right now showing signs of some serious strain: our marriages.

10.

Wonderful Husbands

"Is it true," a young woman asked me recently at a party, "that when you're a mother you love your children *so much* that you don't care about sex anymore?"

IF YOU TALK to women these days, and the conversation turns to marriage, a great many will tell you how lucky they are. How blessed. How grateful. Because (and this seems always to be the phrase) they have "wonderful husbands."

Husbands who bring home the bacon—and fry it up in a pan (on Sundays, when they get up early with the kids). Husbands who love their children desperately and are trying the best they can to break the mold of fatherhood passed down to them by their dads. Husbands who bend. And adapt. And accept to "babysit": for Girls' Night Out, book club night, even the occasional girls' weekend away.

But keep the talk going (change the subject, shift gears) and the conversation inevitably will turn. Someone will say, "I have a wonderful husband, *but . . .*" or "I know we all in this room have wonderful husbands, *but . . .*" or "My husband's an exceptional father, *but . . .*" and then things will go south very fast.

As in:

"He puts a plate in a dishwasher and it's 'What a wonderful husband.'"

Or:

"He said after this past weekend—when he took two naps and went running—'Honey, I'm the <u>best</u> babysitter you have.'"

Or:

"I do have a wonderful husband. . . . This is not a complaint about my husband. But . . . do you think my husband knows if we have milk or not? I think sometimes: What if I got a full-time job, would things fall apart? Would we eat at McDonald's every night? . . . There's a learned incompetence that sets in. I think: if you did this at work, if you did things in such a dufus-y *sort of way, you wouldn't be having a career.*

Or:

"I have a husband who's totally wonderful and a total contrast with my father, who was this crazy person, but my father, crazy as he was, was around a whole lot more than my husband is."

Suddenly all the wonder, all the blessedness, sloughs away. Leaving behind something that looks and sounds a whole lot more like rage.

> MOM #1: *He walks in the door and says,* "I don't even have time to pee." *And I say,* "Yes, but I've scheduled the dentist appointments, gone for haircuts, gone back and forth to school and carpools <u>and</u> I've managed to write all my seminar papers."
> MOM #2: *And only slept three hours . . .*

> MOM #3: *I have to make {my husband} his to-do list. Then I have to ask him to do things. Then it becomes an issue. Then I'm catapulted into the nag category.*
>
> MOM #1: *The mother category.*
>
> MOM #2: *I am so tired of that.*
>
> MOM #3: *But do you care?*
>
> MOM #2: *I don't care anymore. But it's taken years, and therapy.*
>
> MOM #3: *I cared for a while. I don't care anymore*

Many, many women have trouble dealing with their anger head-on. Anger, openly avowed, is an unacceptable emotion. It is considered ugly, *inappropriate,* to directly vent your rage, even a little bit—as *Washington Post* writer Ruth Marcus learned in the spring of 2003, when she was almost universally condemned for a Mother's Day op-ed piece, "What Mommies Want," in which she discussed the rage and desperation that sometimes seized her when she picked her husband's boxer shorts up off the floor. Anger is as tacky, as outdated, overmuch, and unwelcome, as is talking about financial stress or politics.

It is better, safer to laugh it all off, to chortle derisively at the many TV ads that now depict husbands and fathers as hapless household boobs. Like the ad I saw recently in a movie theater that showed a 1950s family gathered for breakfast, Mom serving up homemade waffles, children exquisitely polite, and Dad at the end of the table silently hidden behind his newspaper. *"Get real,"* an off-camera voice broke in—and the image changed to a real-life family at breakfast today: kids eating on the run, everyone snapping and snarling, Mom supervising, shepherding, overseeing, and organizing as she got herself ready for work, sheer chaos all around . . . and Dad at the end of the table silently hidden behind his newspaper.

(*"What's so funny?"* my husband said, as my nervous laughter echoed in the dark room.)

. . .

"THIS GENERATION of women thought it had a new, trustworthy bond with which to replace that archaic deal of prefeminist marriage: flaming, erotic, friendly, egalitarian love," Naomi Wolf writes in the excellent chapter on marriage in her motherhood memoir, *Misconceptions.* "Our generation did not think we were marrying breadwinners; we thought we were marrying our best friends."

Many postboomer mothers who once bought into this vision are ending up, these days, sorely disappointed. Their husbands may be fine fathers; they *are,* usually, breadwinners (thank God, as it turns out), but they're not—not on golf mornings or on laundry day or when the kids need shoes or on the one evening when both of you want to go to the gym—much in the way of "friends." Or lovers. Or "soul mates."

"I can't say these days that our marriage is about love," says a working mother of two in New York. "It's *definitely* not about romance. It's like we run a small business together. We're business partners. And that's okay, so long as the business is working smoothly."

This is not an ideal situation. It can be pretty depressing—if you let yourself think about it too much. (*"I have learned that I am basically going it alone"* was the insight one mother culled after years of therapy.) And so women don't. Think about it. Or fight. Or even feel. "My turning point was: this is just the way it is," says a Washington, D.C., working mother of three who attained a state of peaceful acceptance in her marriage on the day she realized that she no longer *wanted* her husband's help. "I have strengths and he has strengths . . . and all of a sudden I realized: I don't have to be mad at him all the time."

And so, instead of talking about their anger, women talk about other things. How hopeless men are at taking care of children. (*"I asked him to make a play date and he couldn't do it."* . . . *"If he were in charge of dinner, he'd just pour a bowl of cereal."* . . . *"I went out to dinner. I set everything out. For bath time. Bedtime. I came home and they were still running around."*) How lucky they are not to be like men. (*"We've come further than men have." . . . "We're more evolved." . . . "We're better off."*) How lucky their children are to have mothers like them, women who aren't afraid to be *real* women, *real* moms, instead of trying to be man substitutes. (*"We don't want to be mini-men. They're selling their souls very cheaply and their options are not the best and they're losing control and they're losing time for the things that would make them full—like their children."*)

They talk about how much easier life often is when their husbands are away. (*"There's no friction." . . . "No expectations." . . . "Nothing to negotiate." . . . "TV is a better babysitter than Daddy, any day."*)

And they talk about sex. About how, as more highly evolved females, they don't *need* to have sex, don't want to have sex, while their husbands, being *men*, well . . .

> *"Men are a whole different breed, man."*
>
> *"They just need to fuck and come."*
>
> *"My husband says, 'We're abnormal.' I say, 'Honey, we're not abnormal, you're lucky to get as much as you get.'"*
>
> *"My husband's, like, 'Don't worry about me. It's okay. I can go it alone. I'll just masturbate in bed. I'll take a long shower.'"*
>
> *"My husband just had a vasectomy. I thought it would be a good idea and he was almost perfectly willing to do it, but then I started thinking: Is this going to mean we're going to have sex all the time? I thought—shit, I'll have no excuse."*

I broached the uncomfortable topic of sex in my interviews by talking about how other people were talking about sex. *Newsweek,* in 2003, had published a hot new statistic: that up to 20 percent of couples were reporting having sex no more than ten times a year, qualifying them for the official classification of "sexless marriage." Dr. Phil had taken up the issue on his website, proclaiming that "sexless marriages are an undeniable epidemic." *Everyone Loves Raymond* sitcom star Patricia Heaton was urging women to have sex more with their husbands, joking in her memoir, *Motherhood and Hollywood*, "Think about it. Really, what's three minutes out of your week? (I'm counting that as sex twice, Wednesday and Saturday.)" Kate Reddy, heroine of the best-selling British work of "mum lit" *I Don't Know How She Does It,* was brushing her teeth twenty times per molar at night, hoping that her husband would fall asleep and not try to have sex. ("If we don't have sex, I can skip a bath in the morning. If I skip the bath, I will have time to start on the e-mails that have built up while I've been away.") Everyone was reading *The Bitch in the House,* an entire volume of essays organized around the theme of mothers' lack of libido and "inexplicable rage." And Naomi Wolf had put forth the theory, in *Misconceptions,* that our generation of mothers was nursing a "quiet, stubborn knot of resentment" at the "passive aggression" and "almost deliberate obliviousness" of their husbands, and were withholding sex as a way of evening the score.

The women I interviewed were comforted to hear that not having sex was shaping up to be a national trend. But they sharply disagreed with the idea that lack of sex was a sign of something amiss in their marriages. Time and again they told me about real love and lifelong commitment, about spiritual love that transcends mere physical contact, about love on a higher, and deeper, level than sex. They had a great deal to say about long-term intimacy and growth, the nature of matrimony, the absorption of motherhood.

"There's a level of intimacy that has nothing to do with sex that we have that's about our family and our lifestyle."

"Intimacy in the context of a true lifelong partnership—I won't say a romantic partnership but some kind of intellectual partnership—is the most challenging kind of intimacy. The relationship is so permanent and so all-encompassing."

"Because my husband and I know each other so well and are so

comfortable with each other and know *we're sexually attracted to each other, we don't have to have sex a lot, and actually I start to think that it's almost better."*

Until the conversation degenerated utterly and they described how their husbands were masturbating in the shower.

Something was terribly wrong.

Because there was a nasty underside to the giggles of nice-mommy conversations about sex. There was something sinister in the fact that the very same women who would tell me how wonderful their husbands were would, in the next breath, let me (and a roomful of avid listeners) in on the most awful humiliations of their mates' private moments. While praising their neatness, devotion, and quick way with a dishwasher, they would strip them bare and, in the nicest way possible, enjoy their shame.

I am not alone in making this observation. Caitlin Flanagan, reviewing *The Bitch in the House* for the *Atlantic Monthly,* was struck by the degree to which its contributors—like a number of women she'd encountered socially—reveled in dishing the dirt on their most private lives: "What's interesting about these public confessions—and, I suspect, what makes them so satisfying to women—" she wrote, "is that they are utterly humiliating to husbands. . . . Is there anything more wounding to a man, and therefore more cruel and vicious, than a wife's public admission that he is not satisfying her in bed?"

"You're not a woman anymore, you're a mom."
SATURDAY NIGHT LIVE

In 1993, at the height of proclamations about the "death" of feminism and the coming-into-adulthood of a kinder, gentler, and more traditionally minded "postfeminist" generation, social commentator

Wendy Kaminer wrote that it was natural for young women to have turned a cold shoulder to 1970s-era dreams of equality with men. What, after all, was the point of being mad all the time? Better to reclaim True Womanhood (soon to become True Motherhood)—and leave the malcontents to fight it out for themselves. "Given the absence of social and institutional support—family leave and day care—it's not surprising that women would turn for sustenance to traditional notions of sex difference," she wrote. "The belief that they were naturally better suited to child care than men would relieve them of considerable anger toward their husbands. As Victorian women invoked maternal virtue to justify their participation in the public sphere, so contemporary American women have used it to console themselves for the undue burden they continue to bear in the private one."

I think that something very similar is happening in our generation's attitudes to marriage and motherhood today. We have reclaimed the idea of sexual difference (*"Males and females are different, and women respond to different things"*) and use it now as a justification for our exhausting labors (*"That's being a mom. It's 24/7"*). The "fact" that men and women are "just different" has become the rationalization for our society's inability to accommodate the worlds of work and family. And it is the grease that keeps the mechanism of our marriages smoothly functioning.

Women learn that there's no point in being sad or mad or resentful when their youthful dreams of best-friend marriage run aground, because men and women aren't "made" to be friends. It isn't their husbands who have betrayed their hopes by suddenly metamorphosing into *Father Knows Best* types who don't know how to read the instructions on a box of pancake mix. It isn't society that is culpable for stretching the workweek to fifty-plus hours so that one parent has to slave away while the other keeps the family together at home. It is biology, pure and simple. And you can't argue with that.

So, instead of arguing, women shrug and smile, and smugly take the responsibility for, say, pancake-making out of their husbands' hands. They turn their rage into self-righteousness. Channel their resentment into such exquisite heights of über-mommy performance that their husbands' "help" is no longer necessary. Or desirable. And they adopt a desexualized mommy persona (like the woman in the 2003 *Saturday Night Live* skit with her big-butt–hiding "Mom Jeans") that justifies their troubled, sexless marriages. This mommy persona is like a Trojan horse. And sex (or no sex) is a potent stealth weapon in the sad, largely disavowed, new War Between the Sexes.

The phrase "War Between the Sexes" is, of course, a throwback to another generation—one in which women didn't marry their "best friends." But then, so is a significant portion of what passes for normal married life these days.

I think of the way a suburban Maryland mom approached the topic of sex in marriage in one of my interview groups:

> *My friend in my book club said that her grandmother told her: "You know, a happy man is a* drained *man." It's always in the back of my mind. Because compared to us, men are simple: give them a little sex and they're happy. I was driving down the street the other day and I ran into my neighbor. I rolled down my window and I mentioned an article I'd seen recently in the paper. It was about "rekindling the flame" in your marriage. She said, "I haven't seen it. But whatever the article says, it's all about sex." She told me: "If I want to get something for the house, I have sex more that week. All the money issues go away." She said, "This week, I was on a roll:* every other night!"

What's happened to us?

What happened between the mid-1990s, when books like Christina Baker Kline's *Child of Mine* ushered us into maternity with lyrical and hopeful musings on the meaning of motherhood and marriage, and 2002's raging *Bitch in the House?*

Something quite simple. Our generation had the time to fully taste the reality of married life with children. And it wasn't quite what we had bargained for. For one thing, "coparenting" has turned out for most couples to be little more than a pipe dream. Mothers spend four times as much time with their children as do fathers. Working mothers spend twice as much time as working fathers on reading to their children and helping with their homework. And when Dads do help, the quality of time they put in on kid-care is not, often enough, what most moms consider "quality time."

This, at least, was what researchers at the University of Michigan found out in 2001, when they tracked how much time fathers spent with their children each day and how they spent it. What they discovered was that, on weekdays, when the average father spends 63 minutes with his children, 33 of those minutes are used up by family meals or by watching TV. On weekends, when the average father clocks in 166 minutes with his children, 54 of those minutes are spent, once again, on meals and TV—and the rest are spent coparenting with Mom!

Mothers still run the show. They still play the role of the "psychological parent" in most families—"the one who is always mindful of, and feels a direct personal responsibility for, the whereabouts and the feelings of each child, who knows what emotional supports they need, what size shoes they wear, what diseases they've been exposed to, who their teachers are, what kind of work the first grade does . . . who their friends are, who the parents of their friends are, what the current nightmares are, how tightly to bind the baby's blanket, and so on," as a perfectly contemporary-sounding 1976 book on working motherhood put it. Two generations of mothers have come of age since the seventies, but times have changed very little. "I carry the emotional baggage of my children a lot more than my husband does," a part-time government lawyer and mother of four told me. "I fret about their feelings. . . . I worry about the state of their souls, and he says they'll be fine. I assume far too much of the internal emotional life of our family [and] . . . I feel alone in many of my concerns."

Women still do almost all the housework. They know it—*everyone* knows it—even if husbands, sometimes, don't want to admit it. But who are they fooling? Hoots of laughter greeted a 1998 study by the Families and Work Institute showing that, when surveyed, men said they were spending 75 percent as much time on household chores as were their wives. Studies consistently show that while there were big increases in the number of hours men spent on domestic tasks in the 1970s and eighties (from a starting point, let's remember, of just about zero), their contributions plateaued in the 1990s and then generally remained stuck at the "helping-out" level we see today. Working women *alone* do upwards of 70 percent of household chores for their families. Even *househusbands* frequently do less housework than their wives.

Why is this? *Newsweek* asked, in a 2003 story on high-earning alpha women and their husbands. Because, the magazine answered, "Being out of work already threatens their manhood, and taking on 'feminine' tasks like cleaning the toilet might only make them feel worse."

And that strikes right at the crux of the problem.

As unemployed househusbands know (but many women are loath to admit), all the different kinds of work that keep a family functioning are not the same. There is a different status attached to, say, picking boxer shorts up off the floor than there is to bringing home a paycheck. The reversion to traditional sex roles that has occurred in so many households of parents in our generation hasn't come without a price. The more they slip into traditional "feminine" roles, many women find, the more their status declines. The less they earn, the less clout, the less decision-making power they have within their homes. And this often subtle and silently occurring slip in status is, for many, a very bitter pill to swallow. For some, it simply sticks in their throats. And leaves them spitting mad.

"When my husband and I started dating, I made more money than he did," a formerly hydrocharged working mother of two told me. "I had more status than he did, and then all of a sudden—whoosh! I went part-time. I don't think I'm ever getting it back. He now starts conversations with me with the words 'Here's what I'd like you to do.' I want to say, 'You can shove it up your ass.' "

The ideal worker in the boom years when many of us started to have our children was the twenty-eight-year-old (childless) (male) computer whiz who happily put in twenty-hour days in anticipation of launching his new Internet start-up. Everyone else was dragged along for the ride, working longer hours to remain a player in the overheated economy and to earn the money to keep up with the rising cost of living. By the end of the 1990s, Americans were working longer hours than anyone else in the world, including the Japanese. Average working hours for fathers topped 50 per week. Mothers' working hours averaged 41.4 per week.

It usually fell to women to make sure that someone was home, at least some of the time, with the kids. This meant cutting back, slow-pedaling, perhaps even giving up on a career (if family finances permitted), which meant too that the earning power of many mothers dropped substantially. By 1997 alone, among American married couples with children under six, fathers were earning three times as much as their mates.

With this income gap came a status gap, and a power gap within families. The change wasn't generally overt or avowed. It would happen subtly, incrementally. A woman who had once been her husband's peer or his colleague would find herself delegated to the "natural" role of errand-runner. (*"You don't have anything to do today, do you?"*) A woman who had once paid her own way might find herself *asking for money* to buy things for the kids. The sense of humiliation would build slowly, the insults accruing gently. And then they'd snowball: one day she'd wake up to find herself the family maid, the family nag, whose requests for help need not even be acknowledged.

How painful all this can be—how enraging all this can be—varies. It would be a huge mistake to say that all women, or *most* women, experience their status within their marriages as a disappointing, even insulting thing. Much depends upon how invested the women were in their status before they had children, how high they perceived their status to be, and how much that status meant to them. Much depends, too, on what associations they bring to bear upon the role of the traditional, homemaking mom. Stay-at-home or part-time working mothers who grew up seeing their largely at-home mothers treated with real respect and consideration now tend, I think, to see their own position within the family as a less fragile and threatened thing. Those who grew up with denigrated mothers tend more commonly to fear for the worst. And then the notion of fair compensation enters into the equation, too. Much depends on how things look on the marital balance sheet: Is a woman's at-home contribution matched by her husband's work efforts? Are they both pulling their weight in equally arduous ways?

"What I think it comes down to," one working mother of three told me, *"is whether or not you feel like you've gotten a good deal."*

CLEARLY, a lot of women these days feel that they haven't gotten a good deal. Working mothers rail against the "second shift" of housework and child care they must do, largely unaided, when they return home from the office. Stay-at-home moms complain that their care for their children is not recognized for the intensive labor that it is. Their husbands don't acknowledge their needs for breaks, for time alone, even for time spent together as a family.

Most fathers, working and nonworking mothers note, know how to take care of themselves. After work, they head for the gym, or out for drinks; they play golf and nap on weekends. Frequently, their wives have no choice but to "outsource" things like child care and housecleaning as much as is financially possible. This keeps the peace and gives them a break both from their household labors and from belaboring the fine points of their rage with their husbands. And yet, outsourcing is expensive. It diverts money from other spending priorities—*their* spending priorities. "All these things I'm spending money on to keep myself sane are basically taken away from my retirement," says a self-employed mother of three. And, many mothers feel, it's something they just shouldn't *have* to do. "That's always his reaction—get more help," says a mother of four in suburban Maryland. "I've finally gotten to a point where if I need time to myself, instead of expecting my husband to step up I now know to take it during the week when I have the nanny. There was a long time when I resisted that. I felt like I should be getting my time when he was there. [But] I had to do what worked, not what I wanted it to be."

A lot of fathers these days don't feel that they're getting much of a "good deal," either.

Our generation of husbands, for the most part, never wanted to play the role of traditional provider. But with our current culture of do-it-all motherhood and the frequent impossibility of reconciling work and family pushing some wives home, many postboomer men find themselves thrust into the traditional provider role. They can't cut their hours or take paternity leave—not only because such options often don't exist, but also because even when they do, they're frowned upon.

Trying to have a balanced life can be a real liability for working fathers. Research shows that men whose wives work (and who, one assumes, as a result take on a greater degree of fathering duties) actually pay a "daddy penalty"—receiving fewer promotions and earning up to 19 percent less than male professional peers with stay-at-home wives. "Trying to balance work and parenthood is harder for my husband," says a Washington, D.C., businesswoman and mother of two. "The guys at his office do not expect him to take on the responsibilities that he chooses to take on. For the first couple of years he worked there he complained, 'I'm the only guy here who doesn't stand up to his wife.' He was the 'whipped' husband.'"

The way we define motherhood today permits women who are

unhappy in their careers, or stuck in dead-end jobs, or simply not all that inspired or successful to opt out of their working lives for the greater "calling" of child-rearing. Men do not generally feel that they have that option. (Nor do most wives want to give it to them. This was particularly striking among the well-off women I interviewed—*none* of whom would have *dreamed* of having her high-achieving husband cut back on his hours or earning potential.) Men who cut their hours to spend more time with their children are routinely regarded as losers. Men who might want to take risks, try a new tack, or take some time off for a creative project or to recharge their batteries are stopped dead in their tracks by wives who don't want to work more to pick up more income; and they *can't,* after all—they are *moms.*

As a result, many men are stuck in a life of working longer and longer hours to provide for a family whose needs (not to mention whose wants) can barely be met on their salaries. That's not the life they grew up dreaming of. It's not what they signed up for when they married, either.

"It used to be that we were fifty-fifty," said a forty-one-year-old military wife and stay-at-home mother of three. "We were lieutenants, captains together. I think my husband assumed we would go on that way. Now he's forty-four and talks about having to work for the rest of his life. My being home is a real concern for him. He'll be fifty when he retires from the military and it's very frightening for him. He can't start over again."

Many men, forced into provider roles they never hoped for, must end up feeling ripped-off. There isn't much of their financial compensation left over once the household expenses are paid. They don't get much by way of wifely compensation either: their wives are too busy nursing their own resentments to be able to give much in the way of the "consoling and commiserating" that the political scientist Andrew Hacker writes was traditionally considered a world-weary husband's due. (*Wifework* author Susan Maushart calls it "The Wifely Art of Emotional Caregiving.")

Wives today are too frustrated and unfulfilled to care to hear about their husbands' frustrations and lack of fulfillment. For some men—the many men who don't get much satisfaction from their jobs—it must all feel like a raw deal. Particularly since, very often, if they *do* try to get involved in the running of their households, their control-freakish wives find fault with their efforts and take matters into their own hands.

And so the husbands wage war too, retrenching into a defensive posture, matching their role of provider with the kind of age-old husbandly behavior that—once upon a time, at least—brought *their fathers* some peace and quiet. "If *this* is my role," the behavior says, "I'll be damned if I'll play any other."

They become taciturn and uncommunicative; they sloppily cut corners on "helping out" with child care and house chores. They meet their wives' needs with aggrieved indifference, and turn up the volume of the TV after the kids' bedtimes to drown out yet another "litany" of complaint. Or perhaps they hardly come home at all. Researchers say that 55 percent of men actually start spending *more* time at work after they become fathers. ("That's his trump card—'I have to work,'" says a part-time working mother in Washington.) They work longer hours than is strictly necessary. They hang around the office just late enough to ensure that, when they get home, the kids will be in bed and the kitchen will be cleaned up. "My husband comes home for dinner three times a week at seven-thirty, and he calls first and says is their homework done?" says a Washington, D.C., mother of four who works part-time. "He doesn't want to deal with it."

It really seems that in many households these days *no one* is getting a good deal. In two-earner homes, no one—neither husband nor wife—is getting taken care of. And in many one-earner households, no one is fulfilled. Neither husbands nor wives feel that they got what they signed on for. No wonder married life with children has the feel of a labor negotiation: "that fight—of who did what and who did more and who *wins,*" as the Maryland stay-at-home mother of four put it.

"It seems to me that all the couples I know with children are at war," a father of two muttered recently, dodging wife and children for a quiet Sunday-morning talk. "*Everything* has to be negotiated."

It is a chronic, low-intensity battle. Who got to read the whole newspaper? To go to the gym? To go to the bathroom alone? Who has given up more? Who's getting the better deal? Today? This week? This year? In this lifetime?

Sex is another item to fall into the balance sheet. Since so many women lack libido (and perceive their mates' libido as having a life of its own), sex becomes something *for him*—something to add to his "chits pile," to borrow a phrase from Naomi Wolf—and damned if he's going to get it if he hasn't put in any quality face time with the kids. For men, it becomes yet another source of deprivation in their already pleasure-deprived lives. Thus the frequent stories we hear of men feeling displaced in their wives' affections by their children. "My wife gave her body over to another person" is how one man I interviewed put it. Many women make no secret of the fact that they prefer their children's touch to their husband's. As a roomful of women I interviewed enthused:

> "*The love you get from a child can't compare . . .*"
> "*The orgasm is one thing, but the intimacy and the feeling of fulfillment {from a child} . . .*"
> "*It goes on and on and continues. . . .*"
> "*It is so vast. . . .*"

WHERE will it all end?

If current statistical trends, spearheaded by the baby boomers, continue, one out of two of our marriages will end in divorce. But we are a generation so scarred by divorce that I wonder if we won't handle things differently. We are likely to do all that we can do to avoid divorce. Which doesn't mean that we will fix our marriages. It just means that we will *adjust.* Suck it up. Keep things together. And find a fragile peace through living parallel lives.

Already we've become skilled in defusing our resentment—by transforming it into mockery, by sweetening it in girl bonding, by cooling it with the comforts of lowered expectations and benign, condescending acceptance. And above all, by taking recourse to the newly resurgent ideology of "separate spheres," which repairs our dashed hopes and provides an antidote to our anger.

"He can do what he wants; I have my *life set up now"* is the kind of thing I hear around me these days. It is a holding pattern. Not a particularly happy one. And it raises serious questions about just where our current affinity for living apart together in low-intensity "partnership" marriages will lead. You can "outsource" child care, housekeeping chores, and yard work and have it strengthen your marriage. But what if you outsource your need for friendship, connection, understanding, excitement, emotional support, romance . . . sex?

Then you get into dangerous territory. Just as Kate Reddy found out in *I Don't Know How She Does It,* when she came tantalizingly close to having an affair with a client. And as Maggie Owen found out, in Sabine Durrant's *Having It and Eating It,* when she had it off for a time with her gardener. Or as Diane Lane's Constance Sumner learned, in *Unfaithful,* when she jeopardized a beautiful house, a child, and a life of full-time shopping—not to mention her marriage—for the carnal embrace of a young, bohemian antique book dealer.

That these escape fantasies, which push the tantalizing potential of outsourcing to the limit, recur in our popular mom lit (and mom "flix") can't be accidental. Similar fantasies came up time and again in my interviews. There were "crushes"—generally on younger, childless men. The soccer coach. (*"He seemed very tuned in to children and their emotional lives. I could see us angsting together about my son."*) The yoga instructor. (*"He touches me, he touches my hand."*) The rug salesman.

"I'm just very tuned in," admitted a thirty-six-year-old mother of two, married to a "wonderful" husband. "If there's any vibe . . . it feels important."

"I just want to go on a date," a friend sighed as her children crashed around in the basement.

"I want to have sex," another acquaintance told me, while the father of her children held forth at the other end of the room, *"just not with my husband."*

All of this suggests to me that it isn't really true that women, by and large, don't want to have sex. Many just don't want to have sex *with their husbands.* Because they're too tired *of them;* because they're not in the mood *for them;* because they've spent one evening too many paying the bills while the chocolate chip cookies for the next day's bake sale cool—and this, yes this, all this, has given them a perennial headache.

I think it's also true, though, that many women, rather than consciously turning away from their husbands, have turned off their sexual selves. It is a sign of resignation and passive-aggressive protest—the equivalent, in sexual terms, of shrugging and saying, "I don't care." (*"Do you care? I cared for a while. I don't care anymore."*)

I often wonder if our "mommy frumps"—those awful jeans and spit-stained shirts and dreary haircuts we sport like a punitive uniform—aren't a kind of protective shield. Looking crummy all the time, being "just a mom," may be a way to beat back the prospective demons of a sexuality we don't want to deal with, with the sense of possibility it might awaken, reminding us of other times, broader horizons, bigger dreams—and happier marriages. In becoming sexless, we turn off our desires—globally. And we avoid a whole lot of disappointment and frustration.

So we remain "schlubby," safe, untempted, and unchallenged. We don't rock the boat. We don't want to open up the Pandora's box of our desires. There's no point, after all. We wouldn't have the time or energy to deal with what we found there anyway.

Our to-do list is already much too long.

11.

For a Politics of
Quality of Life

Motherhood has been the center of a culture war instead of an economic policy debate.

—ELLEN GOODMAN

WINNERS AND LOSERS

In October 2003, the *New York Times Magazine* ran a cover story titled "The Opt-Out Revolution." In it, reporter Lisa Belkin interviewed a number of women who had opted out of their formerly high-powered careers in favor of staying home with their kids. They'd traded in six-figure salaries, local celebrity, and potential law partnerships in favor of play groups, toddler music classes, and long mornings at Starbucks.

This was important, Belkin said, this was national news, the *Times* implied, because these women, graduates of such prestigious institutions as Harvard, Stanford, and Princeton, were precisely those who, a generation ago, had been expected to grow up and run the world. They'd been "supposed to march toward the future and take rightful ownership of the universe," as Belkin put it. Only they'd seen the universe, and they hadn't found it to their liking. And so, instead of "running the world," they were now running their households.

All of which, the *Times* argued, trotting out the usual turn-of-the-millennium statistics about the surge in stay-at-home motherhood, said a great deal about the choices, the conflicts, and the priorities of women in our generation.

Except that it didn't.

At least, not to me.

HOW MANY WOMEN become CEOs . . . how many make partner in law firms or managing director in investment banks . . . how many graduate from Yale Law School or Wharton . . . how many wealthy, highly educated, and otherwise privileged women are on the fast track? For thirty years now, we, in and out of the feminist movement, in and out of the media, have been keeping tabs on women's progress in our society by watching these numbers. They're not meaningless, of course. They indicate how well women are doing in ascending to the power elite. But do they mean any more than this? And does the focus on the elite—on "winner" women—do most women any good?

I don't think so. Not as far as mothers are concerned.

Here's why: The focus by the media and by many in the mainstream feminist movement on the achievements of the few has neglected the problems of the many. The focus on the motherhood dilemmas of the very successful, which runs through so very much of the thinking about and writing on and media coverage of motherhood in our time, poses the problems relating to motherhood and family life in America in terms that are not only irrelevant to most women but also *harmful to their interests.* And by this I don't just mean that most women can't "relate" to the angst felt by other women, musing over past, present, and future while their six- and seven-figure–earning husbands foot the bills.

(They can't, but that's a very minor part of the problem.)

The major problem is that the experiences of these wealthy women have come, despite their irrelevancy to the vast, vast majority of the population, to *define* the terms through which we understand motherhood in our time.

They determine the vocabulary with which we discuss motherhood—using words like "choice" and "options" and "priorities" and "balance." As though they had universal validity. As though they had any meaning at all in the vast majority of women's lives. And they have inspired the story—the *master narrative,* if you will—that we tell now about women's progress and the problems of motherhood.

That story is that our generation grew up with the greatest number of choices of any generation of women before and continues to enjoy that wealth of choices in motherhood. We can choose to work or stay at home or to do some combination of the two, and we are free to do this largely because we have liberated ourselves from the yoke of feminism, which pushed so many women before us to feel they *had* to keep on striving in the workplace. In other words, we are free to be whoever we want to be.

And yet we are finding (so the story continues) that what we want to be in the workplace is incompatible with who we want to be at home. We can't do it all because we can't *be* it all, worldly ambition and motherly ambition having long proven to be mutually exclusive. And we have learned—and this is the moral of the story—that life isn't perfect. Modern motherhood is full of unresolvable conflicts. Those of us who are smart, who are successful in motherhood, learn to deal with and put the best face on those conflicts. Because they are part of life. They are natural. They will be eternal. And there's nothing you—or your government, or "society"—can do about them. Indeed, these private, close-to-the-bone matters are so far from the realm of what "society" can possibly step in and do (or ought to step in and do) that it's laughable—pitiable, really—to keep going on about how we ought to fight for change and find solutions. To do so partakes, as Marjorie Williams put it, of "an earnestness too deep for satire."

Where does this thinking, which you hear and read *over and over again* these days, lead?

To a brick wall.

Because what happens when you focus constantly on how the ambitions of the so-called best and brightest are incompatible with motherhood is that you end up with the conclusion that *ambition* is incompatible with motherhood. When you explore time and again how hotshot careers can't be balanced with family life, you end up with the conclusion that *work* can't be balanced with family life. And you end up with the overall impression that the problems of motherhood today are simply intractable.

You are forced to come to this conclusion because the kinds of problems that Women Who Should Take Over the World have *are,* for the most part, intractable. You can't conduct a top-flight career on the Mommy Track. You can't scale down a climb to the top (the contradiction in terms is obvious). You can't resolve the conflict between overarching professional ambition and the kind of overarchingly ambitious motherhood that most women with type-A pedigrees seem to want to practice these days.

And yet you *can* accommodate the demands of a more average kind of ambition with motherhood. The kind of ambition that *most* women (and most men) have: which is to work a sufficient number of hours to earn a sufficient amount of money to buy their families a sufficiently good standard of living. Or at least you ought to be able to.

Women in other societies (notably in Western Europe) can. But that's because in other countries society intervenes to make it possible. Other countries believe that lessening the burdens that keep average women and their families from achieving balance in their lives is *precisely* what society can—and ought—to do.

What society and—now, unfortunately, I have to use that dirty word "government"—can do is alleviate the kinds of economic pressures that currently make the fulfillment of a great many mothers' ambitions impossible. Those ambitions are not to be Supreme Court justices, or CEOs, or editors in chief of the nation's top newspapers. They are, rather, to secure a decent quality of life for their families. That is to say: a life in which the bills can get paid, the children can be taken care of, and the future can be—as much as possible—made secure, without every day being lived like the run-up to an Olympic competition. A life, in other words, that bears no resemblance to the kind of high-intensity rat race that those destined for great power and success, whether they're male or female, must *by necessity* contend with because that is the very nature of great success.

Society can't do *anything at all* about the fact that mothers (and fathers) painfully miss their children when they're separated from them for long periods of time, or about the fact that massive professional ambition and massively ambitious parenting are mutually exclusive. (But then: society doesn't have to. The wealthy and successful in our country can already buy themselves wonderful lives, filled with all kinds of "choices" and "options," including those of working a great deal and paying for really top-quality babysitting or day care, or giving it all up and heading home). But what society *can* do—and what our society could and ought to do—is give the vast majority of women, who currently don't have much by way of choices, real options.

Society could make working motherhood something other than an exercise in guilt by backing policies—like government-mandated standards and quality controls—that remove the fear and dread many mothers feel when they leave their children in the care of others.

Society could make stay-at-home motherhood something other than a form of 24/7 vassalage by backing policies that lead to the creation of flexible, affordable, locally available, high-quality part-time day care.

Society could make it possible for mothers to work part-time (something most mothers—though generally not the highest-achieving of high-achieving mothers—say they want to do) by making child care more affordable, by making health insurance available and affordable for part-time workers, and by generally making life less expensive and stressful for middle-class families so that mothers (and fathers) could work less without risking their children's financial futures. Or even, if they felt the need, could stay home with their children for a while.

And society should.

And instead of worrying endlessly over how many first-year female associates at major law firms make it to the level of partner, how many women ascend to the Supreme Court, and how many grace the ranks of the House and Senate, those of us who care about these issues should instead find a way to demand policies that would permit *most* women—the great many, not the few—to improve their lives. We should articulate—and find politicians to promote—a Politics of Quality of Life.

By quality of life I do not mean the ability to buy huge houses and many huge cars. I mean the ability to have a family, provide for your family, and go about the daily rhythms of life without it all becoming a mess and a source of enormous anguish and anxiety.

This seems like a simple thing. But it has until now proven impossible in America, where efforts to create family-friendly policies have for decades been stymied by the Holy War that rages between social conservatives and feminists. This culture war has made pragmatic, real-life thinking about the situation of families in America, and of mothers in particular, almost impossible. On the left, it has been made impossible because the religion of mainstream feminism has permitted no articulation of a vision of women's equality that gives too large a role to motherhood. On the right, it has been made impossible by conservatives' twin religions of free-market economics and Christian fundamentalist "family values."

We are, of course, not the only culture that has ever made a religion out of motherhood. Like us, other countries have a long history of politicizing childbearing and child-rearing. France's powerful pro-family policies today stem from a pronatalist policy put in place at the end of World War Two. The motivation behind that policy was basically to get women to have more babies—hardly a progressive agenda. But other factors came into play later—notably, the French women's movement and economic changes that, as in the United States, made mothers' workforce participation a necessity.

In France, however (unlike in America), these social changes, instead of being denied or demonized, were integrated into society's vision of what modern motherhood should be. This vision has largely held true over the decades whether France was governed by politicians on the left or on the right. The result has been that France's profamily politics are pragmatic, widely accepted, and specifically conceived to enhance mothers' and families' quality of life.

Yet, while France, and, for that matter, most of Europe, has modernized its family politics and philosophy of motherhood, we in the United States have remained in the clutches of a reactionary Motherhood Religion that has never yet undergone a Reformation. The Christian fundamentalist agenda that often drives our policies is so shocking and abhorrent to the rest of the world that, on such international issues as global sex education and AIDS-prevention policies, the United States has at times found itself with no foreign allies other than Muslim fundamentalists. Our callous indifference to the needs of modern families shocks much of the Western world, but in America we are so desensitized to the creep of radical theocracy into our national politics that it passes almost unnoticed. We are so used to fighting the minor battles of the holy war over motherhood in our daily lives that we naturally stake out our positions and dig in our heels, rather than point to the absurdity of the whole enterprise.

And yet it is absolutely absurd. The culture wars between social conservatives and feminists, which take place far from the concerns of most Americans, are a huge and terrible waste of our resources. They have left women holding the bag, with virtually *nothing to show* for themselves, as far as social policy is concerned, after three decades of women's "liberation" *and* of New Right "family-values" activism.

We have a situation where well-off women can choose how to live their lives—either outsourcing child care at a sufficiently high level of quality to permit them to work with relative peace of mind or staying at home. But no one else, really, has *anything.* Many, many women would like to stay home with their children and can't afford to do so. Many, many others would like to be able to work part-time but can't afford or find the way to do so. Many others would like to be able to maintain their full-time careers without either being devoured by them or losing ground, and they can't do that. Many can't work without experiencing agonies of guilt because the quality of child care their salaries can provide for is so low. Many can't stay at home without losing their minds because child care is so expensive they can't afford to get a break.

And, frankly, there is no hope for any of these women on the horizon.

For not only is government activism totally out of favor. Not only has cheap, moralistic nonsense—"pro-fatherhood" initiatives, "pro-virginity" initiatives—replaced substantive efforts to make "family values" a lived reality. Even the burgeoning "motherhood movement" is utterly corrupted by the competing religions of the American left and right, its fledgling agenda hamstrung between distrustful feminists, hostile to anything that they believe overemphasizes a woman's mothering role, and moralists bent on gaining validation for the "calling" of stay-at-home motherhood.

None of this, of course, is officially avowed by the pro-motherhood groups currently forming and growing and finding their voices via the Internet. With names like the Family and Home Network (formerly called Mothers at Home) and Mothers & More (formerly called Formerly Employed Mothers at Loose Ends), these groups have national memberships and purport to unite working and nonworking mothers alike in an ecumenical, pro-family social agenda. Their organizers, I found, were committed to this vision, and strove to make it a reality. But their membership, carried over from their pre–name-change days, was another story. Once you scratched the surface of their pro-unity slogans, all too often, something quite different emerged. Competition. Intolerance. And a big dose of sanctimony. Coming, most notably, from stay-at-home mothers seeking validation for the "sacrifices" they'd made in the name of motherly virtue.

(I witnessed this most horribly when a polite discussion among stay-at-home moms affiliated with one of the groups took a sudden and nasty turn for the worse as the subject of working motherhood arose.

"I don't understand these women who 'dump' their children in day care," said one.

"It's a lot of pushing them around," said another. "It's dishonest. If you have children you have an obligation to raise them." She did a quick calculation of the money an average working mother would have left of her salary after deducting taxes, child care, clothing, etc., and came up with the sum of $5,000.

"So," she concluded, as the others nodded triumphantly, "you're selling your kid *for five grand a year.*")

THE DISUNITY is so bad that a much-touted October 2002 Barnard College symposium, described by its organizers as a "call to a Motherhood Movement," stalled entirely because its participants could not find common ground. One prominent feminist attacked a prominent antifeminist naysayer for supposedly misrepresenting data. Other feminists refused to endorse any statements of purpose that promoted the notion of easing the lives of mothers who leave the workforce. "Motherhood-movement" activists from the stay-at-home camp blocked the proceedings with their quasireligious pro–stay-at-home agenda. The only thing all the demoralized participants could agree on was a need for mothers' "validation."

And yet even that need tripped them up, because what they wanted to have validated was mutually contradictory. Validation for one group necessarily meant demonization of the other. It was politics as clique formation—junior high–style, one disgusted participant told me. "God forbid anyone is doing things differently from us," she said, describing the proceedings. "We can't unite, because if we do it's as though we're admitting that the way we do things isn't absolutely perfect."

The same ideological binding that has stymied the development of a real and practical politics of the family in America has limited the vision of the "motherhood movement." Way too much verbiage is spent on maintaining the illusion of mothers' "choices," too much energy is spent diverting attention from the fact that without help from the government, mothers have only the most paltry options to choose from. Too much energy is being expended on seeking validation—a recognition of mothers' "value" ("we count") and of motherhood as "the most important job in the world" through measures like including unpaid household labor in the GDP. Too much attention has been spent on trying to secure a tax subsidy for stay-at-home moms—an expensive measure whose pointlessness I saw illustrated clearly in France, where one stay-at-home mother of four I knew referred to her $468 monthly government allowance as "sweater money." The only women in France for whom the stay-at-home allowance can conceivably make a meaningful difference are those who are unemployed or partially employed, or tenuously employed in minimum-wage work, earning close to nothing anyway. Earning a little bit less in those circumstances and being able to stay home with the children (with housing vouchers and the like helping make it possible) is certainly better for these mothers than leaving their children with strangers for the sake of a non-lucrative, non–life-enhancing job.

We used to have a program recognizing this in America, too. It was called welfare. That we would abolish that taxpayer-funded program for needy stay-at-home moms and replace it with another simply to provide "validation" for middle-class moms is utterly absurd, financially useless for families, and expensive for society. (In 1999, a $250 tax break for stay-at-home parents with children under the age of one floated around by the Clinton administration was projected to cost $1.3 billion over five years.)

It should not be the business of the government to provide validation for women who lack self-esteem. The needs of families are much too important for this.

A POLITICS OF QUALITY OF LIFE

If we were to desacralize the motherhood issue and drop all the narcissistic and ideological goals that now infuse it, what would families need?

Simply put: *institutions that can help us take care of our children so that we don't have to do everything on our own.* We need institutions made accessible and affordable and of guaranteed high quality by government funding, oversight, and standards.

We need a new set of profamily *entitlements*—standing programs that can outlast election-year campaign promises made by politicians and are more widespread and universally available than the "privileges" sometimes accorded to parents by private employers.

It's time to admit that the idea that businesses will "do the right thing" for American families is a lost hope. More than a decade into the era of "family-friendly policies," more than a third of all working parents in America have neither sick leave nor vacation leave. Many parents are creating their own "family-friendly" career path, and what this much-vaunted assertion of "free choice" implies is taking part-time jobs with few advancement opportunities and often no benefits.

During the late 1990s economic boom, more than five years after the passage of the Family and Medical Leave Act, only 46 percent of U.S. workers were covered and eligible for unpaid leave. And, as the millennium turned, a large number of parents reported not taking advantage of the leave they did have because the culture of their workplace pressured them so strongly against it.

IT COULD BE SAID that making an argument for a set of middle-class entitlements is obscene when the conditions of working-class and poor families in this country are so dire. (And, indeed, they can be horrifying: you need only think of the news stories of working mothers with no child care who, fearing for their jobs, lock their children into their cars—and sometimes land in jail—to understand the impossible stresses of "balancing" the unbalanceable.)

But I believe that the kinds of quality-of-life measures I have outlined are potentially helpful for everyone. I also believe, given the "compassion fatigue" that is, in the politest formulation, said to underlie Americans' hostility toward programs for the poor, you cannot get Americans on board to provide *more* help for the needy until they feel they are getting help too. I think perhaps if so much of the American middle class feels so hostile to "handouts," it's because they themselves feel so beleaguered.

If there's any way to get people to sign on to and pay for a politics of quality of life, it has to come from the creation of a new kind of pro-family consensus of opinion—and in countries like France that consensus has been built through policies that bring something to everyone, to the fortunate as well as to the poor.

PEOPLE COMMONLY SAY there's no way you can make government activism on the part of the family palatable. For one thing, they say, in America, we consider the family to be people's private business, out of the reach of the long arm of government. But the truth is, we already have government programs that meddle in family life—and in very intrusive ways.

The Welfare Reform Act of 1996 had as part of its stated purpose to prevent out-of-wedlock pregnancies and encourage the creation of two-parent families. The Bush administration's 2002 welfare reform reauthorization proposal included $300 million for "demonstration grants" to teach couples how to stay married and avoid having babies out of wedlock. The "pro-fatherhood movement" that took off in the late 1990s used government funds for the specific purpose of restoring men to their "God-given" roles as heads of families.

In truth, the opposition to government programs to help families isn't really about protecting people's private lives from government intrusion. It's about ideology (some kinds of intrusion are bad; some kinds are good). It's also about money. That's why relatively cheap programs that "valorize" a certain form of family life can fly. (A National Fatherhood Initiative flyer once put it, succinctly, "What reduces crime, child poverty, teen pregnancy AND requires no new taxes?") It's also why other more substantive and meaningful initiatives—like the short-lived Clinton administration attempt to rally support for the idea of government-mandated day-care standards—are instantly, and consistently, tabled.

There's no rhyme or reason to this. It's paternalistic, condescending, and, above all, hypocritical. After all, Americans do foot the bill for child care for some people: we spend hundreds of millions of dollars a year funding day care for the children of military personnel (as well we should, and the care is excellent). Many federal workers in Washington, too, have access to excellent on-site day care, some of it subsidized by the government. I think that's great. But why shouldn't the rest of us enjoy similar benefits of our tax money? Aren't we all *entitled*?

. . .

THE COST OF implementing the kind of public policies I advocate is daunting. According to economists Barbara R. Bergmann and Suzanne W. Helburn, authors of 2002's clear-eyed and comprehensive *America's Child Care Problem: The Way Out,* it would cost nearly $50 billion a year ($30 billion more than the federal government currently spends on subsidy programs) simply to solve the problem of caring for preschool-age children in America—chiefly through the form of vouchers to subsidize high-quality early-education programs.

And yet, when the political will is there, we can do seemingly impossible things. Political will brought about welfare reform in 1996. It brought about the New Deal. It brought about the Reagan Revolution. Things can change when the change presented fits the social values of the moment. And there are many indicators now showing that the time may be right for changes that will guarantee American families a better quality of life.

Polling conducted by the Center for Policy Alternatives in 1992, 1996, and 2000 has shown that quality-of-life issues are being rated higher and higher as areas of concern by the American public. Among women, the "time crunch" has surpassed reproductive rights as an area of acute concern.

Quality-of-life issues came to the fore most prominently in the 2000 campaign year, when polling found the "minivan moms" of the turn of the millennium to be considerably more *tired* than the soccer moms of the 1996 election year. And so, in the midst of unprecedented levels of wealth, candidates found themselves talking about the "time famine," and "livability" issues. Even suburban men with young children (minivan dads?) were saying they felt squeezed for time.

The spread of the "simplicity movement" also argues that people are hungry for a kind of slowing-down change. Indeed, 71 percent of women surveyed in 2000 said they would choose a job with more flexibility and benefits over one that offered more pay. Poll results have shown, too, that people are now open to government-directed solutions. In 1999, a *Business Week* poll showed that 74 percent of women and 70 percent of men thought that government should take a larger role to help working families. In 2000, a bipartisan polling team found that a plurality of both men and women said they believed that there should be a government solution to child care. In September 2002, California—a state often considered a bellwether for national political trends—passed the first paid parental-leave law in the country. Polling done nationally at the time showed that 82 percent of women and 75 percent of men said they would support a similar measure in their state. A ballot initiative promoted by Arnold Schwarzenegger to provide universal after-school care for children was also approved by 57 percent of California voters. This from a state that only eleven months later elected Schwarzenegger as governor on a platform of fiscal responsibility.

Clearly, if presented in the right way, quality-of-life policies can garner political support in the most unlikely of places. And the additional $30 billion needed to cover child care is nothing compared with the cost of the Bush tax cuts, which are said now to cost more than $200 billion annually. It's only slightly more (in the stratosphere of the billions) than the $27.2 billion that the tax exemption for Social Security benefits enjoyed by our nation's wealthy currently costs taxpayers. Even if America were, proportionally, to spend as much as France does on subsidized child care and paid leave—increasing our budget outlays by $85 billion a year—*it would still cost less than the Bush tax cuts.*

It isn't really a question of money, it's a question of priorities. And it's a question, too, for Americans, of how we conceive of quality of life.

After all, we already have a politics of quality of life in America.

But it is quality of life defined as luxury spending. It is paid for by tax policies calibrated to permit the wealthy to keep most of their money and spend it on *stuff,* sending their material quality of life skyrocketing, while the middle class, bearing most of the impact of taxation, foots the bill. And it has brought about a culturewide impoverishment of the forms of quality of life that actually generate happiness, as in time with family, leisure time, relaxation, and peace of mind.

There is every reason to think that the kind of material quality of life that was so dramatically fostered by the tax policies and cultural values of the past quarter century are not conducive to happiness. The percentage of people who described themselves as "very happy" fell from 36 to 29 percent between 1970 and 1999. During the boom years, the demands of the 24/7 economy were such that, by 1999, fully two-fifths of all employed Americans were working mostly during evenings, nights, or weekends—and reporting sleep disturbances, stomach problems, perpetual fatigue, and depression. Couples working split shifts— one spouse at night and one during the day—as a way to avoid paying for child care were divorcing at up to five times the rate of other married couples. Even people with lives of relative ease were stressed to the gills: In 2002, a Gallup poll on stress and relaxation time found that families with household incomes of over $75,000 a year were among the "most stressed" households in America. Fourteen percent of Americans, the pollsters found, said they "never have time to relax."

Which form of quality of life our government policies espouse says a great deal about our national priorities. And strikes to the heart of what kind of society we want to be.

For which is more important: the ability to cruise around in ever-larger cars with ever-softer leather interiors and better drink holders? Or the ability to find parking spots and breathe cleaner air?

Which should we "choose": the ability to afford private school (which means buying into the soul-rending process of getting into these schools) or the relief of being able to sign up and show up for a neighborhood public school which is of truly high quality?

Which is more valuable: the ability to afford a $25,000 time share in the Hamptons, or to take an entire month off for vacation?

And which is a better form of parenting: to teach our children the single-minded selfishness they need to thrive in the winner-take-all society—or to change that society so that *everyone wins?*

CHANGING THE RULES
OF THE GAME

At the end of *The Feminine Mystique,* Betty Friedan said, "If women were really *people*—no more, no less—then all the things that kept them from being full people in our society would have to be changed. . . . It would be necessary to change the rules of the game to restructure professions, marriage, the family, the home."

Seven years later, with the women's movement gaining steam, she said, "We have to break down the actual barriers that prevent women from being full people in society, and not only end explicit discrimination but build new institutions."

To do less, she concluded, would be to make the women's movement "all talk."

I would say now: If women are really to be *equal,* no more, no less, then all the things that still keep them from being equal in our society have to change.

Because there is a real gap today between the ideals of gender equality we as a society espouse and the ability of American women to make good on the promises of their freedom. They face compromises that men do not share. Their right to "choose"—to remain true to themselves, to make (and act upon) their own choices—is systematically curtailed when they become mothers. And that's because the structures of our society as they currently exist do not allow mothers to make meaningful choices.

Too many are forced to abdicate the dreams of a lifetime because the demands of the workplace are incompatible with family life.

Others, in the quest to support their families, must "choose" to consign their children to seriously substandard care.

Others must abdicate their dreams of homemaking because it is simply too costly—or the psychological demands of total-reality motherhood are too onerous. And all are, at least on a psychological level, denied that inalienable right of "the pursuit of happiness." Because for a mother to pursue her happiness is in many quarters these days called sheer selfishness.

And though many women can and do manage to accept (or at least adjust to) this situation for themselves, there's a twinge of real sadness that comes out when they talk about their daughters. As a forty-something mother mused one evening to me, "I look at my daughter and I just want to know: What happened? Because look at us: it's 2002 and nothing's changed. My mother expected my life to be very different from hers but now it's a lot more like hers than I expected, and from here I don't see where it will be different for my daughter. I don't want her to carry this crushing burden that's in our heads. . . . [But] what can make things different?"

THE ODD MIX of 1970s feminism and Reaganomics that molded our minds and conditions our politics has not produced a world that is worthy of our daughters. And it has not given us the tools to imagine a world that could be different. After all, most of us in the middle and upper middle class are entirely complicit with the system of winners and losers that condemns us to mother like lunatics. We may, very often, complain about the maddening pace and pressures of our lives, but we rarely stop to question the values that make it all necessary.

And I think that's because the very same values that impoverish the lives of so many women, and families, in our society—untrammeled self-interest, individualism, freedom from government intrusion—are those upon which most successful women's lives (whether working or at-home) are built.

But is the success of the few worth the mess of the many? Do we really need, any longer, to promote the prospects, values, and virtues of natural-born "winners"? And are they necessarily role models?

"The original idea of feminism as I first encountered it, in about 1969, was twofold," Barbara Ehrenreich has written: "that nothing short of equality will do and that in a society marred by injustice and cruelty, equality will never be good enough." Top-achieving women are the heroines of a winner-take-all society. But is the equality to compete, to climb over others to the top of the heap, the only kind of equality we want? What is much more challenging—and meaningful—is finding a way to let *most* women become the people they want to be as they move through the different stages of their lives.

I CAN IMAGINE THAT, because I have not embraced the idea of women's work as tantamount to women's liberation, or the idea of women's workplace success as tantamount to success for the gender, that people will think I'm a reactionary. Or that because I have looked for ways more women can stay home or work part-time I will be interpreted as believing that women *should* stay home, or *should* work part-time. I do not think that at all. Indeed, I do not think that women *should* do anything—other than remain true to themselves so that they can be happy.

And I do not think most women can be happy in our current culture of motherhood. It is just too psychologically damaging.

I think the kinds of "choices" women must now make, the kinds of compromises, adjustments, and adaptations they must accept in the name of "balance" and Good Motherhood, the kinds of disappointments and even heartbreaks they must suck up for the sake of marital harmony, do them a kind of psychological violence. Too often, they end up anxious and depressed, running scared, becoming rigid, shutting down their horizons, and turning a deaf ear to their dreams.

And this is not just a problem of individual women and their privately managed psychological pain. It is a problem of society.

Women today mother the way they do in part because they are psychologically conditioned to do so. But they also do it because, to a large extent, *they have to.* Because they are unsupported, because their children are not taken care of, in any meaningful way, by society at large. Because there is right now no widespread feeling of social responsibility—for children, for families, for *anyone,* really—and so they must take everything onto themselves. And because they *can't,* humanly, take everything onto themselves, they simply go nuts.

I see this all the time. It never seems to stop. So that, as I finish writing this book, I have an image fresh in my mind: the face of a friend, the mother of a kindergartener, who I ran into one morning after drop-off right before Christmas.

Huge dark circles ringed her eyes. Her face was gray, and she rattled, as she spoke, an enormous cup of take-out coffee in her hand.

She was in the midst of organizing a class party. This meant shopping. Color-coordinating paper goods. Piecework, pre-gluing of arts-and-crafts projects. Uniformity of felt textures. Of buttons and beads. Of cookie-cutter shapes and sizes. And the selection of holiday candies that were not made with one very specific (and widely used) shade of red food dye. There were the phone calls, too. From other parents. With criticism, complaints, and "constructive" comments that had her up at night in bed, playing over conversations in her mind and drowning in bile. "I can't take it anymore," she said to me. "I hate everyone and everything. I am going insane."

I looked at her face, saw her eyes fill with tears, and in that instant saw in a mirror the faces of dozens of the women I'd interviewed—women whose voices broke as they told of trying to replicate Martha Stewart's online cupcake decorations, women who went broke paying for soccer and baseball leagues, women who fired off "memos" and "cleared" snack menus with each other via e-mail (not because of allergies, just . . . because . . .)—and, of course, I saw myself.

And I was reminded of the words of a French doctor I'd once seen, in the crazy packing-up-a-household-with-two-children-freelance-deadlines-and-a-husband-shut-down-by-the-stress weeks that preceded our move to America.

I'd come to him about headaches. They were violent. They were constant. And they would prove, over the next few years, to be chronic.

He wrote down the name of a painkiller. (You can get marvelous things over the counter in France.) But he looked skeptical as to whether it would really do me much good. *"If you keep banging your head against the wall,"* he said, *"you're going to have headaches."*

I have thought of these words so many times in my now four years of motherhood in America. I have seen *so many mothers* banging their heads against a wall. And treating their pain—the chronic headache of their lives—with sleeping pills and antidepressants and anxiety meds and a more and more potent, more and more vicious self-and-other–attacking form of anxious perfectionism.

And I hope that somehow we will all find a way to stop. Because we are not doing ourselves any good. We are not doing our children—particularly not our daughters—any good. We're not doing our marriages any good. And we're doing nothing at all for our society.

We are simply beating ourselves black and blue. So let's take a breather. Let's not bang our heads any longer against the walls that hem us in. Let's break down those walls. Free ourselves from the chains in our own minds and spirits, as Friedan urged so many years ago. And let ourselves *be.*

12.

Conclusion

I BEGAN THIS BOOK with one daughter in preschool and the other a baby at home. I am ending it with one a second-grader and the other in a Montessori school. She counts the days until she can start "kindergarten school." I can see the future. And, I fear, it isn't pretty.

Many nights, when I turn out the lights to go up to bed, I look out the window and see our neighbor's son sitting at the dining room table doing his homework. He is eleven.

At least four of my second-grader's girlfriends have told me they are "on a diet."

Many of their older brothers and sisters are being tutored. For everything. Many are on Ritalin. And antidepressants. That's how it is around here, I'm told.

"It's hard to do homework after a 7 P.M. hockey game," I hear.

Particularly when, starting in fifth grade, there are *four hours of home-work a night.*

This is what later childhood looks like from where I sit in Upper Northwest Washington, D.C. It's like an ongoing dress rehearsal for a talent show that never quite begins. And I find myself filled with dread. And I wonder (when I'm not worrying about pencil grips or test scores or my children's ability to say "th"): What is the point?

"What's the endgame?" a frustrated father whose four-year-old daughter is up to her ears in speech and occupational therapy recently asked me.

I wish I could say that I knew. I wish I believed that this game we all play actually had an end, or a point, or some value. Some higher purpose. Some meaning. Something to justify all the stress and the mess that we impose these days upon our children and ourselves.

IT'S BEEN two years since I heard those crucial words "this mess." Two years of talking and writing and reading and thinking and liv-ing at the crucible of all that is messed-up in America today. Noth-ing has changed. The "material"—the fodder for this book—still comes my way, every day. In conversation and on TV. In *Time* maga-zine and the *Atlantic Monthly.* In all the sanctimony and the bad faith that drive the continuing cult of stay-at-home motherhood. In the anger and the frustration of the mothers around me, who live their lives as real women, and not as sinners or saints.

I find myself, when things get *really* tense (report card time, class-mother duties), fantasizing about eventually Opting Out. Running away—back to France—before high school starts, before the anorexia kicks in and the college-application-prep summer camps begin, and the robotic performance of community service starts to eat up our weekends.

The escape fantasy, I know, is ridiculous. The future "France" I've constructed in my mind doesn't exist. School-aged French children are every bit as stressed as their American counterparts, if not more so. Public schooling there is often a soul-crunching experience, and certain popular parenting techniques (*"You're an idiot. . . . You're a slob. . . . Do you want me to hit you again?"*) leave something to be desired. If French children are not being drugged now in order to meet the kind of Olympian performance standards we hold dear, it's probably just a matter of time. Because according to the French newsweekly *Le Point*, French children too are now being reared like racehorses, dragged to an average of three after-school activities per week and filled, from the earliest possible age, with the fear of failure. "A child must not only be seductive," wrote journalists Irène Inchauspé and Valérie Peiffer in January 2004, "he must also be ultrahigh-performing: first in his class, accomplished at sports, and a friend like none other. . . ."

" 'Over the past couple of years I've heard more and more children say that they're worthless,' " they quote one elementary school head as saying. " 'The parents are the most at fault, because the demands they make of their offspring have never been greater.' "

Life for French mothers, in the long term, isn't necessarily such a bowl of cherries either. For there is a price they pay for the wonderful (and expensive) benefits they enjoy: a pervasive and all-but-unchallenged kind of institutional sexism. It can keep women of childbearing age from being hired. And can condemn others to being fired when they fully avail themselves of the "rights" so readily accorded to them.

This happened to a friend of mine just weeks after I featured her in an article for *Working Mother* magazine on the pro-family policies in the French workplace. She e-mailed me about her experience:

> *My boss called me to set a meeting during my maternity leave to let me know, in advance and "between friends," that my work with {a major sportswear company} was going to end when I got back. The job had changed and would now involve a lot of travel, necessitating,*

obviously, a man, for whom children wouldn't be such a great burden. . . . They made sure to tell me that there were only two women in positions of responsibility with the company: one had no children and the other was unmarried, with a twenty-year-old child. . . . I should have known last year when he suggested I switch to work in the public relations department: "It's a good job for a woman," he said. Petits fours and seduction, I can see why he thought so. . . .

Clearly, there is no such thing as earthly paradise.

In my years in Paris, I caught France at its best: in the way it cares for new mothers and babies and educates pre–primary-school children. Here in Washington, I have seen much of America at its worst: at its most competitive and rapacious and amoral and moralizing and just plain *mad.* I've seen that there's a great deal of happy living to be had in a universe that's not ruled, as ours is, by the tyranny of the *should.* And I recognize now just what was so special about my early years of motherhood: I was bathed in a feeling of taken-caredness at pretty much every level of my life. It was a benefits package *conferred upon my children at birth*—and, by extension, upon my husband and me, too. We took it entirely for granted then, and we have mourned its loss ever since.

I know that many people would say that that feeling of taken-caredness, writ large upon the whole of society, is a poison that eats away at people's creativity and drive. There may be some truth to that. My husband used to refer to his ten-weeks-a-year-of-paid-vacation lifestyle as a "velvet coffin." And I always knew that, despite all the comforts of our life in France, I wanted my children to grow up in America. Because I wanted them to tap into my country's energy and forward-looking self-propulsion. And because I wanted them to be American women—as I imagined them, as I dreamed them, to be.

I still believe in that dream of American womanhood: the sense of limitless possibility, that unique potential for unbounded self-creation. I tell my girls this (in so many words) all the time. And I will always tell them that—no matter how many doubts I have to suppress, no matter how much cynicism I have to swallow, no matter how many defeatist escape fantasies I nurture, in the moments when I feel the most impotent.

I hope my girls will never say that I lied to them. I hope they, too, will grow up believing in that most American of dreams. And that society will come together to make it a reality.

Acknowledgments

THIS BOOK would not have come into existence without the energy and encouragement of my agent, Jennifer Rudolph Walsh, who saw its potential and made me believe in mine.

It would not be readable without the stupendous editing skills of Susan Lehman, whose perceptiveness, intelligence, honesty, and humor made working together a dream.

I will always be grateful to Cindy Spiegel, who immediately made me feel at home at Riverhead. Special thanks are due, too, to Lisa Grubka at William Morris for all the time and effort she has put in on my behalf.

THIS BOOK encapsulates a world for me, and I cannot think about it without imagining the faces of all the many, many mothers and fathers, teachers and school administrators, doctors and grandparents and friends, whose words and experiences speak through its pages. I cannot begin to express my gratitude to the dozens and dozens of women (and some men) who participated in interviews in person or via the Internet. Many of these people I never met in person, yet their names on the page look like old friends to me. Their enthusiasm encouraged me; their spirit inspired me; their insights pushed me, time and again, to challenge my preconceptions and refine my thinking.

I wrote this book with the hope of doing justice to their perceptions and their eloquence. I hope that they will recognize themselves in these pages and know just how deeply I feel indebted to them.

They are: Alex Johns, Annie Donovan, Kim Benjet, Deirdre Hamlar, Jill Cochones, Mercedes Lemp, Susan Hasten, Stacy Title, Julie Genn, Heidi Peipkal, Hope Adler, Jessica Honigberg, Kelly Hewitt, Joanne Bamberger, Jill Meyer, Rima Sirota, Dimitra Lambrose, Sandy Lachter, Susan Barron, Jodi Goodman, Janice Kaplan-Allen, Emily Joffe, Jenn Klein, Nancy Brewer, Resa Eppler, Kathy Tolbert, Robin Miles-McLean, Sarah Wartell, Deborah Epstein, Harriet Klontz, Karyn Spriggs, Melissa Turner, Nancy McGuckin, Catherine Ribnick, Rhonda Shore, Tanya Chutkan, Lisa Terry, Tanya Tyler, Anita Walls, Iris Eagleton, Delna Gray, Theresa Saunders, Kristina Chura, Lanette Woodruff, Karlita Webster, Shawna Perkins-Gbla, Maura Sheehy, Mary Finn, Mona El Bayoumi, Karine Elsen, Jayne Jerkins, Saskia Vangroningen, Annie Mahon, Natasha Khan, Camilla Carpenter, Carrie Irvin, Betsy Hildebrandt, Anneke Wertheim, Debra Schenaker, Barbara Cornwell, Pauline Connole, Susan De Ritis, Kelly Miller, Mandy Book, Betsy Cavendish, Colleen Connors, Virginia Murphy, Joey Lampl, Nancy Segal, Karen Kornbluh, Maureen Pallotta, Amy Elsbree, Karen Allyn, Karen Austin, Claire Ferguson, Sharon Hill, Baan Alsinawi, Stephanie Dale, Lisa Tyler, Jeanne Digel, Jeann Lee Gillespie, Beth Miller, Becky Killion, Lutishia Williams, Lisa Williams, Kelly Willenberg, Sarah

Baldwin, Selena Mendy Singleton, Monique VanLandingham, Jack Cremeans, Judy Hanks-Henn, Todd Hedinger, Raheela Anwar, Becky Burgett, Nancy McConnell, Amy Guillet Agrawal, Kristene Smith, Veda Storey, Lynn Tickle, Michele Booth Cole, Louise Sennesh, Robin L. Seitz, Bev Schulz, Sue Sabo, Mary Roos, Susan Roberts, Martha Pardavi-Horvath, Debra O'Shea, Jeanmarie Nielsen, Debbie Newhouse, Ann-Janine Morey, Julia Moore, Patti Micklin, Lori Merrow, Michele Linnen, Tanya Mahoney, Tracey Lawton, Sharon Hill, Kristine Henriksen, Mary Furrie, Sarita Churchill, Barb Chamberlain, Connie Barr, Robbie White, and Christie Highlander. (If any names are missing, I offer my heartfelt apologies.)

Special thanks are due the incredibly generous women who took time they didn't have to organize interview groups and lend their homes for our meetings. They are: Jan Greenburg, Ruth Marcus, Anna Pines, Janet Riessman, and Marcia Rock. Tom Pines very kindly lent us office space. I am very grateful, too, to the organizations Mocha Moms, Mothers & More, and the Family and Home Network for making their members available for interviews.

Denise Kersten generously gave of her time and talents to help me with research. I am grateful to Joan Williams for graciously sharing her expertise, to Jennifer Tucker for making me aware of my blind spots, and to a host of other women, who prefer to remain nameless, for helping me with specific insights into policy, education, and politics. It was a phone call from Melanne Verveer that put this whole project into motion. I will always be supremely grateful to her for it.

I HAVE NEVER UNDERSTOOD how people translate their feelings toward family members into the telegraphic language of acknowledgments and know that my efforts to do so here will undoubtedly be inadequate. There is no limit to the debt I owe my husband, Max

Berley, whose unwavering faith, optimism, and love brighten my dark places and keep me afloat. His intelligence and critical eye define the standard toward which I will always strive.

As for my daughters, Julia and Emilie Berley—they simply make life worth living.

Notes

CHAPTER 1: INTRODUCTION: THE MOMMY MYSTIQUE

20 "New Economy Parents": Rochelle Sharpe, "Nannies on Speed Dial," *Business Week,* Sept. 18, 2000.

21 "Luxury fever": Robert H. Frank, *Luxury Fever: Money and Happiness in an Era of Excess* (Princeton, N.J.: Princeton University Press, 2000).

22 "Nonworking" mothers putting kids in day care: Sandy Banks, "Shoveling Guilt Onto the Working Mom's Pile," *Los Angeles Times,* July 30, 2002.

22 64% of American mothers worked: "Employment Characteristics of Families in 2000," U.S. Department of Labor press release, April 19, 2001.

22 Only a third of married mothers with children under six: Gary Burtless, "Squeezed for Time?," *Brookings Review,* Sept. 22, 1999, pp. 18ff.

22 Fully two-thirds of mothers work less than forty hours: Interview with Joan Williams, director of the Gender, Work and Family Project at American University's Washington College of Law and author of *Unbending Gender: Why Family and Work Conflict and What to Do About It* (Oxford, New York: Oxford University Press, 2000).

22 Mothers who work part-time . . . only seasonally . . . without pay for a family business: Author interview, Department of Labor, Division of Labor Force Studies.

CHAPTER 2: THE *NEW* PROBLEM THAT HAS NO NAME

34 "The old illusions . . .": Nora Johnson, "The Captivity of Marriage," *Atlantic Monthly,* June 1961, pp. 38–42.

35 A recent revolution in the social sciences . . . : William H. Chafe, *The American Woman: Her Changing Social, Economic, and Political Roles 1920–1970* (London, N.Y.: Oxford University Press, 1972), p. 210.

35 "Armed with the accumulated knowledge . . .": Fitzhugh Dodson, *How to Parent* (Los Angeles: Nash, 1970), p. 284.

35 Spock explained: Benjamin Spock, "Working Mothers: Some Possible Solutions for Child Care," *Redbook,* Sept. 1970, p. 34.

36 The sociologist: Philip Slater, *The Pursuit of Loneliness: American Culture at the Breaking Point* (Boston: Beacon Press, 1970), p. 56.

36 "This was to be our life's work . . .": Anne Roiphe, "Seismic Shift," *Ladies' Home Journal,* May 2000, p. 126.

36 They . . . "hollered": Helena Znaniecka Lopata, *Occupation: Housewife* (New York: Oxford University Press, 1971), p. 183.

37 Educated women were *"'touched with a sense of grievance . . .'"*: Bruno Bettelheim, "Growing Up Female," *Harper's Magazine,* October 1962.

38 One young wife . . . a husband complained to *Redbook*: Jhan and June Robbins, "Why Young Mothers Feel Trapped," *Redbook,* Sept. 1960.

38 Pacatal ad: Cited in Eugenia Kaledin, *Mothers and More: American Women in the 1950s* (Boston: Twayne Pub., 1984), p. 181.

38 Betty Friedan, for one: Betty Friedan, *The Feminine Mystique* (New York: Laurel, 1983), pp. 18–19.

39 The ideal that Betty Friedan dreamed of: Betty Friedan, "Up from the Kitchen Floor," *New York Times Magazine,* March 4, 1973, pp. 8ff.

39 "Memo to the American Woman": Patricia Coffin, "Memo to the American Woman," *Look,* Jan. 11, 1966, pp. 15ff.

40 *"I have no time for myself . . ."*: Robbins.

41 Kate Reddy's mind: Allison Pearson, *I Don't Know How She Does It: The Life of Kate Reddy, Working Mother* (New York: Alfred A. Knopf, 2002), p. 33.

44 Tail end of the baby boom: As defined in Kaledin, p. 181.

51 ". . . women have as many occupations open to them as men . . .": Phyllis McGinley, *Sixpence in Her Shoe* (New York: Macmillan, 1964), p. 9.

52 "Locked as we all were then in that mystique . . .": Friedan, "Up from the Kitchen Floor."

CHAPTER 3: THE SACRIFICIAL MOTHER

61 Story of Martha Spice: Gary Dorsey, "A Mother's Journey: For Martha Spice, Motherhood Has Been a Mysterious Odyssey of Genius, Sacrifice and Fulfillment. Now It's Just a Matter of Letting Go," *Baltimore Sun,* May 13, 2001.

63 *"For as long as I can remember . . ."*: Iris Krasnow, *Surrendering to Motherhood* (New York: Hyperion, 1997), p. 9.

63 "An air of Messianic expectation . . .": John R. Seeley, *The Americanization of the Unconscious* (New York: International Science Press, 1967), p. 6.

64 Mothers were responsible . . . collectively, for the very soul of the nation: Ruth H. Block, "American Feminine Ideals in Transition: The Rise of the Moral Mother, 1785–1815," in Nancy F. Cott, ed., *History of Women in the United States: Domestic Ideology and Domestic Work, Part 1* (Munich: K. G. Saur, 1992), p. 21. Also see Cott, Introduction, p. xi.

64 Susannah Wesley cited in Daniel R. Miller and Guy E. Swanson, *The Changing American Parent* (New York: John Wiley and Sons), 1958, p. 11.

65 Puritan ministers railed: Block, p. 21.

65 Wet nurses going against the will of God: Block, p. 4.

65 "An unnatural degenerate": Miller and Swanson, p. 14.

66 "Our soul is to be filled by the child . . .": Ellen Karolina Sofia Key, *The Century of the Child* (New York and London: G. P. Putnam's Sons, 1909), p. 102.

66 The forward-thinking, health-oriented mother: This is Ellen Key, cited in Ann Hulbert, "The Century of the Child: A History of American Scientific Child Rearing," *The Wilson Quarterly,* Jan. 1, 1999. p. 14.

67 "That remotely familiar stranger . . .": Nora Okja Keller, "You'll Get Used to It," in Camille Peri and Kate Moses, eds., *Mothers Who Think* (New York: Villard, 1999), pp. 114–120.

68 An attempt at leaving her baby, etc.: Keller, p. 119.

69 *Parenting* magazine called: Margaret Renkl, "Zen and the Art of Motherhood," *Parenting,* February 2001.

69 "Eros of parenthood": Noelle Oxenhandler, "The Eros of Parenthood," *New Yorker,* Feb. 19, 1996, p. 47.

69 This "set the stage": "50 Simple Ways to Make Your Baby Smarter," *Parents,* April 2002, pp. 132ff.

69 Sign language class: Tina Kelley, "How Do You Say Goo Goo in Sign Language?" *New York Times,* Aug. 12, 2002.

70 "Quality time" even during sleep: Martin E. P. Seligman, "How to See the Glass Half-Full," *Newsweek,* Sept. 16, 2002, pp. 48ff.

70 Six IQ points: Patricia Pearson, "What's the Real Result of Endless IQ Studies? Crazed Moms," *USA Today,* May 13, 2002.

70 "The needs of their babies . . .": cited in Lynn Y. Weiner, "Reconstructing Motherhood: The La Leche League in Postwar America," in Rima D. Apple and Janet Golden, eds., *Mothers and Motherhood: Readings in American History* (Columbus: Ohio State University Press, 1997), pp. 372–373.

71 Stanley Greenspan said: T. Berry Brazelton and Stanley I. Greenspan, *The Irreducible Needs of Children: What Every Child Must Have to Grow, Learn and Flourish* (Cambridge: Perseus Books, 2000), p. xvi.

71 T. Berry Brazelton said: Ibid., p. 12.

71 "Great delight and pleasure . . . ": Ibid., p. 17.

71 70 percent of mothers surveyed: "What Moms Love," *Ladies' Home Journal,* Nov. 1, 2000.

72 "Never hug and kiss them . . . ": John B. Watson, *Psychological Care of Infant and Child* (New York: W. W. Norton and Co., 1928), p. 81.

72 "It is a serious question . . .": Watson, p. 5.

73 "Motherly type": Helene Deutsch, *The Psychology of Women* (New York: Gruner & Stratton, 1944), p. 18.

73 In a despairing book: Edward A. Strecker, *Their Mothers' Sons: The Psychiatrist Examines an American Problem* (Philadelphia: J. B. Lippincott Co., 1945), p. 36.

74 She was, he said, a woman who had "failed . . .": Strecker, p. 13.

74 In 1945, *Ladies' Home Journal* published an article: Amram Sheinfeld, "Are American Moms a Menace?" *Ladies' Home Journal,* Nov. 1945, p. 36. Reprinted in Nancy A.

Walker, *Women's Magazines 1940–1960: Gender Roles and the Popular Press* (Boston and New York: Bedford/St. Martin's Press, 1998), pp. 108–114.

74 "... 'I had a mother ...'": Ferdinand Lundberg and Marynia F. Farnham, *Modern Woman: The Lost Sex* (New York: Harper and Brothers, 1947), p. 3.

74 Mother as "psychological toxin": René Spitz, *The First Year of Life* (New York: International Universities Press, 1965), p. 207.

74 Colic . . . infantile eczema: Ibid., p. 224

75 The "good-enough mother": D. W. Winnicott, The *Maturational Processes and the Facilitating Environment* (New York: International Universities Press, 1965), p. 57.

75 Needs *in the abstract*: Joshua Kendall, "Fierce Attachments: The Controversial Science of Mother-Infant Bonding Gets a New Look," *Boston Globe Online,* June 29, 2003.

76 "On the one hand, infinite amounts of attention . . .": Jessie Bernard, *The Future of Motherhood* (New York: Dial Press, 1974), pp. 90–91.

76 The "young and modern" residents of twelve Midwestern suburbs: Lopata, p. 38.

77 In the late 1960s, only ten percent of children: Suzanne Bianchi, "Maternal Employment and Time with Children: Dramatic Change or Surprising Continuity?" *Demography,* 37:4, 2000, pp. 401–414.

77 Mothers, having "shifted load," seem to be spending more time with children: Ibid., p. 412.

78 "An irreparable loss . . .": Walter Kempler, "The Pampered, Neglected Child," *Today's Health,* March 1969, p. 47.

78 "Fire-department ideology of child rearing": Alice Rossi, "Women Re-entering the Work Force," 1964 article reprinted in *Society,* Jan. 11, 1998, p. 11.

78 René Spitz: Spitz, p. 201.

79 "Please do not . . . conclude that you must spend most of your baby's waking moments playing with him . . . ": Dodson, p. 52.

79 In a 1960 article: Benjamin Spock, "Russian Children Don't Whine, Squabble or Break Things—Why?," *Ladies' Home Journal,* Oct. 1960.

80 "When father returns home in the evening . . .": Haim Ginott, *Between Parent and Child* (New York: Avon, 1969), p. 136.

81 A relatively typical critique of Spockian parenting: Elizabeth Bernstein, "Myths of a Golden Age: Motherhood in the 1950s," *Civil Rights Journal,* Sept. 22, 2000.

82 "Children cause divorces . . .": Silverman and McCawley, in Ellen Peck, "Good Old Motherhood Can Be an Evil, Too," *Today's Health,* March 1972, p. 70.

83 "The heart of women's oppression . . .": Shulamith Firestone, *The Dialectic of Sex* (New York: William Morrow and Company, 1970), p. 81.

83 Women . . . "feel cheated and resentful . . .": Lucy Komisar, "The New Feminism," *Saturday Review,* Feb. 21, 1970, p. 27

83 Books like *The Baby Trap*: See Ellen Peck, *The Baby Trap* (New York: Bernard Geis Associates, 1971).

83 "Tyrannical goddess": Jane Lazarre, *The Mother Knot* (New York: McGraw-Hill, 1976), pp. viii and xviii.

83 As one boomer writer put it: Maureen Smith Williams, "We Can Stop Feeling Sorry for Our Mothers," *McCall's,* August 1980, p. 140.

84 "What I remember most . . .": Erica Jong, "My Surrender to Motherhood," *Glamour,* September 1994, p. 306.

84 "Was I reluctant . . .": Pamela Redmond Satran, "Wanting It All," *Ladies' Home Journal,* May 2000, p. 128.

84 One magazine writer: Maureen Smith Williams, "We Can Stop Feeling Sorry for Our Mothers."

84 "It is time we started to redefine our concept of what makes a good mother . . .": Caryl Rivers, Rosalind Barnett, and Grace Baruch, "How Not to Do to Your Daughter What Your Mother Did to You," *McCall's,* July 1979, p. 105.

84 "The mother's emotional state is a key . . .": C. Christian Beels, "The Case of the Vanishing Mommy," *New York Times Magazine,* July 4, 1976, pp. 28–29.

85 "Girls growing up . . .": Rivers, Barnett, and Baruch.

86 "When work around the house . . .": Bruno Bettelheim, "Why Working Mothers Have Happier Children," *Ladies' Home Journal,* June 1970, p. 24.

86 A University of Michigan study: Cited in Rivers, Barnett, and Baruch.

87 "Even the most interested and able of adults . . . ": Elizabeth M. Whelan, "Should a Career Woman Have Children?" *Harper's Bazaar,* Feb. 1977, pp. 153ff.

88 "Supermomism": Helen De Rosis, "Are You a Supermom?" *Ladies' Home Journal,* August 1974, pp. 54ff.

88 *McCall's* took on: Carole Klein, "The Myth of the Perfect Parent," *McCall's,* September 1975, p. 58.

88 "Simplify your life . . .": Gloria Norris and Jo Ann Miller, "The Working Mother's Anti-Guilt Guide," *Harper's Bazaar,* October 1979.

88 "Mother's Lib": Deborah Mason, "The New Sanity–Mother's Lib," *Vogue,* May 1981, p. 193.

88 "Choice has elevated . . .": Friedan, *The Feminine Mystique* (New York: Laurel, 1983), p. xiv.

88 "Working women don't feel guilty . . .": "Guilty of Feeling Guilt-Free," *McCall's,* Jan. 1994.

89 By 1986, a majority of all women with children under age three were in the workforce: Anne Cassiday, "Profiles in Power," *Working Mother,* June 1999, pp. 22ff.

89 "These mothers know exactly . . .": Greta Walker, "Mothering Is Back in Style," *Ladies' Home Journal,* June 1984.

89 The baby boomer mother as a paragon of nonstop high performance: Lois Leiderman Davitz, "Are You a Better Mother Than Your Mother?" *McCall's,* July 1984, pp. 82–3.

90 Women's magazines celebrating the "Supermom": See, for example, Neala S. Schwartzberg, "Call Me Supermom," *Parents,* March 1986, pp. 79–82.

90 53 percent of employed moms: Margery D. Rosen, "The American Mother: A Landmark Survey for the 1990s," *Ladies' Home Journal,* May 1990, pp. 132ff.

I am generally indebted in this chapter to Jana Malamud Smith's "Mothers: Tired of Taking the Rap," *New York Times Magazine,* June 10, 1990, pp. 32ff.

CHAPTER 4: SELFISH MOTHERS, FORSAKEN CHILDREN

91 "A child forsaken . . .": John Bowlby, *Attachment and Loss,* vol. 1 (New York: Basic Books, 1969), p. 24.

92 Brazelton's "whole thinking" based upon attachment theory: Robert Karen, "Becoming Attached," *The Atlantic Monthly,* February 1990, pp. 35ff.

92   "Children raised in orphanages . . .": Cited in C. Christian Beels, "The Case of the Vanishing Mommy," *New York Times Magazine,* July 4, 1976, pp. 28ff.

93   ". . . *the brink of unthinkable anxiety*": D. W. Winnicott, *The Maturational Processes and the Facilitating Environment* (New York: International Universities Press, 1965), p. 57.

94   We conceived of ourselves: Ladd-Taylor writes that in this period many women were turned against their mothers by well-meaning therapists. She explains that ever since the 1960s, therapists' attitudes toward mothers have been widely influenced by Margaret Mahler's work on a child's "separation and individuation from its mother." She writes (p. 142): "Mahler advised therapists to watch carefully when a mother entered the room. . . . They were to take note of whether she carried the child 'like a part of herself'—which would then brand the mother as being unable to separate from the child—or 'like an inanimate object,' which would label her as the cold-and-rejecting type." Mahler, notes Ladd-Taylor, formed her theories by working with severely disturbed children. So, once again, theories derived from extreme situations were generalized to normal family dynamics.

94   Soon, women's magazines: See, for example, *McCall's,* July 1979, p. 105.

95   "Narrative point of origin": Daniel Stern, *The Interpersonal World of the Infant* (New York: Basic Books, 1985), p. 260.

95   All of which led Mademoiselle: *Mademoiselle,* November 1979, p. 195.

95   Wild exposés: "Surviving the Unbelievable: A First-Person Account of Cult Ritual Abuse," *Ms.,* January/February 1993, pp. 40–45.

95   In some quarters of the feminist movement: See this encapsulated in Gloria Steinem, "Helping Ourselves to Revolution," *Ms.,* November/December 1992, p. 24.

96   Followers of the recovery movement guru John Bradshaw set about finding and reclaiming their "inner children" in the hope of mending the wounds inflicted on their souls by years of parental abuse. Abuse didn't have to be physical or sexual, Bradshaw taught, it could be any form of parental unwillingness or inability to meet a child's "dependency needs." This is from Shari L. Thurer, *The Myths of Motherhood: How Culture Reinvents the Good Mother* (Boston and NY: Houghton Mifflin, 1994), p. 293.

96   Insensitivity as child abuse: Wendy Kaminer, "Feminism's Identity Crisis," *The Atlantic Monthly,* October 1993, p. 51.

96   "All toxic parents . . .": Susan Forward with Craig Buck, *Toxic Parents: Overcoming Their Hurtful Legacy and Reclaiming Your Life* (New York: Bantam, 1989), p. 9.

96   "Cult of the abused Inner Child": Robert Hughes, *Culture of Complaint* (New York: Oxford, 1993), p. 8.

96   Other then-contemporary titles: Erika J. Chopich and Margaret Paul, *Healing Your Aloneness: Finding Love and Wholeness Through Your Inner Child* (San Francisco: HarperCollins, 1990); Jeremiah Abrams, *Reclaiming the Inner Child* (New York: St. Martin's Press, 1990); and Jacqui Bishop and Mary Grunte, *How to Love Yourself When You Don't Know How: Healing All Your Inner Children* (Barrytown, NY: Station Hill Press, 1992).

96   "Blaming parents . . .": Melinda Blau, "Adult Children, Tied to the Past," *American Health,* July 1990, pp. 56ff.

97   "The terrible certainty . . .": Robert Karen, "Becoming Attached," *Atlantic Monthly,* February 1990, pp. 35ff.

98   For an overview of the satanic ritual abuse scare: See Debbie Nathan and Michael Snedeker, *Satan's Silence: Ritual Abuse and the Making of a Modern Witch Hunt* (New York:

Basic Books, 1995); Lawrence Wright, *Remembering Satan: Recovered Memory and the Shattering of a Family* (New York: Knopf, 1994); and Elaine Showalter, *Hystories: Hysterical Epidemics and the Modern Media* (New York: Columbia University Press, 1997).

98   A new generation of young feminists: See, for example, Naomi Wolf, *Fire with Fire: The New Female Power and How it Will Change the 21st Century* (New York: Random House, 1993); Rene Denfeld, *The New Victorians: A Young Woman's Challenge to the Old Feminist Order* (New York: Warner Books, 1995); and Karen Lehrman, *The Lipstick Proviso: Women, Sex, and Power in the Real World* (New York: Doubleday, 1997).

98   Robert Schwartz, brutally murdered by a friend of his daughter, Clara Jane, "often refused to give her rides to school events," claimed a history teacher, whose testimony was invoked by Clara Jane Schwartz's defense team: See Maria Glod, "Sentencing of Scientist's Daughter Delayed; Defense, Seeking New Trial, Says Teacher Could Have Backed Up Claims of Abuse," *Washington Post*, January 22, 2003, p. B2. Schwartz's convictions have been appealed, and a decision on the appeal was pending when this book went to press.

99   "The grieving of a baby . . .": Penelope Leach, *Children First: What Our Society Must Do—and Is Not Doing—for Our Children Today* (New York: Knopf, 1994), p. 87.

99   "The most dramatic recent example of the results of neglecting a small child's needs . . .": Brazelton and Greenspan, p. xii.

100   "Gilded ghettos": George F. Will, "Mothers Who Don't Know How," *Newsweek*, April 23, 1990.

100   Romanian orphans and early brain stimulation: See Sandra Blakeslee, "Behind the Veil of Thought: Advances in Brain Research; in Brain's Early Growth, Timetable May Be Crucial," *New York Times*, Aug. 29, 1995.

101   "Insecurely attached babies": Robert Karen, "Becoming Attached," *Atlantic Monthly*, February 1990, pp. 35ff. For the New York City statistic, Karen quoted Larry Aber, director of the Barnard Center for Toddler Development at Columbia University.

101   ". . . guilt can be healthy": William and Martha Sears, *The Baby Book* (Boston: Little Brown, 1993), p. 14.

102   As *Glamour* once put it: Nancy Eberle, "How Not to Turn into Your Mother," *Glamour*, May 1989, pp. 160ff.

102   "Therapeutic parenting": The phrase is from Frank Furedi, *Paranoid Parenting: Why Ignoring the Experts May Be Best for Your Child* (Chicago: Chicago Review Press, 2002), p. 68.

105   In the late 1960s . . . only 2 percent of children were in group care: Cynthia Fuchs Epstein, *Women's Place: Options and Limits in Professional Careers* (Berkeley and Los Angeles: University of California Press, 1970), p. 109.

105   Jerome Kagan, *Unstable Ideas: Temperament, Cognition, and Self* (Cambridge, Mass.: Harvard University Press, 1989), p. 81.

106   "Infants without love . . . adults full of hate": Spitz, p. 300.

106   "Historical nodes of worry": Kagan, p. 96.

107   A new generation of researchers in the social sciences: See Rossi, "Women Re-entering the Work Force."

107   Margaret Mead: mentioned in many places; for example, Elizabeth Whelan, "Should a Career Woman Have Children?" *Harper's Bazaar*, February 1977, pp. 101ff.

107   "Folklore" and "myth": C. Christian Beels, "The Case of the Vanishing Mommy," *New York Times Magazine*, July 4, 1976, pp. 28ff.

107 "And a growing number of researchers came to agree . . .": See a mini-history of this in Stella Chess and Alexander Thomas, "Infant Bonding: Mystique and Reality," *American Journal of Orthopsychiatry* 52 (2) (April 1982), pp. 221ff.

108 "Nation of victims": The phrase is from Charles Sykes, *A Nation of Victims: The Decay of the American Character* (New York: St. Martin's Press, 1992).

108 For a full cataloguing of the many ways American opinion-makers turned against working mothers in the late 1980s and 1990s, see Susan Faludi's *Backlash: The Undeclared War Against American Women* (New York: Crown, 1991) and Susan Chira's *A Mother's Place* (New York: HarperCollins, 1998). Chira says a "new cult of domesticity" was sweeping the nation, filled with vitriolic attacks on working mothers and "a broader assault on the very idea of women's fulfillment" (p. xvi). Faludi notes that television writers in the late 1980s were so uncomfortable with the idea of working mothers that many new sitcoms simply *killed them* out of their scripts. (*Backlash*, pp. 142–143). As a result, she writes, in 1988, almost 40 percent of American mothers said that they were fearful of leaving their children in day care. The percentage of American mothers who reported feeling confident about their children's day care, a number that had hovered above 70 percent in the early 1980s, dropped, for the first time, by a full 10 percent (*Backlash*, p. 81).

108 No one minded the fact . . . : Faludi, p. 44.

109 "My purpose . . .": quoted in Ellen Ruppel Shell, "Babes in Day Care," *The Atlantic Monthly*, August 1988.

109 "Yuppie empowerment": quoted in Paul Taylor, "New Push on for Parental Leave," *Washington Post*, March 21, 1991, p. A19.

110 After detailing the baby's injuries: Mike McManus, "Mother Cares Best," *Pittsburgh Post-Gazette*, November 16, 1997.

110 A particularly harsh judgment: cited in Betty Holcolmb and Michaele Weissman, "The Nanny Case," *Working Mother*, March 1998.

111 The vast majority of mothers want to work part-time: *Ladies' Home Journal* reported in 1990 that 80 percent of mothers wanted to work part-time. Also see, among many others, "What Do Mothers Really Want?," *Parents*, May 1996, pp. 38ff.

111 For more on the *I Am Your Child* moment, see Furedi, p. 41.

112 Child prodigies as "made, not born": "Did Mozart Have Help?" *Psychology Today*, November/December 1997, p. 10.

112 "In an age where mothers and fathers are increasingly pressed for time . . .": J. Madeleine Nash, "Fertile Minds," *Time*, Feb. 3, 1997 pp. 48ff.

113 It was also later revealed: Jeffrey Kluger, "The Quest for a Super Kid," *Time*, April 30, 2001. pp. 50ff.

113 People close to Hillary Rodham Clinton: author interview.

113 "Cutting-edge science . . .": Barbara Kantrowitz, "Off to a Good Start," *Newsweek*, May 1997 (Spring/Summer Special Edition), pp. 6ff.

114 "Every lullaby . . .": Kantrowitz, p. 6.

114 Hillary Clinton's advice: "Remarks by President Bill Clinton at Early Childhood Development Conference. Also speaking: Hillary Rodham Clinton," Federal News Service, April 17, 1997.

CHAPTER 5: MILLENNIAL MOTHERHOOD

115 "If you are a soccer mom . . .": Neil MacFarquar, "Don't Forget Soccer Dads: What's a Soccer Mom, Anyway?" *New York Times,* Oct. 20, 1996.

116 As her wheels implied: Such was the dizzying schedule of a Silver Spring, Maryland, mother profiled by the *Washington Post* in April 2001. See Bob Thompson, "A Wild Patience Has Taken Me This Far," *Washington Post Magazine,* April 15, 2001, p. W22.

116 "Almost always on-duty": Richard Cohen, "The Parenting Trap," *Washington Post,* July 12, 1998.

117 "New Nesters": Pamela Paul, "The New Nesters," *Redbook,* Feb. 1, 2001, p. 104.

117 "Top Corporate Women . . .": Jane Hodges, "Top Corporate Women are Quitting to 'Have it All,'" *Wall Street Journal,* July 16, 2002.

117 "You Can Afford to Stay Home": See "I Quit My Job to Be a Full-Time Mom," *Mc-Call's,* August 1999, pp. 56ff; Christina Baglivi Tinglof, "You Can Afford to Stay at Home," *Parents,* March 2000, pp. 156ff; "Your Kids vs. Your Job," *Ladies' Home Journal,* October 2000, pp. 66ff.

117 Whose life was "worth" more: This equation, perhaps not coincidentally, was playing out in many states, where mothers' and fetuses' lives were increasingly pitted against each other as the abortion wars raged. See, for example, "Killer moms, working nannies; an increase in arrests of mothers charged with child neglect, some on ridiculous charges, highlights the need for working mothers to stand up for their rights," *The Nation,* Nov. 24, 1997.

118 The way "it's supposed to be": Michelle Conlin, "The New Debate Over Working Moms," *Business Week,* Sept. 18, 2002, pp. 102ff.

118 Psychotic over-achievers . . . shameless self-promoters: See, for example, Jane Hodges, "Top Corporate Women Are Quitting to 'Have it All,'" *Wall Street Journal,* July 16, 2002, and Sarah Mahoney's article, "Charting Your Own Course," in *Working Mother,* August/September 2002.

118 Wealthy women, pretty much exclusively: Author interview with Joan Williams. Also see Louis Uchitelle, "Job Track or 'Mommy Track'? Some do Both, in Phases," *New York Times,* July 5, 2002, p. C5; and Pamela Paul, "The New Nesters," *Redbook,* Feb. 1, 2001, pp. 104ff. Also see Ann Marsh, "Mommy, Me and an Advanced Degree," *Los Angeles Times,"* January 6, 2002.

119 63 percent of women said no to leaving dream jobs: Paul, "The New Nesters."

119 Newsweek started scolding: Laura Shapiro, "The Myth of Quality Time," *Newsweek,* May 12, 1997, pp. 62ff.

119 *U.S. News & World Report*: Shannon Brownlee, "Lies Parents Tell Themselves About Why They Work," *U.S. News & World Report,* May 12, 1997.

120 "No more insidious a drug . . .": Marie Winn, *The Plug-In Drug* (New York: Penguin, 2002), pp. 14–15.

120 Winn joyfully recalled: Winn, p. 189.

120 87 percent of parents: *Parents,* March 2000.

120 90 percent of parents: Maureen Boland, "How to Be a Great Mom—and Have a Life," *Redbook,* May 2001, p. 180

121 "Equal freedom from household tedium": Michelle Hoffnung Garskof, *Roles Women Play: Readings Towards Women's Liberation* (Belmont, Calif.: Brooks/Cole, 1970), p. 1.

121 Housework now was back: Cheryl Mendelson, *Home Comforts* (New York: Scribner, 1999).

122   "Memoirs of a Dot.com Wife": Hope Edelman, "The Myth of Co-Parenting," in Cathi Hanauer, ed., *The Bitch in the House* (New York: William Morrow, 2002), p. 172.

123   Iris Krasnow, *Surrendering to Motherhood* (New York: Hyperion, 1997).

123   "Surrender circles": Julie V. Iovine, "Yes-Dearing Your Way to a Happy Marriage?" *New York Times,* Feb. 8, 2001, p. F1.

123   "American women . . .": Marjorie Williams, "A Working Mom's Comedy," *Washington Post,* Oct. 2, 2002, p. A17.

123   "Coparenting . . .": Lindley Shutz, "A Family Romance," in Christina Baker Kline, ed., *Child of Mine* (New York: Hyperion, 1997), p. 238.

124   Mothers' natural needs: Danielle Crittenden, *What Our Mothers Didn't Tell Us: Why Happiness Eludes the Modern Woman* (New York: Simon & Schuster, 1999).

125   "A model of routine . . .": Lonnae O'Neal Parker, "The Donna Reed Syndrome," *Washington Post Magazine,* May 12, 2002, p. W42.

126   Depression alone: "Study Finds Depression Among New Mothers," *Mental Health Weekly,* May 12, 2003, p. 8.

126   "State of despair": "Modern Mums Suffer Sleep Deprivation," *BBC News,* April 2, 2002.

129   "I felt I could paint . . .": Jacob Santini and Ashley Estes, "Speed Trap," *Salt Lake Tribune,* Sept. 2, 2001, p. A1.

129   "The house, the kids . . .": Lisa Belkin, "A New Drug Demographic: Supermoms," *New York Times,* June 23, 2002.

130   "My children . . .": Carol Christian and Lisa Teachey, "Yates Believed Children Doomed," *Houston Chronicle,* Feb. 23, 2002, p. A1.

131   "I'm a mother . . .": Timothy Roche, "The Yates Odyssey," *Time,* Jan. 28, 2002, p. 42. Also see, among many others, Bill Hewitt, Bob Stewart and Gabrielle Cosgriff, "Life or Death; Does Andrea Yates, on Trial for Murder in Houston, Deserve Mercy for Drowning Her Five Kids?" *People,* March 4, 2002, p. 82; Terri Langford, "Russel Yates Paints Picture of his Wife's 'Traditional Home Life,'" *Dallas Morning News,* March 1, 2002; Megan K. Stack, "Killings Put Dark Side of Mom's Life in Light," *Los Angeles Times,* July 8, 2001, p. A20; Megan K. Stack, "Religious Zeal Infused Yates' Lives," *Los Angeles Times,* March 1, 2002, p. A16.

131   Cultural and epochal specificity of mental disease: Edward Shorter, *From Paralysis to Fatigue: A History of Psychosomatic Illness in the Modern Era* (New York: The Free Press, 1992).

CHAPTER 6: THE MOTHERHOOD RELIGION

133   "None of the studies . . .": Social science studies conducted over the past four decades have consistently shown that whether or not a mother is home full-time with her child or not is not, in and of itself, a determinative factor in her child's development. Studies of the effect of a mother's work—the usual vector that confers self-definition, self-sufficiency, and independence—from the mid-1950s onward have always had the same result: that there is no evidence that work *per se* impacts on children one way or another. (This conclusion occurs throughout the sources I have cited in this book.)

    In 1955, in response to widespread public outrage over the news that one-third of mothers of school-age children were employed, F. Ivan Nye and Lois Wladis Hoffman began to compare the levels of happiness and quality of relationships of children of working and nonworking mothers. After eight years of study, they found no significant differences in school performance, psychosomatic symptoms, or closeness to their mothers between the two groups. (F. Ivan Nye and Lois Wladis Hoffman, *The Employed Mother in America* [Chicago: Rand McNally, 1963]. In 1964, the sociologist Alice Rossi, reviewing the literature that then existed on working motherhood, concluded, "There is a widespread belief in our society that children suffer when they are not cared for, full-time, by their own mothers. Social science does not support this belief. The essential finding of all the studies on children . . . is that the children of working mothers are not different, in any significant way, from [those of] mothers who stay at home." (Alice Rossi, "Women Re-entering the Work Force," reprinted in *Society,* Jan. 11, 1998, p. 11)

In the mid-1970s, Jerome Kagan of Harvard interpreted a series of studies of the effects of nonmother care on young children, controlling out some sources of problems in children by not including families where there was obvious chaos or strain, making sure the day care was of the highest quality, and controlling for class and ethnicity. He then found that there were no significant differences in intelligence, language, social skills, or attachment among children who were taken care of by their mothers, babysitters, or day-care workers—even if they were as young as three months old when they began in nonmother care. (C. Christian Beels, "The Case of the Vanishing Mommy," *New York Times Magazine,* July 4, 1976, p. 28)

In 1988, Ellen Galinsky and Judy David in *The Preschool Years* reviewed the research on the effects of a mother's employment outside of the home and concluded that, all things being equal, a mother's work had no particular effect at all on her children. "Children are not necessarily helped or harmed by the fact that their mothers are employed and they are cared for by others," they wrote. "The impact of a mother's employment depends; it depends upon the children's experiences in their families and in their child-care situations." (Ellen Galinsky and Judy David, *The Preschool Years: Family Strategies That Work* [New York: Times Books, 1988], pp. 365–366)

In 1996, a far-reaching study of 1,300 families followed since 1991 found that there were no differences in degrees of attachment to their mothers among infants taken care of by their mothers or in day care. (Susan Chira, "Study Says Babies in Child Care Keep Secure Bonds to Mothers," *New York Times,* April 21, 1996, p. A1)

Summing up all these studies, *Redbook* has noted, "Research has consistently shown that the key factor in children's well-being is the mother's happiness with what she's doing—whether that's staying home or working outside it." (Lee Connor and A. Lusardi, "Can You Afford to Stop Working?" *Redbook,* November 1996, p. 50) *Parenting* magazine—like *Redbook,* hardly a hard-line champion of working motherhood—said in 2001, "Research conducted over the past five decades shows that a mother's decision to work or stay home isn't a good predictor of how her children will turn out, for better or worse (unless their care is substandard)." (Betty Holcolmb, "Should You Quit Work?" *Parenting,* June/July 2001)

133 (The quality of care . . .): See studies just mentioned. Also those mentioned at the end of the chapter.

133 The self-fulfillment: Susan Chira, "Study Says Babies in Child Care Keep Secure Bonds to Mothers," *New York Times,* April 21, 1996, p. A1.

134 Potentially, even: Here I am indebted to Ruth H. Block, "American Feminine Ideals in Transition: The Rise of the Moral Mother, 1785–1815," in Nancy F. Cott, ed., *History of Women in the United States: Domestic Ideology and Domestic Work, Part 1* (Munich: K. G. Saur, 1992), pp. 16ff.

135 And the notion: For all of this, see Block again and, generally, Maxine L. Margolis, *Mothers and Such: Views of American Women and Why They Changed* (Berkeley and Los Angeles: University of California Press, 1984).

135 And their fears: Margolis, p. 49.

136 Kaiser brochure: Quoted in "Let's Stop Lying About Day Care," *Glamour,* October 1994, p. 114.

136 One contemporary domestic guide: Quoted in Margolis, p. 77.

137 Middle-class necessities: Stephanie Coontz, "Nostalgia as Ideology," *The American Prospect,* April 8, 2002, pp. 26ff.

137 Now women's salaries: C. Christian Beels, "The Case of the Vanishing Mommy," *New York Times Magazine,* July 4, 1976, pp. 28ff.

137 It's commonly believed: "The women's movement shifted public opinion" on working motherhood is how the *New York Times* put it, reflecting a typical view of this, in a recent article on changes in mothering practices through time. (Patricia Cohen, "Visions and Revisions of Child-Raising Experts," *New York Times,* April 5, 2003, p. D7)

137 Manpower Inc.: "The Married Woman Goes Back to Work," *Woman's Home Companion,* October, 1956, pp. 42ff. Reprinted in Nancy A. Walker, *Women's Magazines, 1940–1960: Gender Roles and the Popular Press* (Boston and New York: Bedford/St. Martin's Press, 1998), pp. 87–95.

137 About two-thirds: "The Married Woman Goes Back to Work," p. 88.

137 Over the course of the 1950s: Coontz, "Nostalgia as Ideology," p. 26.

137 By the late 1960s: Mary P. Ryan, *Womanhood in America* (New York: New Viewpoints, 1979), p. 196.

138 In 1971: "A Woman's Place Is on the Job," *Newsweek,* July 26, 1971.

138 By 1972: Margolis, p. 65.

138 The rate increased . . . with each passing year: And it kept on going: by 1978, the first time that the U.S. Census Bureau counted mothers of infants under age one who were at work, 30 percent of mothers of infants were working at least part-time and 41 percent of mothers with a child under two were employed (Weiner, p. 377). By 1984, 60 percent of women with children under eighteen were employed (Margolis, p. 65). By 1998 (the last year for which government data is available), 73 percent of mothers with children over the age of one were employed and 59 percent of mothers of infants—a record high—worked at least part-time.

138 73 percent of mothers with children over age one (and 59 percent of those with infants): "Record Share of New Mothers in Labor Force, Census Bureau Reports," United States Department of Commerce press release, Oct. 24, 2000.

139 Fears of college-educated white men: Susan Faludi explores them at great length in *Stiffed: The Betrayal of the American Man* (New York: William Morrow, 1999).

139 In the job-poor years . . . women's influx into the marketplace stopped: Howard V. Hayghe, "Developments in Women's Labor Force Participation," *Monthly Labor Review,* Sept. 1997, pp. 41ff.

139 Only 10 percent of employers were providing child-care assistance: 1988 U.S. Labor Department statistics, cited in Wendy Kaminer, *A Fearful Freedom: Women's Flight from Equality* (Reading, Mass.: Addison-Wesley, 1990), p. 143.

140 16 percent of dads at home in 1993, from a high of 20 percent: Jerry Adler, "Building a Better Dad," *Newsweek,* June 17, 1996, pp. 58ff.

140 Drop in percentage of mothers with infants in the workforce: This was a trend detected by the U.S. Census Bureau and detailed in its "Fertility of American Women" report released in October 2001. Based on a survey of 30,000 women, the Census Bureau found that between June 1998 and June 2000 the percentage of women in the workplace with infant children declined from 59 percent to 55 percent. See, among many other places, Judith Warner, "Why We Work," *Working Mother,* September 2001, pp. 64ff; and Ann Marsh, "Mommy, Me and an Advanced Degree," *Los Angeles Times,* Jan. 6, 2002.

140 The full-employment economy: Author interview with Harvard University economist Ken Rogoff.

141 Women transitioning from welfare: Sharon Hays, *Flat Broke with Children: Women in the Age of Welfare Reform* (New York: Oxford University Press, 2003).

141 A hopeless cause: author interview with former Clinton administration staffers.

142 "They kind of see me . . .": Marsh, Part 5, p. 1.

145 Mommy Trackable careers: see for example, Laura Meade Kirk, "Mom's Juggling Act," *Providence Journal-Bulletin,* May 12, 2002; or "Mommy Is Really Home from Work," *Business Week,* November 2002.

146 "I work the way I work . . .": Penelope Green, "Family Value," *Vogue,* March 2001, pp. 170ff.

150 "Establishing an advantageous niche . . .": Sarah Blaffer Hrdy, *Mother Nature* (New York: Pantheon, 1999), pp. 110–11.

151 "Striving for status" and "maternal emotions" compartmentalized: Ibid., p. xiii.

152 "The conflict . . .": Ibid., p. 112.

153 "The psychological research . . .": Thurer, p. 291.

154 Three-year-olds with working mothers: Toddi Gutnerhers, "Working Moms: Don't Feel So Guilty," *Business Week,* September 23, 2002.

154 What was really going on . . . poor quality of care: Susan Gilbert, "Two Studies Link Child Care to Behavior Problems," *New York Times,* July 16, 2003, p. A12.

155 "Instead of saying . . .": Quoted in Sandy Banks, "Shoveling Guilt onto the Working Mom's Pile," *Los Angeles Times,* July 30, 2002.

155 One upper-middle-class mother: Quoted in Ryan, p. 202.

CHAPTER 7: A GENERATION OF CONTROL FREAKS

164 Our "entitlement": Barbara Findlen, *Listen Up: Voices from the Next Feminist Generation* (Seattle: Seal Press, 1995), p. xii.

164 Increasing numbers of women in the professions: By 1993, they would earn 35 percent of all MBAs (up from 4 percent in 1972), 42.5 percent of all law degrees (up from 8 percent in 1973), and 38 percent of all doctoral degrees (up from 18 percent in 1970). Statistics cited in Karen Lehrman, *The Lipstick Proviso* (New York: Doubleday, 1997), p. 154.

164 Anorexia and bulimia . . . in 2 percent of women overall . . . in 10 percent of our age group and 20 percent of women on some college campuses: Joan Jacobs Brumberg, *Fasting Girls: The History of Anorexia Nervosa* (New York: New American Library, 1989), p. 12.

165 "The norm . . .": Naomi Wolf, *The Beauty Myth: How Images of Beauty Are Used Against Women* (New York: HarperCollins, 1991), p. 182.

165   Anorexia as "characteristic psychopathology": Brumberg, p. 257.

165   "Even though . . .": Ibid., p. 267.

166   The *real* epidemic: In 1990, Richard A. Gordon, author of *Anorexia and Bulimia: Anatomy of a Social Epidemic* (Cambridge, Mass.: Basic Blackwell, 1990) called the eating disorders a "vocabulary of discomfort" that is expressed at varying levels of volume by different women, taking its loudest and clearest expression in the full-fledged anorexic or bulimic. A woman with an eating disorder, he wrote, "suffers from psychological conflicts that are pervasive in the culture, but are experienced by the patient in particularly acute form," p. 5.

166   A "normative discontent": J. Rodin, L. Silberstein, and R. Striegel-Moore, "Women and Weight: A Normative Discontent," in T. Sonderegger, ed., *Psychology and Gender: Nebraska Symposium on Motivation* (Lincoln: University of Nebraska Press, 1985), pp. 267–307.

166   "Subclinical eating disorder": Michelle Stacey, *Consumed: Why Americans Love, Hate and Fear Food* (New York: Simon & Schuster, 1994), p. 176.

167   One to 2 percent of the population: Daniel Q. Haney, "Study Finds Most Lactose Intolerant People Can Drink Milk," Associated Press, July 6, 1995. According to this story, the numbers generally heard at that time—that as many as 80 percent of Asians, 75 percent of African-Americans, 51 percent of Hispanics, and 21 percent of white people were lactose-intolerant—had been generated after subjects were made to drink an entire quart of milk in one sitting—a deluge of dairy not really comparable with the normal intake of most people at most meals and, the experts said, enough to bring on symptoms of gastric distress in the most lactose-hardy among us. A survey of 5,000 households conducted for the British medical journal *The Lancet* found that while about 20 percent of people surveyed (particularly women) said they suffered from some form of a food intolerance, only 1.4 to 1.8 percent of those people, when tested in a double-blind, placebo-controlled study, actually did. See Elspeth Young, Michael D. Stoneham, Anne Petruckevitch, Jeremy Barton, and Roberto Rona, "A Population Study of Food Intolerance," *The Lancet,* vol. 343, May 7, 1994, pp. 1127–1130.

167   "Every time I'd make a plan . . .": Stacey, p. 176.

169   "Fashionable diagnoses" study: Donna E. Stewart, "The Changing Faces of Somatization," *Psychosomatics,* vol. 31, no. 2 (Spring 1990).

170   Forklift: See "Stroh's Brewery: The Story Behind the Harassment Case," *Ms.,* November/December 1992.

171   Bella Abzug: Quoted in Amy Erdman Farrell, *Yours in Sisterhood: Ms. Magazine and the Promise of Popular Feminism* (Chapel Hill and London: University of North Carolina Press, 1998), p. 18.

171   Sexual violence on TV: Susan J. Douglas writes about this at length in *Where the Girls Are: Growing Up Female with the Mass Media* (New York: Penguin, 1994).

172   "It seemed very dangerous . . .": Quoted in Betsy Israel, *Bachelor Girl: The Secret History of Single Women in the Twentieth Century* (New York: William Morrow, 2002), p. 231.

172   Lucinda Franks: Quoted in Israel, p. 231.

172   "Fear of sexual assault and rape": Maria P. Root, "Reconstructing the Impact of Trauma on Personality," in L. S. Brown and M. Baillou, eds. *Personality and Psychopathology: Feminist Reappraisals* (New York: Guilford, 1992). Cited in Elaine Showalter, *Hystories: Hysterical Epidemics and Modern Media* (New York: Columbia University Press, 1997), p. 61.

172   *Redbook* survey: Cited by Wendy Kaminer, "Feminism's Identity Crisis," *Atlantic Monthly,* October 1993, pp. 51ff.

173   Peak in divorce rate (it has since decreased): Anne Cassidy, "Profiles in Power," *Working Mother,* January 1999, pp. 22ff.

173   Displaced homemakers: Sylvia Ann Hewlett, *A Lesser Life: The Myth of Women's Liberation in America* (New York: William Morrow and Co., 1986), p. 54.

173   "Most therapists . . .": Janet Gardner, "Problems of the New Woman," *Glamour,* June 1978, pp. 220ff.

174   "I still don't know exactly why . . .": Peggy Orenstein, *Flux: Women on Sex, Work, Kids, Love and Life in a Half-Changed World* (Doubleday: New York, 2000), p. 6.

175   "Blow up like zeppelins . . .": Aimee Liu, *Solitaire* (New York: Harper & Row, 1979), p. 80.

175   "If you are a mother . . .": Kim Chernin, *The Obsession: Reflections on the Tyranny of Slenderness* (New York: Harper & Row, 1981), p. 66.

175   "I saw my identity . . .": Anne Glusker, "Go Ahead—Just Tell Me I Have It All," *Washington Post,* May 12, 2002.

177   "Ironic hopelessness": David Leavitt, "The New Lost Generation," *Esquire,* May 1985, pp. 85ff.

177   "The worry about people of our age . . .": David Lipsky and Alexander Abrams, *Late Bloomers: Coming of Age in Today's America, The Right Place at the Wrong Time* (New York: Times Books, 1994), p. 26.

177   "For women in the age of Reagan . . .": Douglas, p. 246.

178   Supreme Court's limited view of abortion rights: Justice Blackmun, in writing the court's majority decision in *Roe,* argued that the right of a woman to seek an abortion was an outgrowth of her right to due process under the law (to have her fundamental right to privacy protected). This was a "negative" argument. It meant that the government couldn't *keep* a woman from exercising her constitutional rights, but neither did it have to make sure she was *able* to exercise her rights. The right to *choose* was established, but not the right to have access to the choice. And this limitation would prove to be the Achilles' heel of the *Roe v. Wade* decision, as in the decades that followed, a series of laws, backed by more recent court decisions, restricted women's access to abortion more and more until, by the 1990s, in some parts of the country, it was all but impossible to get an abortion at all.

180   "In a culture weary . . .": Rickie Salinger, "Poisonous Choice," in Molly Ladd-Taylor and Lauri Umansky, eds. *"Bad" Mothers: The Politics of Blame in Twentieth-Century America"* (New York and London: New York University Press, 1998), p. 385.

181   "Mining the Body": Subtitle is a play on the title from a collection of essays edited by Patricia Foster, *Minding the Body* (New York: Doubleday, 1994).

181   *Roe v. Wade* could have set a precedent: Salinger, p. 384.

182   "Battles for control": Paula Kamen, *Feminist Fatale* (New York: Donald I. Fine, 1991) p. 213.

183   "My body needed to be listened to . . .": Jane Fonda, *Jane Fonda's Workout Book* (New York: Simon & Schuster, 1981) pp. 9–10.

183   "Being strong": Ibid., p. 47.

183   "We might not be able . . .": Roberta Pollack Seid, *Never Too Thin: Why Women Are at War with Their Bodies* (New York: Prentice Hall, 1989), p. 235.

183   Faludi: *Backlash,* p. 71.

184 Politics of haircuts, etc.: See, for example, Findlen, *Listen Up: Voices from the Next Feminist Generation* (Seattle: Seal Press, 1995).

184 Politically hopeless age: The Equal Rights Amendment had died in 1982, just three states short of the 38 needed for ratification, driven to its grave by fear-mongering about mixed-sex bathrooms and drafting women into the military. The Supreme Court and the E.E.O.C., which had been created by the Civil Rights Act of 1964 to investigate discrimination claims, stopped effectively enforcing civil rights laws in the 1980s. The Reagan administration had cut child-care subsidies to poor and middle-income families. The number of women in elected or appointed political posts was dropping. And as the 1990s dawned, 80 to 95 percent of women working in the private sector said they suffered from job discrimination and unequal pay. See Faludi, *Backlash,* pp. xviff.

184 "The terrain . . .": Adrienne Rich, *Of Woman Born: Motherhood as Experience and Institution* (New York: W.W. Norton, 1976), p. 55.

184 "Repossession": The repossession by women of our bodies will bring far more essential change to human society than the seizing of the means of production by workers," wrote Rich (ibid., p. 285).

185 "At a class . . .": Meg Wolitzer, "Mirror Image," *Elle,* May 1994, pp. 192ff.

185 Feminists often: See, for example, Gloria Steinem, *Moving Beyond Words* (New York: Simon & Schuster, 1994), pp. 94ff.

186 "Antipatriarchal rebellion": See, among countless others, Catrina Brown and Karin Jasper, eds., *Consuming Passions: Feminist Approaches to Weight Preoccupation and Eating Disorders* (Toronto: Second Story Press, 1993), p. 29.

186 "Suddenly, a skinny . . .": Steinem, *Moving Beyond Words,* pp. 94–95.

186 "Episiotomies are not a male conspiracy . . .": Renée Rose Shield, *Making Babies in the '80s* (Boston: The Harvard Common Press, 1983), p. 58.

187 "A terrible sense of failure": Claudia Kalb, "Should You Have Your Baby Now?," *Newsweek,* Aug. 13, 2001, pp. 40ff.

187 Trend for home births: Randi Hutter Epstein, "When Giving Birth, Opting to Go It Alone," *New York Times,* May 7, 2002.

187 "Men still set the agenda . . .": Erica Jong, "Women and the Way of All Flesh: Tyranny of Thinness," *Sunday Times,* Feb. 13, 1994.

187 "Anorexia and bulimia . . .": Regina Schrambling, "Fear of Food," *Vogue,* December 1995, pp. 212ff.

CHAPTER 8: RUNNING SCARED

191 "An enlarged sense of vulnerability . . .": Janna Malamud Smith, *A Potent Spell: Mother Love and the Power of Fear* (Boston: Houghton Mifflin, 2003), p. 25.

191 "Skittish, nervous versions of our former selves . . . ": Francine Prose, "What Mothers Are Really Afraid Of," *Redbook,* August 1997, pp. 135ff.

191 Parental fears out of proportion to threats: Sociologist Frank Furedi, in *Paranoid Parenting: Why Ignoring the Experts May Be Best for Your Child* (Chicago: Chicago Review Press, 2002), provides an encyclopedic view of our current culture of fear. He writes, "A survey of US pediatricians carried out in 1995 claimed that parental anxieties were on the rise among their patients—and that these anxieties tended to be significantly out of proportion to any real risks" (p. 6).

194   Pedophiles in day care: See, for example, Hal Karp, "Preschool Perils," *Parents,* October 2002, pp. 125ff.

194   Autism up 273 percent: In California. Laura Fording, "Autism Alert," *Newsweek Online,* May 22, 2003.

194   Milk as "insidious ingredient": Susan Carlton,"Living with Food Allergies," *Parents,* August 1995, pp. 28ff.

194   A "fighting chance": Described in Jane Brody, "Empowering Children to Thwart Abductors," *New York Times,* Jan. 26, 2003.

194   Curing autism by banning dairy: Karyn Seroussi, "We Cured Our Son's Autism," *Parents,* February 2000, pp. 118ff.

195   " 'Look at the neurotic parent . . .' ": Paul Ehrlich, a pediatric immunologist in New York City, quoted in Susan Dominus, "The Allergy Prison," *New York Times Magazine,* June 10, 2001, pp. 63ff.

195   "What oversights . . .": Alvin Rosenfeld and Nicole Wise, *The Overscheduled Child: Avoiding the Hyper-Parenting Trap,* (New York: St. Martin's/Griffin, 2000), pp. 6–7.

196   School violence has dropped: Barbara Kantrowitz, "The New Age of Anxiety," *Newsweek,* Aug. 23, 1999, pp. 39ff.

196   More than half of parents worried . . . 41 percent feared: "What Matters Most: A Newsweek Poll," *Newsweek Special Edition,* May (Spring/Summer), 1997, p. 6.

196   Three-quarters of parent: *Parents* magazine poll, March, 2000; and Furedi, p. 7.

196   Less than one percent of children: Betty Holcolmb and Michaele Weissman, "The Nanny Case," *Working Mother,* March 1998, pp. 18ff.

196   Incidence of food allergies among children under three . . . and for the population at large: Jim Atkinson, "Food Fright," *Texas Monthly,* August 1997, pp. 64ff. Stats on incidence are from this article and also from Dominus.

197   "Two-thirds of parents were worrying . . .": Charles J. Whalen, "The Age of Anxiety," *USA Today Magazine,* Sept. 1996, pp. 14ff.

198   "Many believe . . .": "Do Workplace Woes Signal the End of the American Dream?" *USA Today Magazine,* August 1995, pp. 10ff.

198   "Age of Anxiety": Whalen, p. 14.

198   Our age group: All information in this paragraph is from Ted Halstead, "A Politics for Generation X," *Atlantic Monthly Online,* August 1999. Halstead also notes that real median weekly earnings for men aged 20 to 34 fell by about a third between the years 1973 and the end of the century.

199   "Financialization": Kevin Phillips, "The Cycles of Financial Scandal," *New York Times,* July 17, 2002, p. A19.

200   In 1998, the 13,000 richest . . . had incomes 300 times that of average families . . . top 0.01 percent were earning . . . with top executives earning: Paul Krugman, "For Richer," *New York Times Magazine,* Oct. 20, 2002, p. 62.

200   Families' incomes having fallen almost 4 percent: Sylvia Ann Hewlett and Cornel West, *The War Against Parents* (Boston and New York: Houghton Mifflin, 1998), p. 61.

200   In middle-class families where incomes did rise: Krugman.

200   52 percent of parents were afraid . . . 36 percent feared . . . 35 percent feared: "What Matters Most: A Newsweek Poll," *Newsweek Special Edition,* May (Spring/Summer), 1997, p. 6.

201   Middle-income families' incomes no higher: Robert H. Frank, "Why Living in a Rich Society Makes Us Feel Poor," *New York Times Magazine,* October 15, 2000, pp. 62ff.

201   For families our age: Halstead.

201   "Head for the hills . . . ": Vince Passaro, "Who'll Stop the Drain?: Reflections on the Art of Going Broke," *Harper's Magazine,* August 1998, pp. 35ff.

201   Number of people filing for bankruptcy: Bob Herbert, "Caught in the Credit Card Vise," *New York Times,* Sept. 22, 2003, p. A17.

201   1.3 million filings for bankruptcy: Passaro.

201   And in 2003: Christine Dugas, "Middle Class Barely Treads Water," *USA Today,* Sept. 15, 2003, p. 1B.

202   The crippling burden of debt: Halstead. Much of this was student loan debt, he writes, which had climbed from 1977 to 1997 from a median amount of $2,000 to $15,000.

202   Price of a three-bedroom house in San Francisco: John Ryan, "Endangered Species," *San Francisco Chronicle,* March 5, 2002, p. A17. Also see: Tim Lemke, "Home Owning Elusive for Many," *Washington Times,* May 9, 2003, p. C7.

202   In the 1950s, house payments ate up 14 percent: By 1987 . . . : Frank Levy, *Dollars and Dreams: The Changing American Income Distribution* (New York: Russell Sage Foundation, 1987), p. 68.

202   80 percent of moderate- and low-income homeowners: Dugas.

202   In 2003, a family of four: Jeff Madrick, "Necessities, not luxuries are driving Americans into debt, a new book says," *New York Times,* Sept. 4, 2003, p. C2.

202   Health care costs: Madrick.

202   "The new middle-class poverty": Abby Ellin, "Gambling on Good Health," *New York Times,* Sept. 21, 2003, Sect. 3, p. 8. Also see Dugas: in 2003, the average employee contribution toward health insurance in America was $2,412, up 13 percent since 2002. And Madrick: the cost of health care rose about 8 percent each year from 1973 to 2000, greatly outpacing incomes.

202   "Typical families . . .": Madrick.

203   Cost of care for a preschooler higher than state college tuition: Jody Heymann, *The Widening Gap: Why America's Working Families Are in Jeopardy and What Can Be Done About It* (New York: Basic Books, 2000), p. 50.

203   Families spending 9 to 25 percent of their income: U.S. Department of the Treasury, *Investing in Child Care: Challenges Facing Working Parents and the Private Sector Response,* 1997.

203   Low-income families: "Low-income families spend as much as 35 percent of their incomes on child care—much more than higher-income families," writes Karen Christopher, "Family-Friendly Europe," *American Prospect,* April 8, 2002, p. 59. This entire issue of *The American Prospect* was devoted to "The Politics of Family."

203   Credit card debt as "Band-Aid": "New Report, 'Borrowing to Make Ends Meet,' Finds Credit Card Debt Explosion," press release, *Demos,* Sept. 8, 2003.

203   In 2000, women with children under six were telling pollsters: Results from survey, "Women's Voices 2000," carried out by the Center for Policy Alternatives in partnership with Lifetime Television.

204   Advantageous tax rates . . . infrastructure: Robert H. Frank, *Luxury Fever* (New York: Free Press, 1999), p. 5

204   "It's all too easy . . .": Krugman, "For Richer."

204   "Star system": Robert H. Frank and Philip J. Cook, *The Winner-Take-All Society* (New York: The Free Press, 1995), pp. 3–4.

205   "Winner-Take-All Society": Frank and Cook, p. 2.

205   Obsessive mother/malnourished child: "There's definitely a certain personality type," Dr. Hugh Sampson, chief of the division of pediatric allergy and immunology at Mount Sinai Medical Center, told the *New York Times* in 2001. Some parents, said Sampson, appear to have a strange personal investment in the idea of their children's food allergies. Indeed, the *Times* reported, he said he'd heard of parents who "seem so invested in their child's unproven food allergies that the child ends up dangerously malnourished." In Susan Dominus, "The Allergy Prison," *New York Times Magazine*, June 10, 2001, p. 63.

205   Parents nearly starved baby on "vegan" regime: Greg Retsinas, "Couple Guilty of Assault in Vegan Case," *New York Times*, April 5, 2003, p. D1.

206   Behaviors to be "fixed" by occupational therapy: Stacey Colino, "Problem Kid or Label? Some Say Sensory Integration Dysfunction Is a Legitimate Diagnosis. Others Call It a New Name for a Familiar Behavior," *Washington Post*, Feb. 26, 2002, p. F1.

206   New York City parents: Vickers, Marcia, "Why Can't We Let Boys Be Boys?" *Business Week*, May 26, 2003, pp. 84ff.

207   "Extreme separation anxiety disorder": Shankar Vedantam, "Drug Found to Curb Kids' Debilitating Social Anxiety," *Washington Post*, April 26, 2001, p. A1.

207   50 to 75 percent of children: Furedi, p. 123.

207   "Mommy Panic": Susan J. Kraus, "Mommy Panic," *Redbook*, February 1995, pp. 148ff.

208   "'Embodiment'": Barbara Hey, "Fat and Loathing," *Allure*, May 1996, pp. 144ff.

210   "Grace" of acceptance: "The Inner Life of Executive Kids: A Conversation with Child Psychiatrist Robert Coles," *Harvard Business Review*, November 2001, pp. 63ff.

210   Teacher salaries and SAT scores on the decline: Frank, p. 58.

210   Enrollment in private day schools: Laura Sessions Stepp, "Teaching Timidity to Kids," *Washington Post*, Dec. 6, 2002.

210   Home-schooling: Margaret Talbot, "The New Counterculture," *Atlantic Monthly*, November, 2001, pp. 136ff.

211   What staff there is: Sharon Hays, *Flat Broke with Children* (New York: Oxford University Press, 2003), p. 40.

211   Not all states require: This information is from Hal Karp, "Preschool Perils," *Parents*, October 2002, pp. 125ff.

213   The tax code in the postwar years: Hewlett and West, p. 98.

213   "The most massive government subsidization": Stephanie Coontz, "Nostalgia as Ideology," *American Prospect*, April 8, 2002, pp. 26ff.

213   "Encouraging family formation . . .": Stephanie Coontz, *The Way We Never Were* (New York: Basic Books, 1992, 2000), p. 79.

213   In 1974 . . . In 1999: Halstead.

213   The cost of higher education: Edward B. Fiske, "Student Debt Reshaping Colleges and Careers," *New York Times*, Aug. 3, 1986, Section 12, p. 34.

214   "The welfare state . . .": Levy, pp. 161–163. (63 percent of families in 1973 could be labeled middle-class by his accounting, versus 51 percent in 1996; 13 percent in 1973 had incomes over $80,000, compared with 21 percent in 1996 and the percentage of those termed poor increased from 8 to 11 percent in that period.)

CHAPTER 9: WINNER–TAKE–ALL PARENTING

215 "In the last 20 years . . .": "The Inner Life of Executive Kids: A Conversation with Child Psychiatrist Robert Coles," *Harvard Business Review,* November 2001, pp. 63ff.

215 "Standing on the sidelines . . .": Drew Lindsay, "Kids Just Wanna Have Fun," *Washingtonian,* September 2002.

216 "Sink down into hardship and discomfort": William Damon quoted in Barbara Kantrowitz and Pat Wingert, "The Parent Trap," *Newsweek,* Jan. 29, 2001, pp. 48ff.

218 "A robust economy . . .": *Publishers Weekly,* April 10, 2000, p. 23.

220 "Conquer, conquer, conquer . . .": "The Inner Life of Executive Kids," p. 63.

220 Children loved as "results," etc.: Arlie Russell Hochschild, *The Commercialization of Intimate Life* (Berkeley: University of California Press, 2003), pp. 147–148.

221 "We need to have parents . . .": quoted in Pat Wechsler, "It's 8 PM and Mom's Out Trading," *Business Week,* June 14, 1999, pp. 44ff.

221 "Product development": William Doherty quoted in Austin Bunn, "Terribly Smart," *New York Times Magazine,* March 24, 2002, p. 17.

222 LeaderWorks: Paul Tough, "The Year in Ideas: Dad's Performance Review," *New York Times Magazine,* Dec. 15, 2002, p. 80.

223 Grade-optimizing strategies: Evelyn Porreca Vuko, "Before School Starts, Try This Homework," *Washington Post,* Aug. 20, 2002, p. C10.

224 "It's part of our culture . . .": Educational psychologist quoted by Jane Gross in "Paying for a Disability Diagnosis to Gain Time on College Boards," *New York Times,* Sept. 26, 2002, p. A1.

225 "An especially precious type of equality . . .": Mickey Kaus, *The End of Equality* (New York: Basic Books, 1992), p. 6. Cited in Frank and Cook, p. 228.

225 "Turbo-charged capitalism . . . ": Edward Luttwak, "Turbo-Charged Capitalism Is the Enemy of Family Values," *New Perspectives Quarterly,* March 22, 1995, pp. 10ff.

225 "Corruption" of American life: Kevin Phillips, "The Cycles of Financial Scandal," *New York Times,* July 17, 2002, p. A19.

225 Our "inner Gekko": Paul Krugman, "Greed Is Bad," *New York Times,* June 4, 2002, p. A19.

226 "I hesitate to say . . .": Rachel Cusk, "To Smack or Not to Smack," *New Statesman,* March 12, 2001.

227 Hollywood "balancing act": Jan Lindstrom, "A Delicate Balance: Players Juggle Fast-Track Careers with Motherhood," *Variety,* Nov. 29, 2000, p. A1.

227 Time as a "form of personal capital": Arlie Russell Hochschild, "There's No Place Like Work," *New York Times Magazine,* April 20, 1997, p. 51.

230 First-time depression: Laura Sessions Stepp, "Teaching Timidity to Kids," *Washington Post,* Dec. 6, 2002, p. F1.

230 Increases in eating disorders, alcohol abuse, and other problems: Barbara Kantrowitz and Pat Wingert, "The Parent Trap," *Newsweek,* Jan. 29, 2001, pp. 48ff.

230 Suicide rate for teens up 114 percent: Laura Sessions Stepp, "Perfect Problems: These Teens Are at the Top in Everything. Including Stress," *Washington Post,* May 5, 2002, p. F1.

230 Harris poll: Ibid.

231 Children as young as 11: Stepp, "Teaching Timidity to Kids."

231 "Overuse injuries": Ibid.

231 "No child ever did anything repetitive enough . . .": Dr. Lyle Micheli, quoted in Lindsay.

NOTES

231 "Some five-year-olds . . .": Judy Azzara, "Now More Than Ever: Unspoiling Our Kids," *Education Digest,* November 2001, pp. 16ff.

233 "Selfism": James H. McMillan, Judy Singh and Leo G. Simonetta, "Self-Oriented Self-Esteem Self-Destructs," *Education Digest,* March 1995, pp. 9ff.

234 Princeton University students: Profiled in David Brooks, "The Organization Kid," *Atlantic Monthly,* April 2001, pp. 40ff.

234 Children's immune systems weakened by excessive cleanliness: See Susan Dominus, "The Allergy Prison," *New York Times Magazine,* June 10, 2001, pp. 63ff. Also see: Charlotte Fahrländer Braun, et al., "Environmental Exposure to Endotoxin and its Relation to Asthma in School Age Children," *New England Journal of Medicine* 347, pp. 869–877, Sept. 19, 2002, and Scott T. Weiss, "Eat Dirt—The Hygiene Hypothesis and Allergic Disease," *New England Journal of Medicine* 347, pp. 930–931, Sept. 19, 2002.

235 Psychologists' warnings in 1963: Betty Friedan, *The Feminine Mystique* (New York: Laurel, 1983), p. 30.

235 On breeding "learned helplessness": Arlene Skolnick, "The Myth of the Vulnerable Child," *Psychology Today,* February 1978, pp. 56ff.

235 *"Spielraum"*: Bruno Bettelheim, "The Importance of Play," *Atlantic Monthly,* March 1987, pp. 35ff.

235 "Hand-and-foot disease" and "Frantic Family Syndrome": John Rosemond, "Hey Mom! Get a Life!" *Better Homes and Gardens,* May 1996, p. 106, and "Frantic Family Syndrome," *Better Homes and Gardens,* March 1996, p. 52.

235 "Mach 3" moms: Nick Wishart, "With Kids in Sports, Parents Have to Be on the Go," *St. Louis Post-Dispatch,* July 23, 2001, p. 9.

236 "When free time was actually free . . . : Steven A. Cohen, ed., *The Games We Played* (New York: Simon & Schuster, 2001).

236 "The essential wonder . . .": David Maraniss, "The Sweet Long Days," in Cohen, *The Games We Played,* p. 28.

236 "It was all so much fun . . .": Patricia Heaton, *Motherhood and Hollywood* (New York: Villard, 2002), p. 70.

CHAPTER 10: WONDERFUL HUSBANDS

241 Ruth Marcus . . . almost universally condemned: Author interview. And see Ruth Marcus, "What Mommies Want," *Washington Post,* May 11, 2003, p. B7.

242 "This generation of women . . . ": Naomi Wolf, *Misconceptions* (New York: Doubleday, 2001), p. 261.

243 Hot new statistic: Kathleen Deveny, "We're Not in the Mood," *Newsweek,* June 30, 2003, pp. 40ff.

243 "Sexless marriages": Dr. Phil website: www.drphil.com.

244 "Think about it . . .": Patricia Heaton, *Motherhood and Hollywood* (New York: Villard, 2002), p. 196.

244 Kate Reddy: Allison Pearson, *I Don't Know How She Does It* (New York: Knopf, 2002), p. 9.

244 Mothers' lack of libido and "inexplicable rage": Cathi Hanauer, *The Bitch in the House* (New York: William Morrow, 2002), p. xiv.

244 A "quiet, stubborn knot . . .": Wolf, *Misconceptions,* pp. 236ff.

245 "What's interesting . . .": Caitlin Flanagan, "The Wifely Duty," *Atlantic Monthly,* January/February 2003, pp. 171ff.

246 "Given the absence . . . of support . . .": Wendy Kaminer, "Feminism's Identity Crisis," *Atlantic Monthly,* October 1993, pp. 51ff.

248 Mothers spend four times as much time with children: Carin Rubenstein, "Superdad Needs a Reality Check," *New York Times,* April 16, 1998, p. A23.

248 Working mothers spend twice as much time as working fathers: Andrew Hacker, *Mismatch: The Growing Gulf Between Men and Women* (New York: Scribner, 2003), p. 56.

248 University of Michigan study: cited in Hacker, pp. 55–56.

248 The "psychological parent": excerpt from Jean Curtis's *Working Mothers* (Doubleday, 1976), published in "The 'Psychological Parent,'" *McCall's,* December 1975, pp. 42ff.

249 Hoots of laughter: Carin Rubenstein, "Superdad Needs a Reality Check," *New York Times,* April 16, 1998, p. A23.

249 Studies consistently show: Deveny.

249 Working women alone: Susan Maushart, *Wifework* (New York and London: Bloomsbury, 2002), p. 92. Her source is Ken Dempsey, "Attempting to Explain Women's Perceptions of the Fairness of the Division of Housework," in *Journal of Family Studies,* April 1999 pp. 3–24.

249 "Being out of work . . .": Peg Tyre and Daniel McGinn, "She Works, He Doesn't," *Newsweek,* May 12, 2003, pp. 44ff.

250 Average working hours: According to a 1997 study by the International Labor Organization, fathers were working an average of 50.9 hours a week and mothers 41.4 hours a week. Reported in Barbara Kantrowitz and Pat Wingert, "The Parent Trap," *Newsweek,* January 29, 2001, pp. 48ff. Also see: Harriet B. Presser, "Toward a 24-hour Economy," *Science,* June 11, 1999, pp. 1778ff.

250 Fathers earning three times as much as mothers: Janet C. Gornick, "Reconcilable Differences," *American Prospect,* April 8, 2002, pp. 42ff.

250 Status gap and power gap: As per interviews. Also see: Jena McGregor, "Love & Money," *Smart Money,* October 2003, pp. 75ff.

252 Our generation of husbands: Keith H. Hammonds, "The Daddy Trap," *Business Week,* Sept. 21, 1998, pp. 56ff.

252 Paternity leave frowned upon: Mary Beth Grover, "Daddy Stress," *Forbes,* Sept. 6, 1999, pp. 202ff.

252 "Daddy penalty": Orenstein, p. 285. Her sources are Tamar Lewin, "Men Whose Wives Work Earn Less, Studies Show," *New York Times,* Oct. 12, 1994, p. A1; and Betsy Morris, "Is Family Wrecking Your Career?" *Fortune,* March 17, 1997, p. 71.

253 "Consoling and commiserating": Hacker, p. 4.

253 "The Wifely Art . . .": Maushart, p. 144.

254 55 percent of men: Deveny.

256 Dangerous territory: The un-dangerous alternative, of course, is Girls' Night Out or the book club, as in Rebecca R. Kahlenberg, "A Woman's Place Is with Her Friends," *Washington Post,* March 28, 2002, p. C8.

256 Maggie Owen: Sabine Durant, *Having It and Eating It* (New York: Riverhead, 2002).

257 "Mommy frumps": See *McCall's* article of that title, April 1996, pp. 118ff.

CHAPTER 11: FOR A POLITICS OF QUALITY OF LIFE

258 "Motherhood has been the center . . .": Ellen Goodman, "And the Kids?" *Washington Post,* May 25, 2002, p. A31.

258 "The Opt-Out Revolution": Lisa Belkin, "The Opt-Out Revolution," *New York Times Magazine,* October 26, 2003, pp. 42ff.

258 "Rightful ownership of the universe": Belkin, p. 44.

261 "An earnestness too deep for satire": Marjorie Williams, "A Working Mom's Comedy," *Washington Post,* October 2, 2002, p. A17.

263 Twin religions: This is no exaggeration. House majority leader Tom DeLay has said he was on a mission from God to promote a "biblical worldview" in American politics. (Paul Krugman, "Gotta Have Faith," *New York Times,* Dec. 17, 2002) The Southern Baptist Convention, the largest Protestant denomination in the United States, has adopted as formal policy a statement that a wife should "submit graciously to the servant leadership of her husband." Former secretary of education and drug czar William Bennett has said: "We must attempt to shape a society anchored in . . . the deep enduring truths" of Christian belief. "There is a natural order," he writes, "that we attempt to do away with at the peril of the very fabric of our lives." (William J. Bennett, *The Broken Hearth* [New York: Doubleday, 2001], pp. 170 and 183)

264 France's profamily politics: There is much that we in the United States can learn from Europe about taking a pragmatic rather than a moralistic approach to the issue of motherhood, notably in the way that certain conservative, tradition-bound countries find ways to embrace, rather than run from, modernity. Look at Belgium—where employees can stop work for one year or cut their working hours by up to half for up to five years without losing benefits or risking losing their jobs while receiving a paid allowance of about $500 a month. Universal public education in Belgium begins at age two and a half, and nearly all three-to-four-year-olds are enrolled. Working parents are entitled to a tax deduction worth 80 percent of their child care expenses for children under age three (if the child care is "regulated" and "supervised"), and stay-at-home mothers benefit from a higher per-child family allowance to offset their loss of income. We might look too at Italy, which offers universal preschool, the opportunity for both parents to take up to ten months of leave after the birth of a child, and publicly funded day care centers that, despite giving priority to low-income families, are of such high quality that they actually draw a majority of their children from middle- and upper-income homes. Even the U.K., our spiritual cousin in terms of free-market economics, provides paternity leave to those who will take it. (Source: The Clearinghouse on International Development in Child Youth and Family Policies at Columbia University)

264 The United States has at times found itself with no foreign allies other than Muslim fundamentalists: Stryker McGuire, "New Moral Order?" *Newsweek International,* Dec. 9, 2002, pp. 42ff.

268 A $250 tax break: Robert Pear, "Clinton to Propose Tax Break for Parents Who Stay at Home," *New York Times,* January 19, 1999, p. A15.

268 More than a third of working parents have no sick leave or vacation leave: Karen Kornbluh, "The Parent Trap," *Atlantic Monthly,* January/February 2003, pp. 111ff.

269 46 percent of U.S. workers eligible for unpaid leave under FMLA: Jane Waldfogel, "Family Leave Coverage in the 1990s," *Monthly Labor Review,* October 1999, pp. 13–21.

269 Parents not taking advantage of their leave: In 2000, 78 percent of covered workers who reported needing leave did not take it because they could not afford unpaid leave. And 88 percent of them said they would have taken leave if they had received some pay. U.S. Department of Labor, *Family and Medical Leave Surveys, 2000 Update.*

270   "Demonstration grants": Theodora Ooms, "Marriage Plus," *American Prospect,* April 8, 2002, pp. 24ff.

270   It's about ideology: In 1999, the Republican-dominated House of Representatives was able to find $2 billion to pass the "Fathers Count" Act, which was a five-year block grant to support local fatherhood projects and promote marriage. The late 1990s saw a number of fatherhood groups emerge ranging from local community groups seeking to encourage "responsible fatherhood" to national groups with a theological agenda to get men to reclaim their roles as heads of families. This theologically based, often socially reactionary movement received federal funds and had a direct impact on public policy. After welfare reform did away with AFDC money for poor mothers, some of the Temporary Assistance to Needy Families block grant money that replaced it was spent on profatherhood initiatives. While the mothers were pushed out into the workforce, the fathers were entitled to use the grants to pursue higher education, participate in training programs, and seek higher-paying jobs. In Pennsylvania, a special Health and Human Services grant was used to give them "better access to their children." The 1997 Balanced Budget Act authorized the use of TANF funding to pay for job training for noncustodial parents, effectively transferring money that once would have been spent on mothers to fathers, in an effort to validate their efforts to earn money. (For all this, see: Leslie R. Wolfe, Jennifer Tucker, and Tanya Chin Ross, *Report on the Symposium on Multiethnic Feminist Visions of Fatherhood: Promoting Feminist Family Policy,* Center for Women Policy Studies, December 1999, p. 4. Information also comes from author interview with Tucker.)

270   "What reduces crime . . .": Jerry Adler, "Building a Better Dad," *Newsweek,* June 17, 1996, p. 58.

270   The short-lived Clinton administration attempt: Author interview with a former administration child-care policymaker.

270   Hundreds of millions of dollars for day care in military: In 1997, the cost of providing day care for 200,000 children of military personnel was $273 million, according to Shankar Vedantam, "Clinton Touts Military as Model on Child Care," *Philadelphia Inquirer,* April 18, 1997, p. A3.

270   Subsidized day care for federal workers: "Work/Life Programs are Part of Total Benefits Package," *Federal Human Resources Week,* June 27, 2003.

271    $50 billion a year: Barbara R. Bergmann and Suzanne W. Helburn, *America's Child Care Problem: The Way Out* (New York: Palgrave, 2001), p. 3. They advocate "a large, active, and expensive federal program, providing both finance and a national framework for quality improvement."

271   71 percent of women surveyed: "Women's Voices 2000" poll, carried out by the Center for Policy Alternatives and Lifetime Television. Also see Sonja Steptoe, "Ready, Set, Relax!," *Time,* Oct. 27, 2003, p. 38.

272   74 percent of women and 70 percent of men: Susan B. Garland, "Wooing Minivan Moms," *Business Week,* Sept. 20, 1999, pp. 83ff.

272   A plurality of both men and women: According to "Women's Voices," nearly 60 percent of women say the government should help them find solutions to their child-care problems. A plurality of both women and men now believe there should be a government solution to child care.

272   Schwarzenegger initiative: Michael Finnegan, "Worker's Comp May Test Governor's Battle Tactics," *Los Angeles Times,* March 26, 2004, p. B1.

272 More than $200 billion: The tax cut will cost $291.3 billion in fiscal 2005, according to David Corn, "Where's the Outrage?," *The Nation,* June 4, 2003.

272 $27.2 billion tax exemption: *Analytic Perspective, Fiscal Year 2002,* Office of Management and Budget (Washington, D.C., 2001), Table 5-1.

272 $85 billion a year: Karen Christopher, writing in *American Prospect* (and citing a January 1–15, 2001, *Prospect* article by Janet Gornick and Marcia Meyers) noted that "if the United States were to spend the same share of gross domestic product on subsidized child care and paid leave as France does, we would need to increase expenditures by at most $85 billion yearly. This seems a huge outlay, but it is only about 3 percent of President George W. Bush's recently proposed $2.1 trillion budget for 2002 and far less than the annual cost of his tax cut." See "Family-Friendly Europe," *American Prospect,* April 8, 2002, pp. 59ff.

273 Tax policies calibrated to permit the wealthy to keep most of their money: Paul Krugman writes, "The major tax cuts of the past 25 years, the Reagan cuts of the 1980s and the recent Bush cuts were both heavily tilted towards the very well off . . . more than half the Bush tax cut will eventually go to the top one percent of families." This all was accompanied by tax policies that impoverished those with less money (the one major tax increase in recent decades, the increase in payroll taxes in the 1980s, affected working class families most deeply). See "For Richer," *New York Times Magazine,* October 20, 2002, pp. 62ff.

273 A culturewide impoverishment: That idea is from Frank.

273 Percentage of people who describe themselves as "very happy" fell: David Leonhardt, "If Richer Isn't Happier, What Is?," *New York Times,* May 19, 2001.

273 Couples working split shifts: Harriet B. Presser, "Toward a 24-Hour Economy," *Science,* June 11, 1999, pp. 1778ff.

273 A Gallup poll: Jeffrey M. Jones, "Parents of Young Children Are Most Stressed Americans," Gallup News Service, November 8, 2002.

274 "If women were really *people* . . .": Betty Friedan, quoting *The Feminine Mystique* in "Up From the Kitchen Floor," *New York Times Magazine,* March 4, 1973, pp. 8ff.

274 "All talk": Friedan cited in Lucy Komisar, "The New Feminism," *Saturday Review,* February 21, 1970, pp. 27ff.

276 *"The original idea of feminism . . .":* Barbara Ehrenreich, "Why We Lost the ERA," *Atlantic Monthly,* October 1986, pp. 98ff.

278 Chains in our own minds: "[C]hains in her own mind and spirit," Friedan wrote in *The Feminine Mystique,* p. 31.

CHAPTER 12: CONCLUSION

281 French children too are being reared like racehorses: Irène Inchauspé and Valérie Peiffer, "A Quoi Rêvent Nos Enfants?" ("What Do Our Children Dream Of?") *Le Point,* January 2, 2004, pp. 44ff.

Bibliography

Bass, Ellen, and Laura David. *The Courage to Heal: A Guide for Women Survivors of Child Sexual Abuse.* New York: Perennial Library, 1988.

Belkin, Lisa. *Life's Work: Confessions of an Unbalanced Mom.* New York: Simon & Schuster, 2002.

Bennett, William J. *The Broken Hearth: Reversing the Moral Collapse of the American Family.* New York: Doubleday, 2001.

Bergmann, Barbara R., and Suzanne W. Helburn. *America's Child Care Problem: The Way Out.* New York: Palgrave, 2001.

Bernard, Jessie. *The Future of Motherhood.* New York: Dial Press, 1974.

Bialosky, Jill. "How We Became Strangers." In Cathi Hanauer, *The Bitch in the House.* New York: William Morrow, 2002, pp. 111–121.

Block, Ruth H. "American Feminine Ideals in Transition: The Rise of the Moral Mother, 1785–1815." In Nancy F. Cott, ed., *History of Women in the United States: Domestic Ideology and Domestic Work, Part 1.* Munich: K. G. Saur, 1992, pp. 3–28.

Bowlby, John. *Attachment and Loss.* New York: Basic Books, 1969.

Brazelton, T. Berry, and Stanley I. Greenspan. *The Irreducible Needs of Children: What Every Child Must Have to Grow, Learn, and Flourish.* Cambridge: Perseus Books, 2000.

Brown, Catrina, and Karin Jasper, eds. *Consuming Passions: Feminist Approaches to Weight Preoccupation and Eating Disorders.* Toronto: Second Story Press, 1993.

Bruch, Hilde. *The Golden Cage: The Enigma of Anorexia Nervosa.* Cambridge: Harvard University Press, 1978.

Brumberg, Joan Jacobs. *Fasting Girls: The History of Anorexia Nervosa.* New York: New American Library 1989.

Caplan, Paula J., and Ian Hall-McCorquodale. "Mother-Blaming in Major Clinical Journals." *American Journal of Orthopsychiatry* 55 (3), July 1985, pp. 345–353.

Caplan, Paula J. "Mother-Blaming." In Molly Ladd-Taylor and Lauri Umansky, eds., *"Bad" Mothers: The Politics of Blame in Twentieth-Century America.* New York and London: New York University Press, 1998, pp. 127–144.

Chafe, William H. *The American Woman: Her Changing Social, Economic, and Political Roles, 1920–1970.* London and New York: Oxford University Press, 1972.

Chafe, William H. *Women and Equality: Changing Patterns in American Culture.* New York: Oxford University Press, 1977.

Chafe, William H. *The Paradox of Change.* New York: Oxford University Press, 1991.

Chernin, Kim. *The Obsession: Reflections on the Tyranny of Slenderness.* New York: Harper & Row, 1981.

Chess, Stella, and Alexander Thomas. "Infant Bonding: Mystique and Reality." *American Journal of Orthospychiatry* 52 (2), April 1982, pp. 213–221.

Chira, Susan. *A Mother's Place.* New York: HarperCollins, 1998.

Christensen, Kate. "Killing the Puritan Within." In Cathi Hanauer, *The Bitch in the House.* New York: William Morrow, 2002, pp. 73–84.

Cohen, Steven A., ed. *The Games We Played: A Celebration of Childhood and Imagination.* New York: Simon & Schuster, 2001.

Coontz, Stephanie. *The Way We Never Were.* New York: Basic Books, 2000.

Cott, Nancy F., ed. *History of Women in the United States: Domestic Ideology and Domestic Work, Part 1.* Munich: K. G. Saur, 1992.

Crittenden, Ann. *The Price of Motherhood: Why the Most Important Job in the World Is Still the Least Valued.* New York: Metropolitan Books, 2001.

Crittenden, Danielle. *What Our Mothers Didn't Tell Us: Why Happiness Eludes the Modern Woman.* New York: Simon & Schuster, 1999.

Davis, Flora. *Moving the Mountain: The Women's Movement in America Since 1966.* New York: Touchstone, 1991.

Denfeld, Rene. *The New Victorians: A Young Woman's Challenge to the Old Feminist Order.* New York: Warner Books, 1995.

Deutsch, Helene. *The Psychology of Women.* New York: Gruner & Stratton, 1944.

Dodson, Fitzhugh. *How to Parent.* Los Angeles: Nash Pub., 1970.

Douglas, Susan. *Where the Girls Are: Growing Up Female with the Mass Media.* New York: Penguin, 1994.

Doyle, Susan. *The Surrendered Wife: A Practical Guide to Finding Intimacy, Passion, and Peace with a Man.* New York: Fireside, 2001.

Durrant, Sabine. *Having It and Eating It.* New York: Riverhead Books, 2002.

Edelman, Hope. "The Myth of Co-Parenting: How It Was Supposed to Be. How It Was." In Cathi Hanauer, *The Bitch in the House.* New York: William Morrow, 2002, pp. 171–180.

Ehrenreich, Barbara. *The Hearts of Men.* New York: Anchor, 1983.

Epstein, Cynthia Fuchs. *Woman's Place: Options and Limits in Professional Careers.* Berkeley and Los Angeles: University of California Press, 1970.

Epstein, Sue. "Mothering to Death." In Molly Ladd-Taylor, and Lauri Umansky, eds., *"Bad" Mothers: The Politics of Blame in Twentieth-Century America.* New York and London: New York University Press, 1998, pp. 257–262.

Faludi, Susan. *Backlash: The Undeclared War Against American Women.* New York: Crown, 1991.

Faludi, Susan. *Stiffed: The Betrayal of the American Man.* New York: William Morrow, 1999.

Farrell, Amy Erdman. *Yours in Sisterhood: "Ms." Magazine and the Promise of Popular Feminism.* Chapel Hill and London: University of North Carolina Press, 1988.

Figes, Kate. *Life After Birth: What Even Your Friends Won't Tell You About Motherhood.* New York: St. Martin's Press, 2001.

Findlen, Barbara. *Listen Up: Voices from the Next Feminist Generation.* Seattle: Seal Press, 1995.

Finnamore, Suzanne. *The Zygote Chronicles.* New York: Grove Press, 2002.

Firestone, Shulamith. *The Dialectic of Sex.* New York: William Morrow and Company, 1970.

Fonda, Jane. *Jane Fonda's Workout Book.* New York: Simon & Schuster, 1981.

Forward, Susan, with Craig Buck. *Toxic Parents: Overcoming Their Hurtful Legacy and Reclaiming Your Life.* New York: Bantam, 1989.

Foster, Patricia, ed. *Minding the Body: Women Writers on Body and Soul.* New York: Doubleday, 1994.

Frank, Robert H. *Luxury Fever.* New York: The Free Press, 1999.

Frank, Robert H., and Philip J. Cook. *The Winner-Take-All Society.* New York: The Free Press, 1997.

Friday, Nancy. *My Mother/My Self: The Daughter's Search for Identity.* New York: Delta, 1977.

Friedan, Betty. *The Feminine Mystique.* New York: Laurel, 1983.

Furedi, Frank. *Paranoid Parenting: Why Ignoring the Experts May Be Best for Your Child.* Chicago: Chicago Review Press, 2002.

Galinsky, Ellen, and Judy David. *The Preschool Years: Family Strategies That Work.* New York: Times Books, 1988.

Garskof, Michele Hoffnung. *Roles Women Play: Readings Towards Women's Liberation.* Belmont, Calif: Brooks/Cole Pub., 1971.

Ginott, Haim G. *Between Parent and Child.* New York: Avon, 1969.

Goldin, Claudia. *Understanding the Gender Gap: An Economic History of American Women.* New York and Oxford: Oxford University Press, 1990.

Gordon, Richard A. *Anorexia and Bulimia: Anatomy of a Social Epidemic.* Cambridge: Basil Blackwell, 1990.

Green, Arnold. "The Middle-Class Male Child and Neurosis." *American Sociological Review* II(1), 1946, pp. 31–41.

Greenberg, Dan. "How to Be a Jewish Mother: A Very Lovely Training Manual." Los Angeles: Price Stern Sloan 1964, 1975. Reprinted in Molly Ladd-Taylor and Lauri Umansky, eds., *"Bad" Mothers: The Politics of Blame in Twentieth-Century America.* New York and London: New York University Press, 1998, pp. 271–272.

Greer, Germaine. *The Female Eunuch.* New York: McGraw-Hill, 1971.

Hacker, Andrew. *Mismatch: The Growing Gulf Between Men and Women.* New York: Scribner, 2003.

Hanauer, Cathi. *The Bitch in the House.* New York: William Morrow, 2002.

Hanauer, Cathi. "Breastfeeding: The Agony and the Ecstasy." In Christina Baker Kline, *Child of Mine.* New York: Hyperion, 1997, pp. 181–191.

Hays, Sharon. *The Cultural Contradictions of Motherhood.* New Haven: Yale University Press, 1996.

Hays, Sharon. *Flat Broke with Children: Women in the Age of Welfare Reform.* New York: Oxford University Press, 2003.

Heaton, Patricia. *Motherhood and Hollywood.* New York: Villard, 2002.

Herrick, Amy. "Mortal Terrors and Motherhood." In Christina Baker Kline, *Child of Mine*. New York: Hyperion, 1997, pp. 72–84.

Hewlett, Sylvia Ann. *A Lesser Life: The Myth of Women's Liberation in America*. New York: William Morrow and Co., 1986.

Hewlett, Sylvia Ann, and Cornell West. *The War Against Parents*. Boston and New York: Houghton Mifflin, 1998.

Heymann, Jody. *The Widening Gap: Why America's Working Families Are in Jeopardy and What Can Be Done About It*. New York: Basic Books, 2000.

Hochschild, Arlie Russell. *The Commercialization of Intimate Life: Notes from Home and Work*. Berkeley and Los Angeles: University of California Press, 2003.

Hrdy, Sarah Blaffer. *Mother Nature*. New York: Pantheon, 1999.

Hughes, Robert. *The Culture of Complaint*. New York: Oxford, 1993.

Hulbert, Ann. *Raising America: Experts, Parents, and a Century of Advice About Children*. New York: Knopf, 2003.

Hull, N. E. H., and Peter Charles Hoffer. *Roe v. Wade: The Abortion Rights Controversy in American History*. Lawrence: University Press of Kansas, 2001.

Israel, Betsy. *Bachelor Girl: The Secret History of Single Women in the Twentieth Century*. New York: William Morrow, 2002.

Kagan, Jerome. *Three Seductive Ideas*. Cambridge: Harvard University Press, 1998.

Kagan, Jerome. *Unstable Ideas: Temperament, Cognition and Self*. Cambridge: Harvard University Press, 1989.

Kaledin, Eugenia. *Mothers and More: American Women in the 1950s*. Boston: Twayne Publishers, 1984.

Kamen, Paula. *Feminist Fatale*. New York: Donald I. Fine, 1991.

Kaminer, Wendy. *A Fearful Freedom: Women's Flight from Equality*. Reading, Massachusetts: Addison-Wesley, 1990.

Kaus, Michey. *The End of Equality*. New York: Basic Books, 1992.

Keller, Nora Okja. "You'll Get Used to It." In Camille Peri and Kate Moses, eds., *Mothers Who Think*. New York: Villard, 1999.

Key, Ellen Karolina Sofia. *The Century of the Child*. New York and London: G. P. Putnam's Sons, 1909.

Kline, Christina Baker. *Child of Mine*. New York: Hyperion, 1997.

Kling, Cynthia. "Erotics 102: Staying Bad, Staying Married." In Cathi Hanauer, *The Bitch in the House*. New York: William Morrow, 2002, pp. 123–131.

Komarovsky, Mirra. *Women in the Modern World: Their Education and Their Dilemmas*. Boston: Little, Brown, 1953.

Krasnow, Iris. *Surrendering to Motherhood*. New York: Hyperion, 1997.

Ladd-Taylor, Molly, and Lauri Umansky, eds. *"Bad" Mothers: The Politics of Blame in Twentieth-Century America*. New York and London: New York University Press, 1998.

Lasch, Christopher. *The Culture of Narcissism*. New York: W. W. Norton, 1950.

Leach, Penelope. *Children First: What Our Society Must Do—and Is Not Doing—for Our Children Today*. New York: Knopf, 1994.

Lehrman, Karen. *The Lipstick Proviso: Women, Sex and Power in the Real World*. New York: Doubleday, 1997.

Levy, David. *Maternal Over-Protection*. New York: Columbia University Press, 1943.

Levy, Frank. *The New Dollars and Dreams: American Incomes and Economic Change*. New York: Russell Sage Foundation, 1998.

Lipsky, David, and Alexander Abrams. *Late Bloomers: Coming of Age in Today's America, The Right Place at the Wrong Time.* New York: Times Books, 1994.

Liu, Aimee. *Solitaire.* New York: Harper & Row, 1979.

Lopata, Helena Znaniecka. *Occupation: Housewife.* New York: Oxford University Press, 1971.

Lundberg, Ferdinand, and Marynia F. Farnham. *Modern Woman: The Lost Sex.* New York: Harper and Brothers, 1947.

Maduro, E. S. "Excuse Me While I Explode: My Mother, Myself, My Anger." In Cathi Hanauer, *The Bitch in the House.* New York: William Morrow, 2002, pp. 3–13.

Maraniss, David. "The Sweet Long Days." In Steven A. Cohen, ed., *The Games We Played: A Celebration of Childhood and Imagination.* New York: Simon & Schuster, 2001.

Margolis, Maxine L. *Mothers and Such: Views of American Women and Why They Changed.* Berkeley and Los Angeles: University of California Press, 1984.

Mathews, Glenna. *Just a Housewife: The Rise and Fall of Domesticity in America.* New York: Oxford University Press, 1987.

Maushart, Susan. *The Mask of Motherhood: How Becoming a Mother Changes Our Lives and Why We Never Talk About It.* New York: Penguin, 1999.

Maushart, Susan. *Wifework: What Marriage Really Means for Women.* New York and London: Bloomsbury, 2001.

McDonnell, Jane Taylor. "On Being the 'Bad' Mother of an Autistic Child." In Molly Ladd-Taylor and Lauri Umansky, eds., *"Bad" Mothers: The Politics of Blame in Twentieth-Century America.* New York and London: New York University Press, 1998.

McGinley, Phyllis. *Sixpence in Her Shoe.* New York: Macmillan, 1965.

Mendelson, Cheryl. *Home Comforts.* New York: Scribner, 1999.

Miller, Alice. *The Drama of the Gifted Child.* New York: Basic Books, 1990.

Miller, Daniel R., and Guy E. Swanson. *The Changing American Parent.* New York: John Wiley and Sons, 1958.

Mogel, Wendy. *The Blessing of a Skinned Knee: Using Jewish Teachings to Raise Self-Reliant Children.* New York: Penguin, 2001.

Nathan, Debbie, and Michael Snedeker. *Satan's Silence: Ritual Abuse and the Making of a Modern Witch Hunt.* New York: Basic Books, 1995.

Nye, F. Ivan, and Lois Wladis Hoffman. *The Employed Mother in America.* Chicago: Rand McNally and Co., 1963.

Orbach, Susie. *Fat Is a Feminist Issue.* New York: Arrow, 1978, 1988.

Orbach, Susie. *Hunger Strike.* New York: Penguin, 1986, 1993.

Orenstein, Peggy. *Flux: Women on Sex, Work, Kids, Love and Life in a Half-Changed World.* New York: Doubleday, 2000.

Pearson, Allison. *I Don't Know How She Does It.* New York: Knopf, 2002.

Peck, Helen. *The Baby Trap.* New York: Bernard Geis Associates, 1971.

Peri, Camille, and Kate Moses, eds. *Mothers Who Think: Tales of Real-Life Parenthood.* New York: Villard, 1999.

Pollitt, Katha. "'Fetal Rights': A New Assault on Feminism." In Molly Ladd-Taylor and Lauri Umansky, eds. *"Bad" Mothers: The Politics of Blame in Twentieth-Century America.* New York and London: New York University Press, 1998, pp. 285–298.

Pollitt, Katha. *Reasonable Creatures: Essays on Women and Feminism.* New York: Vintage, 1995.

Putnam, Robert D. *Bowling Alone: The Collapse and Revival of American Community.* New York: Simon & Schuster, 2000.

Radl, Shirley L. *Mother's Day Is Over.* New York: Charterhouse, 1973.

Rich, Adrienne. *Of Woman Born: Motherhood as Experience and Institution.* New York: W. W. Norton, 1976.

Riesman, *The Lonely Crowd: A Study of the Changing American Character.* New Haven: Yale University Press, 1950.

Roiphe, Katie. *The Morning After: Sex, Fear and Feminism on Campus.* Boston: Little, Brown, 1993.

Rosenfeld, Alvin, and Nicole Wise. *The Over-Scheduled Child.* New York: St. Martin's Press, 2000.

Rossi, Alice C. "Equality Between the Sexes: An Immodest Proposal." In Michele Hoffnung Garskof, *Roles Women Play: Readings Towards Women's Liberation.* Belmont, California: Brooks/Cole Pubs., 1971, pp. 145–164.

Rutter, Michael. *Maternal Deprivation Assessed* (Second Edition). New York: Penguin, 1972, 1981.

Ryan, Mary P. *Womanhood in America.* New York: New Viewpoints, 1979.

Salinger, Rickie. "Poisonous Choice." In Molly Ladd-Taylor and Laura Umansky, eds., *"Bad" Mothers,* pp. 381–402.

Salzman-Webb, Marilyn. "Woman as Secretary, Sexpot, Spender, Sow, Civic Actor, Sickie." In Michele Hoffnung Garskof, *Roles Women Play: Readings Towards Women's Liberation.* Belmont, California: Brooks/Cole Pubs., 1971, pp. 7–24.

Sears, William and Martha. *The Baby Book.* Boston: Little, Brown, 1993.

Seeley, John R. *The Americanization of the Unconscious.* New York: International Science Press, 1967.

Seid, Roberta Pollack. *Never Too Thin: Why Women Are at War with Their Bodies.* New York: Prentice-Hall, 1989.

Schlessinger, Laura. *The Proper Care and Feeding of Husbands.* New York: HarperCollins, 2004.

Shield, Renée Rose. *Making Babies in the '80s: Common Sense for New Parents.* Cambridge: Harvard Common Press, 1983.

Shorter, Edward. *From the Mind into the Body: The Cultural Origins of Psychosomatic Symptoms.* New York: The Free Press, 1994.

Shorter, Edward. *From Paralysis to Fatigue: A History of Psychosomatic Illness in the Modern Era.* New York: The Free Press, 1992.

Showalter, Elaine. *Hystories: Hysterical Epidemics and Modern Media.* New York: Columbia University Press, 1997.

Shutz, Lindley. "A Family Romance." In Christina Baker Kline, *Child of Mine.* New York: Hyperion, 1997, pp. 232–242.

Slater, Philip. *The Pursuit of Loneliness: American Culture at the Breaking Point.* Boston: Beacon Press, 1970.

Smith, Janna Malamud. *A Potent Spell: Mother Love and the Power of Fear.* New York: Houghton Mifflin, 2003.

Spitz, René A. *The First Year of Life.* New York: International Universities Press, 1965.

Spock, Benjamin. *Baby and Child Care.* New York: Pocket Books, 1963.

Stacey, Michelle. *Consumed: Why Americans Love, Hate and Fear Food.* New York: Simon & Schuster, 1994.

Steinem, Gloria. *Moving Beyond Words.* New York: Simon & Schuster, 1994.

Steinem, Gloria. *Revolution From Within: A Book of Self-Esteem.* Boston: Little, Brown, 1992.

Stern, Daniel. *The Interpersonal World of the Infant.* New York: Basic Books, 1985.

Strecker, Edward A. *Their Mothers' Sons: The Psychiatrist Examines an American Problem.* Philadelphia: J. B. Lippincott Co., 1945.

Sykes, Charles. *A Nation of Victims: The Decay of the American Character.* New York: St. Martin's Press, 1992.

Thompson, Clara. "The Role of Women in this Culture." *Psychiatry* (1941) 4, pp. 1–8.

Thurer, Shari L. *The Myths of Motherhood: How Culture Reinvents the Good Mother.* Boston and New York: Houghton Mifflin, 1994.

Walker, Nancy A. *Women's Magazines, 1940–1960: Gender Roles and the Popular Press.* Boston and New York: Bedford/St. Martin's, 1998.

Watson, John B. *Psychological Care of Infant and Child.* New York: W. W. Norton, 1928.

Weiner, Lynn Y. "Reconstructing Motherhood: The La Leche League in Postwar America." In Rima D. Apple and Janet Golden, eds., *Mothers and Motherhood: Readings in American History.* Columbus: Ohio State University Press, 1997.

Williams, Joan. *Unbending Gender: Why Family and Work Conflict and What to Do About It.* Oxford, New York: Oxford University Press, 2000.

Winn, Marie. *The Plug-In Drug: Television, Computers and Family Life.* New York: Penguin, 2002.

Winnicott, D. W. *The Maturational Processes and the Facilitating Environment.* International Universities Press, 1965.

Wolf, Naomi. *The Beauty Myth.* New York: Anchor, 1992.

Wolf, Naomi. *Fire with Fire: The New Female Power and How It Will Change the Twenty-first Century.* New York: Random House, 1993.

Wolf, Naomi. *Misconceptions: Truth, Lies, and the Unexpected on the Journey to Motherhood.* New York: Doubleday, 2001.

Wright, Lawrence. *Remembering Satan: Recovered Memory and the Shattering of the Family.* New York: Knopf, 1994.

Young, Cathy. *Ceasefire! Why Women and Men Must Join Forces to Achieve True Equality.* New York: The Free Press, 1999.

Index